D0094820

אש שחור על גבי אש לבן

Black Fire on White Fire:

Essays in Honor of Rabbi Avi Weiss

Edited by Daniel R. Goodman

YESHIVAT CHOVEVEI TORAH RABBINICAL SCHOOL

ISBN: 978-1-60280-282-7

Published by KTAV Publishing House
527 Empire Blvd.
Brooklyn, NY 11225
(718)972-5449
Web: www.ktav.com
e-mail: orders@ktav.com

Printed in the United States of America

Contents

President's Introduction — *vii*
Asher Lopatin

Foreword — *ix*
Shlomo Riskin

Haver Ha-Ir: A Model of Rabbinic Leadership — *1*
Marc D. Angel

Tefillin As Covenantal Symbol and Enactment — *11*
Saul J. Berman

"The Jewish People are My Family–A *Kavvanah* for the *B'rakhah* of *Retseih*" — *37*
Jeffrey S. Fox

Tritsch-Tratsch Polka:
A Cinematic Triptych in Honor of Rabbi Avi Weiss — *43*
Daniel Ross Goodman

Educating in the Divine Image — *62*
Chaya Rosenfeld Gorsetman

Checking Up on America's "Tentative Orthodox" Jews — *74*
Jeffrey S. Gurock

The Open Torah of Maimonides: Rambam on Halakhah, Ethics and Humanity — *88*
Eugene Korn

Beit Din's Presence in the Mikveh Room for Conversion: A Case Study in Values and Worldview in the Psak of Rav Ovadya Yosef — *97*
Dov Linzer

The Scribal Art of Rabbi Meir: A Study in Metanomianism 110
Bezalel Naor

Speaking Truth to Power: What Avi Weiss Said to
Jimmy Carter and Its Implications for the World Today 121
Walter Reich

"The Last Years Were the Most Difficult" A First-Person
Account of a Mission to the Soviet Union in March 1986 131
Jonathan D. Sarna

Some Comments Relating to Halakhic Feminism 141
Daniel Sperber

The Rabbinic Doctrine of "The Righteous Decrees and
God Fulfills" 162
Dov Weiss

Seven Who Matriculated: Orthodox Rabbis and the
Universities They Attended 185
Dov S. Zakheim

החוויה הדתית המצוות החברתיות א
יובל שרלו

Dedicated by
Avram & Rhoda Freedberg
in memory of their parents

George & Ziporah Freedberg

Sidney & Dorothy Bernstein

ASHER LOPATIN

President's Introduction

IN SOME WAYS, this festschrift is long overdue. How can the modern, intellectual Torah community not celebrate in words one of the great thinker-practitioners of our era? Rav Avi thought about the subject of women at prayer. He felt the pain of women denied spiritual opportunities, and he wrote the eponymous book about it. And he introduced innovative changes at the Hebrew Institute of Riverdale to bring these ideas, feelings, and yearnings into Orthodox Jewish practice. Rav Avi worked tirelessly for Soviet Jewry, and then he wrote about it in *Open Up the Iron Door*. Rav Avi lives spiritual activism, and he wrote the book on it as well. And, of course, Rav Avi thought about an Open Orthodoxy, he wrote its manifesto, and he started organizations and Modern Orthodox *yeshivot* to make openness and sensitivity to the world a reality. Words, written and spoken, have been an integral part of Rav Avi's life of deeds and thought. How can we not have a volume of brilliant writers and thinkers celebrate him in words?

But Rav Avi has always emphasized that his pride and joy comes not from what he writes or even does, but rather, from the accomplishments of his family, his students, and the colleagues who share his vision for Orthodoxy. Rav Avi has made this clear in so many ways. He has boasted that Yeshivat Chovevei Torah has pictures of students on its walls rather than teachers or Jewish leaders because our investment is in the future leaders of Orthodoxy and the broader Jewish world, not those of the present or past.

Given this, being the dedicatee of a festschrift undoubtedly makes Rav Avi uncomfortable. Thus I realized when I became President of YCT that I was blessed to inherit a project that had to happen, but I also knew that we faced questions of how to make it appropriate for such a unique and inspiring person. With the energy of Rav Avi's numerous *talmidim* who worked on the festschrift before I came, and with the direction and thoughtfulness of Professor Jeffrey Gurock, we found the perfect editor to bring this work to fruition: Rabbi Daniel Goodman, *talmid* of Rav Avi, YCT *musmakh*, indefatigable champion of the project, and ultimate believer in the power of the intellect and the pen.

Coordinating with Mati Friedman, Executive Vice President of YCT, Rav Daniel pulled together an incredible group of articles from world-class thinkers, and in so doing, he compiled a volume that answers the contradiction of a festschrift for Rav Avi. The festschrift is made up of twelve articles by Rav Avi's students, congregants, and beloved colleagues, as well as Rav Avi's "*rebbeim*": Rav Dov Linzer, shlit"a, and Rabbi Dr. Professor Dov Weiss. Much of the inspiration for, and the Torah contained in, this volume came from Rav Avi himself, and it is offered here in words of love and respect. The format is based on the YCT journal, *Milin Havivin*, so it reflects Rav Avi's desire to promote the works of the *talmidim*, and it contains articles from Rav Avi's earliest comrades-in-arms as well as more recent allies in his quest to move Modern Orthodoxy back to its open-minded and caring roots. This festschrift is a celebration of Rav Avi's thought and actions, but it has been realized in a way that reflects his desire to highlight the works and actions of others.

In the true spirit of Rav Avi Weiss, may this festschrift be more than a celebration of one man. May it go beyond words, authors, and readers. May it be a call to action for positive impact in this world, for opening up the iron doors, and for creating in our hearts a spirit of activism and devotion to God and to *Am Yisrael*.

Rabbi Asher Lopatin
President,
Yeshivat Chovevei Torah Rabbinical School
March 2017

SHLOMO RISKIN

Foreword

THE PUBLIC PERSONA of Rabbi Avi Weiss is that of a zealous activist, a charismatic leader who has led countless public demonstrations—from New York to Washington to Bergen-Belsen to the Vatican to Buenos Aires to Oslo, amidst the raucous fanfare of media publicity and from which he was often detained and even incarcerated—for the sake of wresting Jewish and human rights from the oppression of senseless bigotry and murderous hatred. And in his passionate zeal, Rabbi Weiss sometimes overlooked the "due process" of legal fine-tuning. (Indeed, both of us were jailed, albeit in rather comfortable quarters, I must admit, for chaining ourselves to the gate of the United Nations headquarters in Manhattan in protest against the international silence in the face of inhuman Communist suppression of Jews behind the Iron Curtain.)

However, an investigation of our Talmudic sources would suggest that our Sages were critical of the zealots and their actions—that Pinchas who slayed the cohabiting tribal prince did not act in accordance with the will of the Sanhedrin, and that had the zealot sought due process and legal sanction for his activity, it would have been denied! (See Jerusalem Talmud, *Sanhedrin* 9:7, and Babylonian Talmud, *Sanhedrin* 82a).

And even a study of the Bible itself would result in a negative assessment of zealotry, given the Divine response to the three zealots featured in our Sacred Text: God bestows upon Pinchas His Covenant of Peace (Numbers 25:12) ,when peace is the last option sought by the typical zealot; God reveals to Elijah the zealot at the end of his ministry that God (Y-HVH) is not to be found in rushing wind, clapping thunder, or fiery flame, but is rather to be glimpsed in the still, small sound of human sensitivity (I Kings 18:11, 12), whereas most zealots prefer the public pyrotechnics of magic-like machina-

---

RABBI SHLOMO RISKIN is the Chief Rabbi of Efrat and Chancellor and Rosh Yeshiva of Ohr Torah Stone Institutions: a network of high schools, Yeshivot Hesder for men and for women, and graduate programs for the training of rabbis, educators, and women spiritual leaders for world Jewry. He is the author of 11 books of commentary on the Bible, theology, and halakhah for Modern Orthodoxy.

tions; and God teaches Moses (the zealot who impulsively slew the cruel Egyptian taskmaster) that His true name is Eternal Love (Y-HVH), Compassion, Freely-Given Grace, Forgiving Patience . . . (Ex. 34:5, 6), while most zealots favor strict punishment and violent vengeance.

But now our question looms even larger: if God is truly the Master of the still, small sound of love and peace, why does He then choose for His prophets those individuals who seem emotionally disposed to passionate zealotry, to violent vengeance? Why did He choose Pinchas, Elijah and Moses in the first place?

I would suggest that, generally speaking, people of forgiveness, brotherly love and peace are rarely passionate about these ideals; it is usually the extremists amongst us, the rabid heretic hunters and the fanatic religionists seeking world domination for their god, who are most vocal, most obsessive and most active in pursuit of their goals. Hence, God chooses His most passionate servants, but only those whom He knows will ultimately utilize their passion positively for the sake of peace, freedom and love of humanity.

Hence, God chose Moses because he must teach his people to passionately desire freedom from Egyptian enslavement and to impart to them a Torah of love and peace—freedom and tranquility—but which admittedly could not then and cannot today be achieved in a world yet unredeemed without sacrifice and war against evil (*milhemet mitzvah*). God chose Pinchas because he was first and foremost a man of peace, a descendant of Aaron the consummate lover of peace; it was Pinchas who had been chosen to broker a peace agreement with the two and one half tribes living in Trans-Jordan and thus prevent a civil war in Israel (Joshua 22), a war against Moses which he similarly prevented earlier by his act of zealotry (see my *Torah Lights: Bamidbar*, 207-215; Maggid, 2012).

And God chose Elijah because his great expertise lay in bringing about the most significant peace of all, peace between the generations, peace within families, the forerunner of peace within Israel which will lead to peace within the world. In the words of Malakhi, last of the Hebrew prophets: "Behold I shall bring to you Elijah the Prophet before the great and awesome day of the Lord (the day of redemption). He shall restore the hearts of the parents to those of the children and the hearts of the children to those of the parents. . . ." (Malakhi 3:23, 24). And as our folk tradition has it, Elijah never died but was rather "translated" into heaven, and often "visits" human beings on earth; he is particularly present at every gathering of national familial connection, at every circumcision ceremony and at every Passover Seder.

Rabbi Avi Weiss is not merely a zealous activist, passionately hell-bent on destroying whatever he believes to be evil; Rabbi Avi Weiss is rather a *spiritual* activist passionately heaven-bent on repairing a broken world in the Kingship of the Divine. His weaponry is not the brandished *sword* but is rather the inspirited *word*, the "*ruah me'mallelah*" which emanates from the Image of God within each of us. (Targum, Gen. 2:7.) His emotional motivation is not hatred and vengeance but is rather love and forgiveness born of repentance. He is a valiant warrior against injustice because he wishes to help recreate a world of peace and freedom wherein every human being, Jew and Gentile, man and woman, can realize his or her potential as a child of the Divine. He is indeed a zealous *spiritual* activist.

Shlomo Riskin
Efrat, Israel
November 2015

MARC D. ANGEL

Haver Ha-Ir: A Model of *Rabbinic Leadership*

This essay is dedicated to my longtime friend Rabbi Avi Weiss, in appreciation of his impressive service to the Jewish people as a genuine Haver Ha-Ir.

AMONG THE TITLES that rabbinic literature ascribes to Torah scholars is *Haver Ha-Ir*. This phrase denotes someone of great learning, integrity and commitment to the welfare of the community.[1] Rabbi Benzion Uziel noted: "The rabbi of a community is called by our Sages *Haver Ir* because he tends to the needs of the public and gathers them for prayer and Torah study."[2]

The *Haver Ha-Ir* model of rabbinic leadership deserves careful attention. The rabbi is literally to be a "friend" of the city, a person who is engaged in people's lives, who strives to make society a better place. He is to feel personal responsibility for the spiritual and material wellbeing of the community. The *Haver Ha-Ir* is not an aloof scholar nor an otherworldly mystic, but is with the people and for the people.

We may explore the *Haver Ha-Ir* model by considering the teachings of four rabbinic figures of the modern period: Rabbi Benzion Uziel (1880-1953); Rabbi Joseph B. Soloveitchik (1903-1993); Rabb Haim David Halevy (1924-1998); and Rabbi Nahum Rabinovitch (1928-).

Rabbi Benzion Uziel: Yishuvo shel Olam

Rabbi Uziel was the pre-eminent Sephardic rabbi and *posek* of his generation. Born and raised in Jerusalem, he distinguished himself as an outstanding

RABBI DR. MARC D. ANGEL is Founder and Director of the Institute for Jewish Ideas and Ideals, jewishideas.org. He and Rabbi Avi Weiss are co-founders of the International Rabbinic Fellowship. Author and editor of 34 books, Rabbi Angel's recent publications include his commentary on *Pirkei Avot*, published by Koren (2015); *The Crown of Solomon and Other Stories* (2014); and *Maimonides: Essential Teachings in Jewish Faith and Ethics* (2012).

Torah scholar and communal leader. He was the Sephardic Chief Rabbi of Israel from 1939 until his death in 1953. A prolific author, he is well known for his volumes of responsa, *Mishpetei Uziel*.[3]

At a rabbinic conference held in Jerusalem in 1919, Rabbi Uziel urged his colleagues to take an active role in the development of Jewish life in the land of Israel. He called on them to live and work among the people, to share their worries and aspirations, and to be an integral part of their lives. "This is our duty to our God and to our nation: to walk in the midst of the people, in the work of the people, to join ourselves in the task of building in all its forms, very carefully watching for the soul of the nation." It is incumbent upon rabbis to conduct themselves "with words of pleasantness and with love for each individual Jew." The religious message is best conveyed by establishing rapport with the public, by working with them and respecting them. "Let us walk on our path together with all the people, to love and appreciate, to learn and to teach the Torah of Israel and its tradition in the presence of all."[4]

During Israel's war of independence in 1948, a group of yeshiva students approached Rabbi Uziel and asked him to arrange exemptions for them from military service. They claimed that their study of Torah should take priority to serving as soldiers. Rabbi Uziel rebuked the students sharply. He told them that religious Jews, including yeshiva students, were obligated to share in the defense of the nation. If they were to influence society to live according to Torah, they themselves had to set an example that the public would respect and wish to emulate.[5]

Among the concepts that Rabbi Uziel emphasized in his teachings was the imperative to work for the general wellbeing of society—*yishuvo shel olam*. Judaism demands that its adherents live moral and upright lives. Religious Jews must feel troubled by any injustice in society and must strive to defend and protect the oppressed. Striving to create a harmonious society is not merely a reflection of social idealism; it is a religious mandate. "We are all workers and employees, each person according to his physical and intellectual abilities and talents; we are workers in the workplace to improve human life, to raise the level of culture and to fulfill the human charter for which we have been created and through which we live: to bring peace and truth, and the love of compassion and truth, throughout our world."[6]

Each person who works honestly and efficiently is thereby helping to build a better world and is participating in *yishuvo shel olam*. Individuals who only seek their own interests, even if they are honest in their dealings, are not living up to the proper religious standard. A religious person should be constructive, honest, and concerned for the welfare of others.

The concept of fostering *yishuvo shel olam* not only relates to individuals; it is also a responsibility of the Jewish people as a whole. Just as we learn and benefit from other nations, so we are to contribute our own talents and energies for the advancement of humankind. Rabbi Uziel wrote:

> Each country and each nation that respects itself does not and cannot be satisfied with its narrow boundaries and limited domains. Rather, they desire to bring in all that is good and beautiful, that is helpful and glorious to their national [cultural] treasury. And they wish to impart the maximum flow of their own blessings to the [cultural] treasury of humanity as a whole . . . Happy is the country and happy is the nation that can give itself an accounting of what it has taken from others; and more importantly, of what it has given of its own to the repository of all humanity. Woe unto that country and nation that encloses itself in its own four cubits and limits itself to its own narrow boundaries, lacking anything of its own to contribute [to humanity] and lacking the tools to receive [cultural] contributions from others.[7]

Rabbi Uziel noted that the Jewish people have contributed vastly to the idealism and morality of the world. Likewise, Jews have learned much from other nations. On balance, though, we have given far more than we have received:

> As much as Israel drew from others . . . far, far more did it give of its own to others: Torah and light, purity of heart and the holiness of life, righteous justice and true ethics; love and appreciation of its Torah, a Torah for the world; the words of its prophets and sages from generation to generation, all of whom were imbued with an elevated love of the God of the universe and all who were created in His image, of all His creations of nature, a wise ethics, words of peace and truth."[8]

Yishuvo shel olam is an obligation to seek the benefit of humanity. This entails not only a responsibility for the physical wellbeing of others, but also a commitment to expand human knowledge, technology, and general culture. *Yishuvo shel olam* is

> a precondition and vital need for our attaining our proper way in life. In the settlement and building of the world, knowledge is increased. From our knowledge of the mysteries of nature, our eyes are opened to new and very wide horizons, from which we will arise and announce the wonders of God, Creator of the universe, and the ways of His wondrous and hidden providence, all of which are love, justice, kindness and compassion.[9]

When Rabbi Uziel became Sephardic Chief Rabbi of Israel in 1939, he delivered a radio address to the nation. He stressed the need for all residents of the land to work together in harmony. "Our first task is the establishment of true peace and strong unity among all segments of the people, its communities and ethnic groups, its organizations and parties; to call 'peace, peace to those who are far and near' among ourselves; and peace with all our neighbors in the land, of all religions and peoples."[10] Later in his address, he spoke in Arabic to the Arab population:

> We reach our hands out to you in peace, pure and trustworthy. We say: the land is stretched out before us, and with joined hands we will work it, we will uncover its treasures, and we will live on it as brothers who dwell together. Know and trust that the word of God will rise forever. Make peace with us and we will make peace with you. Together all of us will benefit from the blessing of God on His land; with quiet and peace, with love and fellowship, with goodwill and pure heart we will find the way of peace.[11]

In his role as a *Haver Ha-Ir*, Rabbi Uziel was a role model of rabbinic leadership that was imbued with a keen sense of responsibility to individuals, to society, to people of all backgrounds. His grand religious vision sought unity and harmony in a world often characterized by dissension and violence.

Rabbi Joseph B. Soloveitchik: Moral Courage

Rabbi Soloveitchik, the Rav, was the pre-eminent Orthodox rabbinic thinker of twentieth century America. For many years, he taught Talmud at Yeshiva University and signed the rabbinic ordinations of thousands of disciples. He was the *posek* of the Rabbinical Council of America, the Union of Orthodox Jewish Congregations and the Religious Zionists of America. He was the founder of the Maimonides Day School in Boston. Through his classes, public lectures and writings, he has had singular impact on the recent generations of Modern Orthodox Jews.

In his own rabbinic career, he drew inspiration from the teachings of his illustrious grandfather, Rabbi Hayyim of Brisk. When R. Hayyim was asked to describe the function of a rabbi, he replied: "To redress the grievances of those who are abandoned and alone, to protect the dignity of the poor, and to save the oppressed from the hands of his oppressor."[12] In reporting these words of his grandfather, Rabbi Soloveitchik notes:

> Neither ritual decisions nor political leadership constitutes the main task of halakhic man. Far from it. The actualization of the ideals of

> justice and righteousness is the pillar of fire which halakhic man follows, when he, as a rabbi and teacher in Israel, serves his community.[13]

Whereas some religions have an otherworldly focus, Judaism—as represented by Halakhic man—is concerned primarily with this world. The goal is to bring comfort to those who suffer, justice to those who are oppressed, and kindness to those who are neglected. "Halakhic man is characterized by a powerful stiff-neckedness [*sic*] and stubbornness. He fights against life's evil and struggles relentlessly with the wicked kingdom and with all the hosts of iniquity in the cosmos. His goal is not flight to another world that is wholly good, but rather bringing down that eternal world into the midst of our world."[14]

To wage a battle for righteousness requires tremendous courage. One must be prepared to confront powerful opponents, people who wish to maintain their own control over others. "Halakhic man does not quiver before any man; he does not seek out compliments, nor does he require public approval."[15]

Rabbi Soloveitchik refers to an incident in the life of his grandfather, R. Hayyim of Brisk. It happened once that two Jews died in Brisk on the same day. In the morning, a poor shoemaker died. Later, a wealthy and prominent member of the community passed away. According to halakhah, the one who dies first must be buried first. However, the members of the burial society decided (after they had apparently been given a handsome sum from the rich man's heirs) to attend to the rich man's burial first. When R. Hayyim learned of this, he sent a message to the burial society to desist from their disgraceful behavior. The members of the burial society refused to heed R. Hayyim's directive, and they continued to prepare for the burial of the wealthy man. "R. Hayyim then arose, took his walking stick, trudged over to the house of the deceased, and chased all the attendants outside. R. Hayyim prevailed—the poor man was buried before the rich man. R. Hayyim's enemies multiplied and increased. Thus have true halakhic men always acted, for their study and their deeds have blended together beautifully, truly beautifully."[16]

Halakhah is unequivocally dedicated to fostering righteousness. The hallmark of great halakhic sages has been their lofty ethical standards and their deep respect for the dignity of others:

> To recognize a person is not just to identify him physically. It is more than that: it is an act of identifying him existentially, as a person who has a job to do, that only he can do properly. To recognize a person means to affirm that he is irreplaceable. To hurt a person means to tell

> him that he is expendable, that there is no need for him. The Halakhah equated the act of publicly embarrassing a person with murder.[17]

Halakhic Judaism is the antithesis of mystical quietism that views pain and suffering in a passive, fatalistic manner. Rather, the halakhah "wants man to cry out aloud against any kind of pain, to react indignantly to all kinds of injustice or unfairness."[18]

In one of his *teshuvah* lectures, the Rav elaborated on the connection a Jew must feel toward *Knesset Israel*, the community of Israel that transcends time and place. "The Jew who believes in *Knesset Israel* is the Jew who lives as part of it wherever it is and is willing to give his life for it, feels its pain, rejoices with it, fights in its wars, groans at its defeats and celebrates its victories."[19]

The *Haver Ha-Ir* must have moral courage so as to set an example to others. For Rabbi Soloveitchik, "heroism is the central category in practical Judaism."[20]

Rabbi Haim David Halevy: Kevod HaBeriyot

Rabbi Haim David Halevy was a prolific author and teacher, a gifted halakhic scholar, a devotee of kabbalah and a creative thinker who applied Torah wisdom to the dilemmas of the modern world. From 1972 until his death in 1998, he served as Sephardic Chief Rabbi of Tel Aviv.

For a number of years, Rabbi Halevy conducted a popular Israeli radio program, *Asei Lekha Rav*, in which he answered a wide range of questions posed to him by listeners. He later wrote up and elaborated on his responses, publishing them in a series of volumes also entitled *Asei Lekha Rav*. In the first responsum in Volume One of this series, Rabbi Halevy noted that a rabbi was not simply a decisor of rabbinic law who ruled on what was forbidden and what was permitted. "Rather he is also—and perhaps mainly—an advisor to everyone in his community for all questions, small and large."[21]

A recurring theme in his voluminous writings was the respect due to fellow human beings. Sensitivity to the needs and feelings of others is a basic feature of proper religious life. An example of this sensitivity is evident in a responsum he wrote relating to wedding ceremonies.

Some rabbis had the practice of reciting the wedding blessings and then taking a sip of wine themselves. They then gave the wine to the groom and bride for them to drink from the wine cup. Rabbi Halevy ruled that rabbis should not drink from the cup before giving it to the couple. Some people feel uncomfortable drinking from a glass from which someone else has drunk. Even if many people do not mind drinking from the cup of others, "aren't we obligated to worry about even the one in a thousand who is particular, and who will drink the wine and feel hurt?"[22] Rabbi Halevy added that when he recited Kiddush at home, he would pass it to family members who did not mind drinking from a shared cup. But whenever he had a guest at the table, he poured from the Kiddush cup into a separate cup from which he drank. He would then pass the Kiddush cup to the others so that they could pour a bit of wine into their own clean cups.

In another case, Rabbi Halevy dealt with the following situation. On a Shabbat, a large group of family and friends attended a synagogue to celebrate with a bridegroom. Among the guests was a young man, who had become blind through an injury in battle while serving in the Israel Defense Forces. The family requested that this blind young man be given an *aliyah*, but the rabbi of the synagogue cited the *Shulhan Arukh* who ruled that a blind person may not be called to the Torah. The blind soldier told the rabbi that he was called to the Torah in his regular synagogue, but the rabbi was not swayed. Feeling angry and humiliated, the soldier and some members of his family left the synagogue.

When Rabbi Halevy heard of this case, he was deeply pained. The young soldier, who had sacrificed so much on behalf of his country, was treated shabbily. If the soldier told the rabbi that he had been receiving *aliyot* in his regular synagogue, the rabbi should have given credence to this. "How careful one must be when it comes to *kevod haberiyot*, who were created in the image of God." Rabbi Halevy noted that the Sephardic community generally did not accept the ruling of the *Shulhan Arukh* (*Orah Hayyim* 139:3) forbidding *aliyot* to blind people, but rather followed the opinion of other rabbinic authorities permitting this practice.[23]

Rabbi Halevy was asked if non-observant Jews should be allowed to participate in the celebration of finishing the writing of a Torah scroll. Usually, a qualified scribe would write the entire Torah, leaving the last few letters to be filled in by the sponsors or donors of the writing of the scroll. Rabbi Halevy permitted non-observant Jews to participate in this happy occasion. "If we prevent them from doing this, there is a fear of complaints, Heaven forbid, since the general practice [is to let non-observant Jews participate]." How embarrassing it would be for the non-observant people to be turned away from participating in this mitzvah. It would be a public humiliation that could deepen their alienation from religious observance.[24]

Rabbi Halevy criticized a practice of some religiously observant Jews to publicly scream at those who were violating Shabbat or other ritual laws. These pietists are vocal in their protest of laxities in ritual observances, yet "they remain quiet and take things in normal stride when they see social and ethical breakdowns in many areas of our public life, when people swallow each other alive, and the moral thread of our life is broken."[25] For Rabbi Halevy, religious Jews should demonstrate concern for all society and for the general moral health of society.

Rabbi Halevy's concern for society included his concern for the well-being of non-Jews. He argued that Christians and Muslims were not to be considered as "idolaters," nor were they to be subjected to Talmudic rulings that related to idolaters. "Providing their sustenance, visiting their sick, burying their dead, comforting their mourners are all to be performed because of the human ethical imperative, not specifically [only] for the sake of peace."[26] Relationships between Jews and non-Jews, whether in Israel or the Diaspora, were to be governed by the moral obligations that bound all human beings.

Rabbi Nahum Rabinovich: Shutafut

Rabbi Nahum Rabinovich has served as Rosh Yeshiva of Yeshivat Birkat Moshe in Maale Adumim for many years. A respected *posek* and thinker, his teachings provide important insight into the role of a *Haver Ha-Ir*.

Rabbi Rabinovich draws on the halakhic idea that members of a community are in a partnership relationship. They each share equally in rights and obligations. Since societies include members with different views, the notion of *shutafut*, partnership, is very important. Instead of each individual or group struggling in an adversarial manner against those with different opinions, all members of society should recognize that they are partners in the same venture. In spite of differences, they need to find ways of working together for the betterment of society as a whole. "In order to reach a practical agreement and cooperation among various groups of society, it is necessary to open doors of genuine dialogue among these groups. Dialogue among the various groups in society will enable them to overcome the deep rifts and conflicts that exist and that are growing."[27]

Rabbi Rabinovich pointed out that the religiously observant community had a responsibility to society as a whole, not merely to their own religious enclaves. Since the religious, along with all other citizens, are partners with equal rights and obligations, they need to be concerned with issues beyond their own neighborhoods. For example, since the Torah was given to all Jews, it is incumbent upon the religious education leaders to recognize their responsibility to the entire public. They should work in harmony with the general education system in order to meet the needs of all students, not only the students in the religious school system. They need to work for the inclusion of Torah values, without diminishing the need for students to study science and technology and other subjects that are essential for the social and economic life of the nation.

> We must create religious schools not only for children [from religious families] but also for children whose parents want them to excel in computers, mathematics, vocations and other fields. In these schools children will also learn Torah. . . . Religious education can draw to itself a large portion of children in Israel, if only it would know how to approach the various groupings of society.[28]

As another example of how the religious community should be working in partnership with other segments of society, Rabbi Rabinovich points to economic issues. All society is impacted negatively by rampant inflation. Why then are the religious parties not front and center in dealing with this problem? Shouldn't rabbis throughout the land be preaching and teaching about the ills of inflation, the sufferings of the poor, etc.? Why should economic issues be relegated to the domain of the "secular" community, when this is an area that impacts on society as a whole?[29]

Another striking example: seat belts. Many Israelis are killed or injured in automobile accidents each year. Some years ago, a suggestion was made to make wearing seat belts a legal requirement. This would save lives and reduce injuries. Yet, before a seat belt law was enacted in Israel, there were delays so that studies could be made to determine the effectiveness of seat belts. Yet, such studies had already been made in other countries and the evidence was clear that seat belts are an important safety feature. Why was so much time lost before enacting the law in Israel? Why wasn't this issue high among the priorities of the religious community? "The time has come for us to recognize that confronting such issues is a moral and religious obligation, and we must be the acute prodders in confronting situations which involve safety to life."[30]

Rabbi Rabinovich notes that

> the light of Torah cannot be revealed or shown as long as Torah manifests itself as the Torah of a particular group, but only when the Torah is the Torah for all society. The challenge at the door of the sages of Torah is to demonstrate how great is the power of Torah for arranging the life of the community at large. . . . We have the genuine opportunity to spread Torah among large segments of the Israeli public, and ultimately to almost all the residents of the State, if only we can succeed to break the sectarian or religious party muzzle. This will not be an easy task, and there are those on all sides who wish to protect their narrow interests and who strive to strengthen those muzzles. Nevertheless, we must undertake this task."[31]

For Rabbi Rabinovich, the principle of *shutafut* is at the heart of creating a vibrant and healthy society. Each member of society needs to feel a sense of partnership with all other members of society. Breaking into small self-contained "interest groups" undermines the general harmony of society.

The *Haver Ha-Ir* model of leadership entails a grand religious vision, courage, respect and a sense of partnership with all members of society. The rabbi, as an exemplar of this model of leadership, must strive not merely to study and teach Torah, but to *live* Torah.

NOTES

1. See *Encyclopaedia Talmudit*, Jerusalem, 1978, volume 12, columns 532-536.
2. *Sha'arei Uziel*, Jerusalem, 5751, Volume 1, 52.
3. For more on Rabbi Uziel, see Marc D. Angel, *Loving Truth and Peace: The Grand Religious Worldview of Rabbi Benzion Uziel* (Northvale, NJ: Jason Aronson, 1999).
4. *Mikhmanei Uziel*, Tel Aviv, 5699, 328.
5. Reported by Shabbetai Don Yihye, *HaRav Benzion Meir Hai Uziel: Hayav uMishnato* (Jerusalem: Histadrut HaZionit, 5715), 227.
6. *Hegyonei Uziel*, Vol. 1, Jerusalem, 5713, 206-7.
7. *Hegyonei Uziel*, Vol. 2, Jerusalem, 5714, 127.
8. Ibid., 128.
9. Ibid., 109.
10. *Mikhmanei Uziel*, 424.
11. Ibid., 429.
12. Joseph B. Soloveitchik, *Halakhic Man*, trans. Lawrence Kaplan (Philadelphia: Jewish Publication Society, 1983), 91.
13. Ibid.
14. Ibid., 41.
15. Ibid., 89.
16. Ibid., 95.
17. Idem, "The Community," *Tradition* 17:2 (1978), 16.
18. Idem, "Redemption, Prayer and Talmud Torah," Ibid., 65.
19. Idem, *Al haTeshuva*, ed., Pinchas Peli (Jerusalem: 5736), 98.
20. "The Community," 13.
21. Rabbi Haim David Halevy, *Asei Lekha Rav*, Tel Aviv, 5736, 1:1. For more on Rabbi Halevy, see Marc D. Angel and Hayyim J. Angel, *Rabbi Haim David Halevy: Gentle Scholar and Courageous Thinker* (Jerusalem: Urim, 2006).
22. *Asei Lekha Rav*, 8:74.
23. Ibid., 6:20.
24. *Mayyim Hayyim*, 2:57.
25. *Asei Lekha Rav*, 8:32-35.
26. Ibid., 9:33.
27. Nahum Rabinovich, *Mesilot Bilvavam* (Maale Adumim: Maaliyot, 5775), 372.
28. Ibid., p. 393.
29. Ibid., p. 396.
30. Ibid., p. 397.
31. Ibid., p. 400.

SAUL J. BERMAN

Tefillin As Covenantal Symbol and Enactment

FIFTY YEARS AGO I had the good fortune to study the Laws of Tefillin with Rabbi Joseph B. Soloveitchik, ZT"L, at RIETS of Yeshiva University. His integration of law and philosophy in this area, as in so many others, penetrated deeply in my consciousness. I therefore, acknowledge the general influence, without ascribing to him any of the detailed teachings contained in this article.

I. Introduction

One of the most meaningful yet perplexing of all of the covenantal Commandments of the Torah is that of Tefillin. The very idea of wearing a sign of the covenant between the individual and God directly on the body is of enormous power in affirming the relationship. On the other hand, the complexity of the objects and the actions entailed in the fulfillment of the Commandment creates a sense of mystery which some find engaging and others might find alienating.

Let's begin with a list of questions and oddities related to the objects and actions.

> **Q.1.** The Torah commands the use of two *batim* (boxes, literally "houses"), one placed on the muscle of the arm, the other on the very front of the head just above the hairline, each containing the four portions of the Torah in which the commandment of Tefillin is found. Why are the four Torah portions written on a single rolled parchment to be inserted into the *bayit* on the arm, while the same four portions are written on separate pieces of parchment to be folded into distinct compartments within the *bayit* on the head?

RABBI SAUL J. BERMAN is Professor of Jewish Studies at Stern College of Yeshiva University; Adjunct Professor at Columbia University School of Law; and for 2009-2010 served as Berkowitz Fellow in The Tikvah Center for Law and Jewish Civilization at New York University School of Law.

Q.2. Why is the distinct inner structure reflected in the external structure? That is, why is it that the *bayit* on the arm is visibly a single unit, while the *bayit* on the head is visibly divided into four segments?

Q.3. Why is the *bayit* placed on the arm prior to the positioning of the *bayit* on the head?

Q.4. Why is the *retzuah* (leather strap) of the *bayit* on the arm wrapped around the forearm seven times?

Q.5. Why is it common custom to cover the Tefillin on the arm?

Q.6. Why is the wrapping of that *retzuah* interrupted before completion, wrapped around the middle of the hand, and the *bayit* then placed on the head, before completion of the wrapping of the *retzuah* around the fingers and palm?

Q.7. Why does the *bayit* on the head have forms of the Hebrew letter Shin marked in the leather on both sides of the *bayit*?

Q.8. Why does the Shin on one side of the *bayit* have four heads instead of the "correct" three?

Q.9. Why is it common custom specifically to not cover the *bayit* worn on the head?

Q.10. Why is there a common custom that the *retzuot* which descend from either side of the *bayit* on the head are of two different lengths, one ending approximately at the navel, the other at the groin?

Q.11. What is the significance of the particular manner of wrapping of the *retzuah* around the fingers and middle of the hand?

Q.12. Why, when wrapping around the hand, do we recite the verses of Hosea 2:21-22?

Q.13. What is the import of the rabbinic debate as to whether the mitzvah of Tefillin should be counted as a single divine commandment or as two separate commandments (one for the application of each Bayit) in the listing of 613?

Q.14. What is the significance of the Rabbinic debate as to the proper order of the four Biblical passages within the *batim*?

Q.15. In which direction within the *bayit* on the head are the four Biblical passages arranged, and why is that significant?

II. The Components of Covenant

A rational approach to the Commandment of Tefillin emerges from an understanding of the nature of the covenant to which the Tefillin are symbol and testimony (*ot* and *zikaron*). Through that approach, we will discover an appropriate response to all of the questions previously listed. We need to begin with an analysis of the four Torah passages in which the commandment of Tefillin is found: Exodus 13:1-10; Exodus 13:11-16; Deuteronomy 6:4-9; and Deuteronomy 11:13-21.

A. Exodus 13:1-10, "*Kadesh Li. . . .*"

This passage follows immediately after the declaration that God had taken the Jewish People out of the land of Egypt (Ex. 12:51). The purpose of the passage is to begin to lay out the components of the covenantal relationship between God and the Jewish people which would now result from the Exodus. And so, God commands Moses to tell the Jewish people, "consecrate unto Me (*kadesh li*) every first-born, man and beast, the first issue of every womb among the Israelites is Mine" (Ex. 13:2). That is, the primary purpose of the Exodus was to empower the individual Jew to be dedicated to the mission of holiness. This mission is exemplified in the holiness of the first born who are to serve as the models of constant service to God, who is the ultimate paradigm of holiness. That very mission is symbolized by the Tefillin to be worn by every Jew (or every Jewish male), as the passage concludes, "And this shall serve you as a sign on your hand and as a reminder on your forehead—in order that the teaching of the Lord may be in your mouth. . . . " (Ex. 13:9)

This first stage of the covenantal relationship between God and the Jewish people, in which the Exodus is motivated by the Divine desire to transform the spiritual identity of the individual Jew, is an echo of what God had promised he would do for the Jewish people. In Exodus 6:6-7, God uses four distinct terms to describe how he will achieve the Exodus. Those four terms, *vehotzeiti* (I will take you out), *vehitzalti* (I will rescue you), *vega'alti* (I will redeem you), and *velakahti* (I will take you), were the subjects of intense rabbinic discussion, and are commonly understood to have served as the basis for the rabbinic enactment of the requirement of drinking four cups of wine at the Passover Seder. The first of those terms has reference to God "taking out" the Jews from their state of "*sivlot*," which, as Sforno notes, is not the state of physical enslavement, but rather is the state of inner emotional and spiritual colonization ("*shi'bud*").

That is why the very first command which God makes of the Jewish People is that they set aside a lamb to be sacrificed as the Pascal offering. That command required of the Jews that they sever their inner emotional and spiritual connection to Egyptian religion and culture, in which such conduct would be an abomination. Those who were unable to free themselves from the assimilation to Egyptian values to which they had been exposed even as slaves would ultimately not be able to make the transition to worshippers of the Lord, and would never leave Egypt.

Why is it that the prohibition against eating *hametz* is distinctively emphasized in this paragraph, in verses 3 and 7? Indeed, we can well understand why verses 6 and 7 of chapter 13 focus on the duty to eat Matzah. After all, Exodus 12:34 had already introduced us to the hasty departure of the Jewish people from Egypt, during which there was not enough time for the breads to leaven. The symbolic meaning of Matzah was then clear. But what was the purpose of avoiding *hametz*? Why even in Exodus 12:15, 19 and 20 does the Torah so emphatically forbid *hametz*—forbidding us to eat it, to own it, to possess it, or even benefit from it—in addition to an affirmative requirement to destroy some of it? There is only one other substance which the Torah forbids in the same full dimensions as it forbids *hametz* on Pesach—and that is the goods used in idolatrous worship. We are forbidden to eat of pagan sacrifices, forbidden to own idols or even to possess them, forbidden to benefit from such idols, sacrifices, or even their places of worship, and mandated to destroy idols within the land of Israel.

What is the significance of this conjunction of prohibitions related to pagan idolatry and related to *hametz*? Let's return to the symbolic significance of Matzah for a moment. Even before the Torah told us in Exodus 12:34 of the import of Matzah as the symbol of the hasty departure from Egypt, the symbol of our liberation, we were commanded to eat Matzah with the Pascal offering, in Exodus 12:13, 17, 18 and 20. What meaning did Matzah have before it was the symbol of liberation? We actually preserve a powerful sense of the pre-liberation meaning of Matzah—it is *Lechem Oni*, the bread of Affliction. That is, before the Exodus, Matzah was the bread which slaves ate, because they were not given the leisure to fully bake their food—they ate barely edible bread that had not risen. Matzah was slave food. As we to this day declare as we expose the Matzah at the start of our Sedarim, "*Ha lachma anya . . .* " "this is the bread of affliction which our ancestors ate in the land of Egypt."

But if Matzah was slave food, what was *hametz*? *Hametz* was the food of masters! *Hametz* was the food which symbolized all that was bloated and excess in the slave-based economy and corrupt culture of pagan Egypt! No wonder then that Torah demanded of us not just that we eat Matzah, that we remember what it was like to be slaves and then to be liberated, but that we fully and completely rid ourselves and our homes of all that smacks of the evils of the idolatrous culture of Egypt, symbolized by *hametz*. The Torah is telling us that we can't achieve covenant with God by trying to pile holiness on top of debasement. We need first to rid ourselves, our hearts, our minds and our souls of the degraded values and beliefs of pagan religion and culture before we can build a life of holiness on a secure foundation. Thus, we need to rid ourselves of *hametz* in extreme ways before we can use Matzah to point us in other directions.

That's why the paragraph of "*Kadesh Li*," in which the first reference to Tefillin is found, reminds us of the prohibition against *hametz*. The very first element of the symbolic meaning of Tefillin is that it serves as a sign and as a reminder that the process of entry into covenantal relationship with God requires the utter transformation of the individual's inner emotional and spiritual identity: divesting oneself of all pagan emotional and spiritual beliefs, feelings and values in order to ready the mind, the heart and the soul for undertaking the covenantal mission of holiness.

B. Exodus 13:11-16, "*Vehaya ki yeviakha. . . .*"

This passage, following immediately upon the first, with a further elaboration of the commandment of the offering of first born of cattle as well as first born of Jewish male children, introduces us to the second layer of transformation implicit in the covenantal relationship. In this passage, we are commanded as individuals to develop a relationship to the material world in which our property and our productive energies are consciously devoted to the achievement of God's purposes. The manifestation of this covenantal quality resides in the offering or the redemption of the first born of herds and flock. It is to this strange behavior that the inquisitive child responds and asks, "*mah zot?*" ["what does this mean"] (Exodus 13:14). The child is not responding, as in the Midrash and in the Haggadah, to the oddities of the Seder night, but to the oddities of parental behavior in their productive lives.

The child has seen the labor of his parents in the shepherding of the flocks, in their protective conduct and their care of each and every animal. She has observed the sacrifice of time, energy and resources in growing the herds and the flock. Now, the child observes the parents taking the first born of all of their animals and either sacrificing, killing or redeeming them. Such inconsistent behavior requires explanation, and so the child asks, "*mah zot?*" The parental answer is powerful: all that we are and all that we have, our very freedom as Jews, our land and our possessions, all derive from God's manifestation of His power in liberating us from Egypt. We respond, the parents continue, in two ways. First, in gratitude we offer up to God a portion of our cattle, and thereby a portion of our productive energies. Secondly, we symbolically represent this element of our covenantal awareness by wearing Tefillin as the symbolic sign and reminder of what we are striving to achieve in this aspect of our relationship to God.

This dimension of the covenant is also anticipated in the second of the four terms of redemption used in Exodus 6:6-7. The second phrase used in that passage is "*vehitzalti etkhem me'avodatam*," "I will rescue you from their (slave) labors." This is not a further reference to relief from emotional and spiritual colonization, as in the first of these four terms, "*vehotzeiti*." Rather, this is a direct reference to the rescue from the physical labor which the Torah had previously described as "*bepharekh*"—crushing, or bitter (Exodus 1:14), or as the rabbis understood it, degrading or purposeless. This is the rescue of the material self, of the productive self, from meaningless existence.

What does this rescue entail? Firstly, it requires the radical alteration of our notion of ownership of property. The Torah consistently reminds us that ultimate ownership is vested only in God Himself. As creator of the universe, all that it contains, all material existence, is His to dispose in accordance with His will—to cause to flourish or to destroy. Only God has rights in material existence with no correlative duties—absolute ownership. By contrast, in the Torah there is essentially no human absolute ownership, only possessory, fiduciary authority to varying degrees. All human relationships to material existence, either as to property or as to persons, reflect limited rights, accompanied by correlative duties. Biblical Hebrew itself is a fundamental tool in promoting this consciousness through its lack of a single word which expresses total human ownership, while many words or phrases express the limited rights of a possessor. Thus, Jacob says to Esau, ". . . *yesh li kol*. . . ." "I have all" (Gen.33:11), after having specifically acknowledged that "God has favored me." That is, Jacob was saying that he recognized where ultimate ownership resided, and expressed his connection to his property in terms of a possessory relationship. In his claim that he has "*kol*," the Torah is playing Jacob's words off against its own prior declaration in Gen 24:1, that "God blessed Abraham with all (*baKol*). Thus, all property, all human possession, derives from God's blessing. Interestingly, Jacob, used the same phrase, "God has favored me," in regard to his children (Gen. 33:5), with the Torah thus clearly setting the stage for a fundamental biblical countercultural teaching, of the absence of parental ownership rights in children. "*Yesh li*" is thus a possessory term, not implying the absolute powers of total ownership.

Even the term "*adon*," "master" is used by theTorah specifically in relation to the master of a Jewish servant—in whom the Torah clearly vests no rights of disposal, only rights to service, combined with correlative duties (Exodus 21:4). Similarly, the use of the term "*adon*" as a description of the master of a female Jewish indentured servant (as in Exodus 21:8) is distinctively associated with the expectation of marriage, the denial of the master's rights to sell her to others, or to deny her marital rights if he does marry her and subsequently takes yet another wife. The rights of this master are limited, and are clearly accompanied by a set of duties. It is not accidental that when the Torah in this same chapter treats the status of the non-Jewish slave (Exodus 21:26-27), the owner is not even honored with the title "*adon*," and his rights in his slave are vigorously limited by the verses which mandate the liberation of the slave, either male or female, upon the slave being assaulted by the owner in a manner which results in loss of an eye or even a tooth.

It is striking that that very same passage in the Torah also used transactional terms to describe the acquisition and sale of indentured servants: "*ki tikneh eved ivri*," ["when you acquire a Hebrew slave"] (Exodus 21:2), and "*vekhi yimkor ish et bito le'amah*," ["when a man sells his daughter as a slave"] (Exodus 21:7). The use of these transactional terms, "*kana*" and "*makhar*," specifically in regard to the acquisition or sale of fellow Jews into servitude, is a powerful indication that these terms themselves are not indicative of absolute ownership. Rather, the words "*kana*" and "*makhar*" are merely terms which indicate the transfer of rights in an agreement, a transaction between persons, without reference to the particular rights being transferred, and without reference to the accompanying duties which are being assumed. But the underlying assumption remains that there are no acquisitions of rights by persons, over either property or persons, which are not accompanied by correlative duties—that is, there is no absolute ownership vested in humans.

As for the use of the term "*ba'al*" (or "*ba'alut*" in modern Hebrew) to express the notion of ownership, such is clearly not reflective of the use of that term in the Torah where it appears primarily in relation to the status of a husband (e.g. Exodus 21:3). Whatever disadvantages a wife might have under Biblical Law, she is not the property of her husband! A husband is granted no right to injure or assault his wife, no right to steal or damage her property, and certainly no right to transfer her by sale or rental to another person. In fact, statutory regulation of the marital relationship is quite sparse in Torah, and a primary focus is on the husband's duties to provide food clothing and sexual satisfaction to his wife, rather than on his rights (e.g. Exodus 21:10). Aside the consensual sexual relationship, the Torah provides a husband with no greater rights over his wife's person or property than what he might acquire in any legal contractual relationship with another unrelated person. "*Ba'alut*" in Torah is a complex relationship involving many presumptions as to the intent of parties and as to their mutual rights and duties when they enter into the marital relationship, but it is unequivocally not ownership.

This awareness of the limited nature of human ownership is central to the second dimension of the covenantal relationship between God and each individual Jew. But beyond this understanding of the relationship to material "stuff," the covenantal consciousness extends to the nature of the productive capacity as well. The offering of first-born cattle in our passage is just one instance of a broad pattern in Torah in which the first product of virtually all productive engagement must be offered to God in recognition that God was and remains the primary source of all productive capacity in life. Thus, the first fruits need to be offered, the first sheaves of the grain harvest need to be offered, the first born of cattle as well as the first born of human male children need to be offered or redeemed, the first month needs to be acknowledged and the first day of the New Year needs to be sanctified. All productive energies in the material world need to be consciously linked to the recognition of God as the source of all productive transformation of the material world.

It is this expanded consciousness of the nature of the relationship between the individual and his material being that occupies central place in this second dimension of the covenantal relationship. That's why the paragraph of "*Vehaya ki yeviakha*" reminds us of the commandment of wearing Tefillin. The very first element of the symbolic meaning of Tefillin is that it serves as a sign and as a reminder that the process of entry into covenantal relationship with God requires the utter transformation of the individual's inner emotional and spiritual identity; divesting oneself of all pagan emotional and spiritual beliefs, feelings and values in order to ready the mind, the heart and the soul for undertaking the covenantal mission of holiness. This second element in the symbolic meaning of Tefillin is that it serves as a sign and a reminder ("*ot*" and "*totafot*") that the process of entry into covenantal relationship with God also requires the utter transformation of the individual's consciousness, and thereby of his outer conduct, in regard to the material world of objects and persons—the realization that everything ultimately belongs to God, even the very human powers which were utilized in the productive process.

C. Deuteronomy 11:13-21, *Vehaya im shamo'a. . . .*

The thrust of this paragraph in the Torah is simple and unequivocal—the continued material existence of the Nation Israel in its Land is dependent upon the nation fulfilling its covenantal responsibilities to God. As it is wont to do, the Torah spells out the contract in the form of "*Tenai kaful,* " presenting "both sides of the conditions" and their consequences, in the form of: If. . . , then . . . ; But if . . . , then . . . .

Thus, an outline of the two alternatives presented to the Jewish people is as follows:

THE FULFILLED COVENANT	THE BREACHED COVENANT
v. 13. If	**v. 16.**Beware, **If**
you listen	your heart is seduced
And Love God	and turn away from God
And worship Him	and worship foreign gods
With all your heart	
And all your body;	and bow your bodies to them.
v.14. Then	**v. 17. Then** God will be angry with you
I will provide timely rain	There will be no rain
And you will harvest your crops	The Land will not yield its produce
v. 15. Your cattle will have pasture	
And you will eat and be sated.	You will be banished from the Land

The passage concludes with a Divine instruction as to what is needed in order to assure the continuous and eternal material existence of the Jewish nation on its Land, as follows:

v. 18. You must firmly establish this understanding of your covenantal responsibilities in your inner identity, your heart and soul, and in your outer being, your body, through the following instrumentalities:

1. Bind these ideas (of covenant) on your arm and on your head (Tefillin).
2. **v. 19.** Study these ideas and
3. Teach them to your children.
4. Recite these ideas twice daily, night and morning.
5. **v. 20** Write these ideas on the doorposts of your homes and cities.

It is vital to note that the instrumentalities through which the assurance of the material well being of the nation Israel can be achieved, the instrumentalities of continuity, are all forms of externalization of inner convictions. The inner state alone, knowledge and beliefs and feelings are insufficient to assure National continuity—they need to be expressed in ways that allow for transmission, through words declared aloud and taught and written in public places, through symbolic objects which represent the ideas, worn visibly on the body.

This in turn is the essential meaning of the third term of liberation used by God in Exodus 6:6, "*vega'alti*," ["I will redeem you"]. *Geulah* is the transformation of a band of individuals or of families into a Nation. *Geulah* is the shift from individuals with commonly held beliefs to a Nation which can actualize its vision of truth and justice in its own homeland in expression of its own autonomy and self-governance. *Geulah* arrives at the point in time when inner convictions as to values and virtues are transformed into public policies through which the ideals of the polity are implemented in the daily life of the society. *Geulah* is a demonstrative state in which all peoples can see that a Nation-State exists with its own unique identity, seeking to achieve God's vision of Holiness beyond the confines of individual lives, but expressed in the very character of the State.

It is precisely that striving for holiness in the material fabric of the Nation in its outer, public identity and character, that constitutes the third dimension of the covenant between God and the Jewish People.

Maimonides, in Book III, chapter 27 of The Guide to the Perplexed presents a vital argument about the nature of Mitzvot. Rambam there contends that every single commandment of the Torah serves some human purpose, disputing the position of those who maintained that some of the Mitzvot were a-rational—having no purpose other than to demonstrate human obedience to God. Rambam further contends that all Mitzvot serve one or more of three general purposes. One purpose is to inculcate Truth and to help people avoid belief in falsehoods; thus e.g., the command to believe in the Unity of God and the prohibition against belief in various forms of magic. A second purpose is to help people inculcate noble virtues and to help them avoid the development of debased personality qualities; thus, e.g., the commands to love neighbors and immigrants, and the prohibition against hating others in our hearts. The third purpose inherent in God's commandments, Rambam contends, is to make possible the development of a just social order and to avoid cruelty and injustice in society.

The Rambam denominates the first of these purposes as the striving for the perfection of the soul, while the latter two purposes he describes as the process through which Torah attempts to aid us in the achievement of the perfection of the body—of the material reality of human social existence. In a striking comment, he asserts that while the perfection of the soul is an innately more noble aspiration, the perfection of the body has priority in time—it must be achieved first in order for the perfection of the soul to become possible. Thus, according to Rambam, all spiritual strivers must recognize that the achievement of a just society, one in which Torah principles of responsibility and fairness, of kindness and justice, of tolerance and of the shared human nature of being created in the Divine image, are honored and actualized, is a precondition for the achievement of perfection of the soul.

The very first expectation of the covenantal relationship between God and the Jewish people was the striving for Individual Spiritual transformation. The second expectation was the striving for Individual Material transformation. Now we can see the shift which takes place as we approach the third dimension of the covenantal relationship: it demands of us a striving for National Material transformation. If the first layer required us to discover holiness in our integration of God's qualities in our inner lives, and the second demanded that we manifest holiness in our understanding of our relationship to the material world of objects and persons, then this third layer calls upon us to unfold the qualities of God's holiness in the ways in which we seek justice in the material governance of autonomous Jewish society.

D. Deuteronomy 6:4-9, *Sh'ma . . . . Ve'ahavta . . . .*

The fourth passage of the Torah which contains the commandment of the wearing of Tefillin is, for Jews, perhaps the most famous single paragraph of the entire Torah. Its opening sentence, "Hear Yisrael, the Lord our God, the Lord is One," has been recognized through the ages as the Divine call to the Jewish People to accept the belief in the absolute Unity of God. This verse stands together with the first of the Ten Commandments as the central starting point of National Jewish spiritual awareness. It is for that reason that the verse became the cry of Jewish martyrs throughout the ages.

Why do I assert that this passage represents National Jewish awareness rather than Individual or personal spiritual understanding? The word "Yisrael" appears in the Torah with two meanings. It is the name which the "man" who wrestles with him grants to Jacob after his return to the land of Canaan (Genesis 32:28), and which God confirms to him after his return to the town of Beth El (Genesis 35:10). Yisrael thereafter becomes the name of the Nation (Genesis 48:20) which is used regularly throughout the rest of the Bible, in alternation with the terms B'nai Yisrael or Beit Yisrael. So, while

Yisrael can throughout time refer either to Jacob-Yisrael or to the Nation-Yisrael, it never appears as the identification of an individual Jew unless he is identified as "*Ish Yisrael*" ["A man of Yisrael"] (e.g., Numbers 25:8, Deuteronomy 27:14), or once as "*Ish HaYisraeli*" and "*Isha HaYisraelit*" (Leviticus 24:10-11). In this latter form, the word Yisrael is still a reference to the Nation. The more frequent term used in Torah to describe an individual Jew is "*Ivri* (e.g., Exodus 2:11, Deuteronomy 15:12). No wonder then that Jonah, being asked for his national identity responds, "*Ivri anokhi*," "I am an Ivri…." (Jonah 1:9).

What exactly is the covenantal mutuality which is constituted in this paragraph? The covenant is actually fully contained in the first two sentences. The following three sentences are the instructions as to how this covenant shall be represented and transmitted, parallel to the similar structure in the paragraph of "*Vehaya im shamo'a*." In explaining the opening verse, virtually all Jewish commentary operates with the assumption that the Unity of God is taught as a way of clarifying that despite the fact that God manifests Himself through many diverse qualities and characteristics, He remains One. This verse is in effect the balance to God's expression in the following conversation between Moses and God. In Exodus 33, Moses asks God for the ability to "know" Him, to experience His direct "Presence" (Exodus 33:13 and 18). God's response is to reveal to Moshe the thirteen Divine Names which express His relational qualities: *Hashem, Hashem, El, Rahum, Hanun, Erekh Apayim, Rav Hesed, Emet; Notzer Hesed LeAlaphim, Nosei Avon, (Nosei) Phesha, (Nosei) Hata'ah, Nakei.* (While there is much rabbinic debate as to exactly where in the passage the Divine Names actually begin and end, the above list is the most commonly accepted list, and is deeply embedded in Jewish liturgical texts.)

The meaning of these Names is somewhat clouded, but broadly, they refer to the following qualities manifest in God's relationship to the world: God is Productive, Adaptable, Powerful, Nurturing, Loving and Patient; He Individualizes Kindness, is Truthful, manifests Gratitude, is Tolerant of Wrongdoing, Tolerant of Rebellion, Tolerant of Error, and is Just. Both the Ten Commandments and Sh'ma respond to the possible false conclusion that there are multiple deities by declaring at the outset that despite this multiplicity of Qualities, God is One. But the opening declaration of the Sh'ma is then predicated on our prior awareness of the problem; that is, on our prior awareness of this very multiplicity of Divine *Midot*.

The significance of the disclosure of these Divine qualities resides not only in our being enabled to achieve correct understanding of God, but in our awareness of the fact that God desires us to emulate these qualities in our relationship to the world. It is this which Rambam was expressing when he referred to one of the three fundamental purposes of the whole of Torah as being the formation of human *Midot*—personality qualities. Human *Midot* need to be formed in direct imitation of the Thirteen Divine *Midot*!

The Jewish liturgical emphasis on the Thirteen Divine qualities, *Midot*, is not just a mantra to be repeatedly chanted or sung. The repetition of these verses in the Selichot, the penitential prayers of the month of Elul, and the Ten Days of Repentance, in the evening services at the start and end of Yom Kippur, on holidays before the reading of the Torah, and for some even in the daily Tahanun (penitential prayer following the Amidah), is the essential declaration of the Torah's Agenda for Jewish National Spiritual Transformation.

The correlative Jewish duty which emerges from the affirmation of the Unity of God, and from God's having revealed to us the *Midot* through which he relates to all of existence, is the body of the second sentence of this paragraph— "*Ve'ahavta* . . . ": "you shall love the Lord your God with all your heart, all your body and all your possessions." Rambam in *Mishneh Torah* (*Yesodei HaTorah* 2:2), and in *Sefer HaMitzvot* (Positive Commandment 2), emphasizes that the love of God derives from the knowledge of God's word and of his actions in the material world. The love which flows from such knowledge then demands expression through our representing the Goodness of God to the rest of the world. A lover is driven to want others to understand and love the object of his own love. This then is the covenantal mutuality of the Sh'ma—The One God reveals His essential *Midot* to us, and we, in our Love of Him, enact His *Midot* in the community of nations in a way that brings others also to share our Love of God. This is the culminating element in our covenantal relationship with God.

This very same mutuality is expressed in the fourth and final expression of redemption in Exodus 6:7: "*Velakahti etkhem li le'am* . . . " "And I will take you unto Me as a nation, and I shall be unto you as God, and you shall know that I am the Lord your God. . . ." The word "*velakahti*," "I will take you," is the word which the Torah uses to describe the consummation of a marriage. Thus, for example, the Torah provides an exemption from military service in a discretionary war for a man who has entered into contract of marriage, "*eiras isha*," but not yet consummated the marriage, "*velo lekaha*." (Deuteronomy 20:7). (The rabbinic term for the second ceremony, marking the permissibility of consummation, is "*Nessuin*.") The verse in Exodus 6:7 continues to indicate that this relationship is characterized by "knowing

God," an indication of the intimacy achieved in union, as in Genesis 4:1, "and Adam knew his wife Chava, and she became pregnant and gave birth to Cain. . . ."

Having propounded the elements of the covenant in verses 4 and 5, the paragraph of Sh'ma then continues with a Divine instruction as to what is needed in order to assure the achievement of this Jewish National Spiritual transformation, as follows:

1. **v. 6**: Make this covenantal affirmation part of your inner identity.
2. **v. 7** : Teach this vision to your children, and
3. Recite the affirmation twice daily, each night and morning.
4. **v. 8** Bind this affirmation (of Covenant) on your arm and on your head (Tefillin).
5. **v. 9** Write it on the doorposts of your homes and cities.

Tefillin then serves as one of the essential instrumentalities through which all four of the dimensions of the Covenant between God and the Jewish people is manifest.

1. *Individual Spiritual*. The very first expectation of the covenantal relationship between God and the Jewish people was the striving for Individual Spiritual transformation. That first layer required us to discover holiness in our integration of God's qualities in our inner lives.

2. *Individual Material*. The second expectation was the striving for Individual Material transformation, demanding that we manifest holiness in our understanding of and our relationship to the material world of objects and persons.

3. *National Material*. The third dimension of the covenantal relationship demands of us a striving for National Material transformation. This third layer calls upon us to unfold the qualities of God's holiness in the ways in which we seek justice in the material governance of autonomous Jewish society.

4. *National Spiritual*. The fourth dimension of our covenantal relationship to God is focused on the National Spiritual transformation. This culminating component, in which we achieve a degree of Love of and Unity with God which is comparable in the human sphere to marital consummation, is expressed in the way in which we enact God's *Midot* in the community of nations in a way that brings others also to share our Love of God.

III. *Tefillin As Covenantal Enactment*

How then is all of this embodied in the symbolic actions of wearing Tefillin on our bodies? As we turn now to that issue, we will attempt to resolve all of the questions about the oddities of the Tefillin which we raised at the beginning of this paper.

The binding of the Tefillin on the upper arm, close to the heart, is the symbolic representation of awareness of the personal inner Jewish covenant that exists between that individual and God, as represented in the Torah passages contained within the *bayit*. The act of binding the *bayit* in place is a commitment to shape inner feelings and consciousness in a way that reflects the vision of holiness taught in the covenant.

The *retzuah*, the strap, which runs through the base of the *bayit* is then wound seven times around the forearm, because it links the inner holiness of the individual to his use of his material senses and powers in the concrete world. Thus, the winding seven times serves as a reminder of the created world, formed by God in seven periods of time, and thus as a representation of the human powers of productivity through which we humans continue the Divine process of moving the world in the direction of God's holiness. The act of winding the strap represents the dedication of those powers to use in expression of the inner values of holiness. (This answers question 4: Why is the *retzuah* (leather strap) of the *bayit* on the arm wrapped around the forearm seven times?)

It is obvious then why this element of the binding of Tefillin remains covered. The essence of the covenant being symbolized thus far has to do with the personal nature of the covenant, both in its inner and in its outer components. The individual covenant with God, both in its spiritual dimension and in its material dimension, require Tzni'ut, humility—that is, the knowledge of one's proper place in God's world. That's why the Sages are so expansive in their application of the concept of Tzni'ut. Of course there is Tzni'ut in dress and in sexual conduct, but they also identify the propriety of Tzni'ut in how one walks and talks, in how a home is designed and furnished, in how one relates to his or her own bodily functions, and even how one conducts government and war. In all of the realms of normal life, the knowledge of how the covenant with God impacts on both the spiritual and the material, on both the inner and the outer elements of life, is the essence of Tzni'ut. It is precisely that attentiveness to the impact of the covenant that enables one to be "*hatzne'a lekhet im Elokekha,*" to "walk humbly with your God" (Micah 6:8). It is that wisdom of the boundaries of the covenant which is both the reward and the source of Tzni'ut—humility (viz. Proverbs 11:2).

(This answers question 5: Why is it common custom to cover the Tefillin on the arm?)

With the first two elements of the covenantal relationship having been enacted in the positioning of the Tefillin on the arm, we are ready to move to the placement of the Tefillin on the head. The Rabbis insist that the verse in Deuteronomy 28:10, "All the Nations of the earth will see that the name of God is proclaimed upon you, and they will be in awe of you," is a hidden reference to the Tefillin upon the head. Why do they make this particular association? The Rabbis understood that the *bayit* of the Tefillin upon the head was an embodiment of that element of the covenant between God and the Jewish Nation through which the Jewish Nation testified publicly to the national transformation of its material being achieved through its implementation of the values of God's holiness in its national character. That's why the *bayit* of the Tefillin of the head has inscribed on both sides the letter Shin, the first letter of the Divine Name "Shaddai." The letter is written in both forms of writing, the three-headed writing jutting out from the surface, and the three-headed letter carved into the surface, therefore appearing as if it has four heads. (This answers question 7: Why does the *bayit* on the head have forms of the Hebrew letter Shin marked in the leather on both sides of the *bayit*? And question 8: Why does the Shin on one side of the *bayit* have four heads instead of the "correct" three?)

It is precisely because the intent of the *bayit* on the head is to communicate outward, publicly, to the external world, that it may not be covered, in contrast to the *bayit* on the arm which is intended to represent the private elements of the covenant and is therefore covered. That also explains why the straps descending from the *bayit* on the head, by custom, extend to the stomach and the sexual organ—for the activities of eating and sexual conduct are essential elements of the way in which a nation manifests its connectedness to the realm of holiness in Divine governance. The values which are manifested in the consumption of foods, and the values which inhere in sexual conduct, are distinctive markers, evident to the entire world, of the holiness quotient of a culture. The Jew, placing Tefillin on his head, with the *retzuot* marking the public linkage between the National Material dimension of the covenant and his personal conduct in these areas of life, affirms the holiness to which he and the nation aspire. (It is not accidental that the Torah emphasizes the holiness of the Jewish People, and provides the distinctive motive clause of "for I the Lord your God am Holy," particularly for these two areas of human conduct, the dietary laws and sexual behavior; viz. Leviticus 11: 44-45, and 20:26.) (This answers question 9: Why is it common custom specifically to not cover the *bayit* worn on the head? And question 10: Why is there a common custom that the *retzuot* which descend from either side of the *bayit* on the head are of two different lengths, one ending approximately at the navel, the other at the groin?)

In the context of the private covenantal awareness, the individual placing the *bayit* of the Tefillin on his arm is presumed to know that the box contains four separate Torah portions, each of which addresses a different dimension of the covenantal relationship. Therefore, the *bayit* itself has a single open area within it, all the four *parshiyot* are written on a single strip of parchment which is rolled, inserted into the open compartment and then sewn closed. However, the public role of the *bayit* worn on the head requires that the structure itself manifest to the observer that it contains four separate Torah passages. Therefore, the folds in the animal skin which forms the *bayit* separate the interior into four narrow compartments which are evident in the outer structure. Each of the four Torah passages is written on a separate strip of parchment, consisting of exactly four lines, which is then folded and inserted into one of the four compartments of the *bayit*, which is then sewn closed. (This answers question 1: The Torah commands the use of two *batim* (boxes, literally "houses"), one placed on the muscle of the arm, the other on the very front of the head just above the hairline, each containing the four portions of the Torah in which the commandment of Tefillin is found. Why are the four Torah portions written on a single rolled parchment to be inserted into the *bayit* on the arm, while the same four portions are written on separate pieces of parchment to be folded into distinct compartments within the *bayit* on the head? And question 2: Why is the distinct inner structure reflected in the external structure? That is, why is it that the *bayit* on the arm is visibly a single unit, while the *bayit* on the head is visibly divided into four segments?)

One further element of the *bayit* on the head requires explication. In which direction in the *bayit* are the four passages arranged, from right to left or left to right? Since Hebrew is written from right to left, one would assume that the order of the passages would be from right to left of the person wearing the Tefillin. What are we to make then of the fact that the correct order is from left to right of the person wearing them? Interestingly, a parallel question arises in regard to the order of arrangement and lighting of the ascending number of candles each of the eight days, to fulfill the rabbinic commandment of Chanukah lights. In that instance, the codes of Jewish Law record two alternative practices. In the most common custom, lights are added each day from right to left, and then lit from left to right, with the "newest" location being thus lit first each night. In a second custom, the lights are added each day from left to right, and then are lit from right to left, so that in this practice as well, the light in the "newest" location is lit first on each day.

Why this alternation of direction in each of the customs? The central issue is that the lighting of lights for Chanukah has a dual purpose. The lighting is intended to serve as a reminder to those within the household, of the miraculous nature of the Divine aid which enabled the Jewish forces to defeat the Syrian Greek armies, and to restore the purity of the desecrated Temple (symbolized by the miracle of the oil and with all of the attendant associations with the significant notions of national and religious liberty). But this act of lighting is also intended to communicate our faith in the covenant between God and the Jewish people outward to the general population. Much of the law regulating this act of lighting is dictated by the need to assure that this dual purpose is achieved. It is for this reason that the lights must be lit in a place which is visible to bypassers; that they must be lit after dark but before pedestrian traffic ceases; that we recite two separate blessings, one over the mandated nature of the act and the other over the "*pirsum ha'nes*," the publicizing of the miracle. It is for this reason that the lights cannot be lit in a circle, so that passersby will be able to discern separate lights (as in the menorah of the Temple) rather than seeing them as a large torch of lights.

It is for this reason that the alternation of direction is essential. Right to left is the direction of communication, but since Chanukah lights need to communicate both within to those lighting, and outward to those observing, two separate acts are emphasized: the addition of lights and the lighting of the lights, one done from right to left of those within the home, and one done from right to left of the observers from outside. Thus, the actions emphasizes to the person performing the act that his or her intention is to achieve both forms of communication.

With this we can now return to the practice in regard to the arrangement of Torah passages in the *bayit* on the head. The order is not, in reality, from left to right. It is from right to left—but the right to left of the observer rather than of the bearer of the Tefillin. For, as we have seen, the central purpose of the *bayit* on the head is to communicate to the external world, to the observer, that the covenantal relationship between God and the Jewish People is intended to transform the outer conduct of the Jewish Nation in its relationship to the material world—in its manifestation of holiness, of God's values, enacted in relation to persons and to property. (This answers question 15: In which direction within the *bayit* on the head are the four Biblical passages arranged, and why is that significant?)

Having begun the process of putting on the Tefillin with the *bayit* on the upper arm and the *retzuah*, the strap, on the forearm, why is it the practice to interrupt that winding at the palm to put the other *bayit* on the head before returning to complete the wrapping of the *retzuah* around the fingers and then up to the palm again? For that matter, why didn't we just begin the performance of the mitzvah by placing the Tefillin on the head and then place the Tefillin on the arm in a single sequence, without interrupting in the middle?

The wearing of Tefillin is not simply a symbolic reminder of the covenant, it is a daily symbolic reenactment of the process by which the Jewish People entered into that covenant through their experience of the events surrounding the Exodus. The sequence of events which shaped that transformation of individuals and tribes into a Holy Nation is exactly what God promised that he would do in Exodus 6:6-7, when he said, …*vehotzeiti* (I will take you out), *vehitzalti* (I will rescue you), *vega'alti* (I will redeem you), and *velakahti etkhem li le'am* (I will take you unto me as a nation). As we have previously seen, these four terms of redemption represent the four separate stages of the process of transformation, which are reflected also in the four paragraphs of the Torah in which the command of Tefillin is found, and which are enclosed within each of the *batim* of the Tefillin. The order of these terms is not random. The order represents a necessary sequence in the process of transformation, as follows:

– *vehotzeiti* (I will take you out), represents individual spiritual transformation;

– *vehitzalti* (I will rescue you), represents individual material transformation;

– *vega'alti* (I will redeem you), represents national material transformation; and

– *velakahti* (I will take you unto me) represents national spiritual transformation.

Each of these stages occurred in the historic experience of the Jewish people at the time of the Exodus. Individual spiritual transformation was represented by the setting aside and then the offering of the sheep as Pascal lamb. Individual material transformation was experienced in the actual departure from Egypt. National Material redemption was the experience of the Jewish Nation crossing the Sea of Reeds and seeing the Egyptian army drowned behind them. And, as we have seen, these first three stages in the process of transformation are symbolically embodied and reenacted in the first three actions in the placement of Tefillin, the tying of the *bayit* on the arm; the winding of the *retzuah* around the arm; and the binding of the *bayit* on the head. That is why the Tefillin on the arm had to precede the placement of the Tefillin on the head. (This answers question 3: Why is the *bayit* placed on the arm prior to the positioning of the *bayit* on the head?)

The fourth term of redemption, *velakahti etkhem li le'am* (I will take you unto me as a nation), representing National Spiritual Transformation, is fulfilled in the Giving of the Torah to the Jewish People at Mt. Sinai, which marked the culmination of the process of redemption—the entry into the contract of marriage between God and the Jewish Nation. This component of the covenantal relationship is enacted in the mitzvah of Tefillin by the winding of the *retzuah* around the fingers, as marital rings, while reciting the verses in Hosea 2:21-22, in which God declares his eternal marriage to the Jewish Nation, "I espouse you to Me forever, I espouse you to Me with righteousness and with justice and with goodness and with mercy. And I espouse you to Me with faithfulness, and you shall know the Lord." The winding of the strap around the fingers represents the three Divine declarations of espousal, and their accompanying Divine virtues to be achieved through the marriage. The phrase "and you shall know the Lord," "*veyada'at et Hashem*," is enacted by the completion of the wrapping of the strap around the back of the hand to form the Hebrew letter Shin, thus inscribing God's name directly on the body. In varied Ashkenazic and Sephardic customs, one or another representation of the name of God is inscribed, or worn, on the body through combinations of letters formed on the *bayit*, in the knots of the *retzuot* and/or in the windings of the *retzuah* on the arm or hand. This binding of God's name on the body suggests our attempt to achieve the closest we can come to bodily marital union with God.

This concluding stage of the process of redemption, of the total transformation of the descendents of Jacob into the Nation Israel, could only happen after the first three stages had been achieved. Therefore, in the Tefillin reenactment of the process of redemption, the winding of the *retzuah* around the fingers could only happen after the third element had been performed—that is, after the *bayit* on the head had been properly situated and experienced. (This answers question 6: Why is the wrapping of that *retzuah* interrupted before completion, wrapped around the middle of the hand, and the *bayit* then placed on the head, before completion of the wrapping of the *retzuah* around the fingers and palm?, question 11: What is the significance of the particular manner of wrapping of the *retzuah* around the fingers and middle of the hand? and question 12: Why, when wrapping around the hand, do we recite the verses of Hosea 2:21-22?)

A chart of the elements of the process of redemption which we have been analyzing will help us see them more clearly, and will identify a singular oddity which will in turn introduce us to the final stages of our deliberation.

THE PROCESS OF REDEMPTION

Term of Redemption	Event of Redemption	Stage in the Process	Enactment in Tefillin	Torah Passage in the Tefillin
Vehotzeiti	Pascal lamb	Individual-Spiritual	*bayit* on arm	*Kadesh*
Vehitzalti	Exodus	Individual-Material	*retzuah* on forearm	*Vehaya ki yeviakha*
Vega'alti	Sea of Reeds	National-Material	*bayit* on head	*Vehaya im shamo'a*
Velakahti	Torah at Sinai	National-Spiritual	*retzuah* on fingers	Sh'ma

The single oddity which becomes evident in this chart is the disparity between the order of the elements of redemption as presented in the four terms of redemption, and in the actual putting on of the Tefillin, as opposed to the order of those same four elements as reflected in the biblical sequence of the paragraphs in which the mitzvah of Tefillin is commanded. The first two paragraphs in the Tefillin are in proper sequence as they appear in the text of the Torah, and they correspond perfectly to the initial two terms of redemption and their meanings in Exodus 6:6. But, Sh'ma appears in Deuteronomy 6:4-9, while *Vehaya im Shamo'a*, appears only later, in Deuteronomy 11:13-21, and so they appear in the order of passages in the *batim* of the Tefillin; Sh'ma comes third, not last. The passages in the Tefillin reflect precisely the same content, the same inner meaning as the four terms of redemption, but in the order of their presentation in the Torah, it appears that National Spiritual transformation precedes rather than follows National material transformation!

The order of passages which is most commonly present in Tefillin in contemporary times is the one in which in fact Sh'ma precedes *Vehaya im shamo'a*, since the sequence of passages is determined by their order in the Torah. This, however, was not always universally accepted as the ideal order. The evidence from Qumran and Masada indicates the possibility that during the first century before the Common Era, at least two versions of the order of passages in Tefillin were present. While there is no conclusive evidence related to the Talmudic period, during Gaonic times there was recognition that while the biblical sequence was the common order in Palestinian

Tefillin, the order commonly used in Babylonian and Spanish communities shifted the order of Sh'ma and *Vehaya im shamoa*. The Palestinian order is consonant with the later position of Rashi, the great early medieval Ashkenazic commentator to both Torah and the Talmud, and of Rambam, the great Sephardic codifier of Jewish Law and seminal Jewish philosopher. However, Rashi's grandson, Rabbi Jacob Tam, held in consonance with the Babylonian practice: that the order of the latter two passages is to be inverted, so that Sh'ma would come last, after *Vehaya im shamo'a*, instead of third. What is this ancient and persistent debate about?

In regard to individual redemption, there seems to be no debate that inner, spiritual transformation needs to precede outer, material transformation in order for the covenantal purposes of holiness to be achieved. Put differently, to gain a stable and transmittable material change which embodies the Divine qualities of holiness, the inner person must be transformed. Without *kavannah*, a sense of purposive spiritual drive, outer behavior of a mechanical nature has little if any sustainability. Therefore, not only the Jews who had been enslaved in Egypt, but every generation of Jews have to work on their inner, spiritual identity in order to eventually achieve a full and meaningful transformation of their external, material existence. This is reflected in the order of the first two Terms of Redemption and the events which they echo; it is reflected in the order of the passages of *Kadesh* followed by *Vehaya ki yevi'akha*; and it is reflected in the order of the elements in the putting on of Tefillin.

But the matter may not be so simple and clear when it comes to the way in which national redemption is to be achieved. The sequence of Tefillin passages in the Torah, with Sh'ma preceding *Vehaya im shamo'a*, suggests that the order of transformation for the nation is identical to that of the order necessary for the redemption of the individual—that spiritual change must precede material change; inner change must precede outer change. On the other hand, the latter two Terms of Redemption suggest that the national experience may have to be different—that here, the outer, material transformation needs to take place before the inner, spiritual transformation can become rooted in the nation. Not only the Terms of Redemption, but the events which they reflect—the splitting of the Sea of Reeds, followed by the giving of the Torah at Sinai—confirm the shift in the necessary order in regard to the national experience. Similarly, the actual way in which Tefillin are placed on the body, with the *bayit* being placed on the head before the *retzuah* rings are wound around the fingers, suggests a radical reordering in the quest for national redemption as opposed to individual redemption.

The Babylonian approach to the order of passages in the Tefillin, the approach then adopted by Rabbenu Tam and preserved in some practices to this day, is an attempt to bring all four columns of our Process of Redemption chart into conformity. By the slight shift of the order of the last two Torah passages, by placing *Vehaya im shamo'a* before the paragraph of Sh'ma—out of the order in which the passages appear in the Torah itself—this approach of Rabbenu Tam, and his antecedents, has the effect of enabling the inner message of the order of passages conveying the same message as the actions of putting on the Tefillin. This alteration results in the uniformity of expression that national redemption differs from individual redemption: that the former requires the outer, material transformation to take place before the inner, spiritual redemption can be completed.

Without belaboring the point, it is important to recognize that in at least one other essential area of religious life this consciousness of the difference between individual and national transformation is prominent. The weekday Amidah consists of three sections: it starts with three blessings of Praise, it then contains thirteen blessings of Petition, and closes with three blessings of Gratitude. All three of those elements—praise, petition and gratitude—are necessary according to Rambam in order to fulfill the Divine commandment of daily prayer. The middle section is divisible into two sections of six blessings each, and a single summation. Each smaller section of six is further divisible into two sets of three. What then is the content of these sets? The first set of six relates to Individual needs, while the second set relates to National needs. The first three Individual needs are inner, spiritual in character: wisdom, repentance and atonement. The next three Individual needs are outer, material in nature: resolving conflict, health and wealth. The second set of six relate to the needs of the Jewish Nation. They too are divisible into sets of three. Here, the first three relate to National material needs: ingathering of exiles, the establishment of justice and national defense. The next three National needs are the inner, spiritual ones: human models of holiness, Jerusalem as the spiritual center, and the messianic kingdom.

Thus, the weekday Amidah which we repeat three times a day, six days each week, embodies within itself precisely the same distinction between Individual and National Redemption that is reflected in the terms of redemption, in the Events of redemption from Egypt, and in the manner of putting on the Tefillin. No wonder then that Sages during the Second Temple period, others in Babylon and in Spain, and later even in Franco-Germany, might have felt that conceptual consistency required a departure from the order of passages in the Torah, so that the physical structure of the

Tefillin would bear a message consistent with the way they were placed on the body, and consistent with the essential text, the Amidah, which would be recited while the Tefillin were being worn.

Interestingly, it was a modern Gaon, Rabbi Abraham Isaac HaKohen Kook, who saw the relevance of this distinction to the reality of Jewish life. In commenting on the disparity in the Amidah between the order of petitions for Individual needs and those for National needs, Rav Kook argued that the reality of pre-state Palestine demonstrated the perceptiveness of the Amidah. In fact, he maintained, the elements of building of the material state, the ingathering of the exiles, the creation of a just society and the protection of the people from their enemies, were precisely the preconditions for the eventual spiritual flourishing of the Nation. Therefore, he contended, those whose entire life's work appeared to be focused purely on material matters were in reality the essential builders of the foundation for the spiritually perfected Nation that would rise on the very foundation which they laid. His call for profound respect for the seminal work of the "irreligious" *Halutzim* went unfortunately unheeded amongst many of the "religious."

But what then of Rashi and Rambam and the host of others before and after them who insist that the preferable order of the passages in the *batim* of the Tefillin needed to be in consonance with their order of presentation in the text of the Torah, with Sh'ma preceding *Vehaya im shamo'a*? Their position, I believe, is straightforward and equally reasonable. Who says that there is only a single path to the achievement of Jewish National Redemption?! They can easily acknowledge that the four Terms of Redemption, the Events of the Exodus—and even the behavioral pattern in placing the Tefillin on the body—all represent a single, uniform approach to the achievement of the elements of transformation needed for National Redemption. However, the very fact that the latter two passages in each of the *batim* of Tefillin are in the correct biblical order of Sh'ma followed by *Vehaya im shamo'a* demonstrates that National Redemption can also be achieved through the Inner, Spiritual transformation preceding the Outer, Material transformation. The historical events surrounding the Exodus reflect one possible redemptive sequence. But, is it not possible, they might contend, that an alternative pattern is demonstrated in the events recounted in the Books of Ezra and Nehemiah, in which the Spiritual transformation of the Nation, evidenced by the rejection of idolatry and the separation from the pollution of foreign wives, are the essential preconditions for the Material establishment of the Second Jewish Commonwealth?

That being the case, there is particular elegance in the *batim* of the Tefillin representing in their ordering of the biblical passages an alternative approach to the achievement of National Redemption from the approach indicated in the actions of putting on the Tefillin. The diversity of approaches is then built directly into the objects and actions of the mitzvah.

Rambam and Rashi might further argue that one ought not claim even in regard to the achievement of Individual Redemption that the particular sequence indicated, of Inner, Spiritual transformation preceding Outer, Material transformation, is the only or preferred mode of achieving the goal. After all, the Torah itself provides an alternative model when it records the response of the Jewish people to the offer of the Torah at Sinai. The People's response of "*Na'aseh venishma*," "we will obey and we will hear," was understood by the Sages to indicate a readiness for outer, behavioral change to precede inner comprehension of the meaning and purpose of the Divine commandments. It is precisely this understanding which led the Sages to their assertion that "*mitokh shelo lishmah, ba lishmah*": that the performance of mitzvah acts as pure external behavior lacking inner spiritual meaning was still of transcendent value, and would ultimately lead to the desired state of inner transformation as well. This alternative model for Individual Redemption also needs to be sustained as a viable option, just as alternative models for National redemption need to be affirmed. (This is the answer to question 14: What is the significance of the Rabbinic debate as to the proper order of the four Biblical passages within the *batim*?)

There remains one further question to explore. The *Sefer Halakhot Gedolot* lists the two parts of the commandment of Tefillin, the binding on the arm and the binding on the head, as a single mitzvah. By contrast, in his *Sefer HaMitzvot*, Rambam lists each of them as a separate Divine commandment (Positive commandments 12 and 13.) Nahmanides, in his commentary to Rambam's *Sefer HaMitzvot*, explains this debate on essentially technical grounds, with *Halakhot Gedolot* maintaining that in each of the four appearances of this commandment, the two elements always appear in a single verse, and that while the fulfillment can happen with one *bayit* in the absence of the other, that is no different from the ability to perform the mitzvah of tzitzit with only white strings, without the tekhelet. By contrast, Rambam maintains that the two *batim* are separate mitzvot because they are fulfilled in two separate acts, with each being able, therefore, to be done without the other; in contrast to tzitzit, where a single act of putting the garment on with its attendant strings, whether just white or white and blue, necessitates its being only a single mitzvah.

There is, I believe, a further conceptual foundation to this debate between *Halakhot Gedolot* and Rambam. In our prior analysis, we demonstrated that the Tefillin on the arm is essentially an enactment of that element of the covenant with God which has to do with Individual Redemption, while the Tefillin on the head has to do with National Redemption. The central conceptual question which then arises is, are those two forms of redemptive transformation separable elements of the covenant between God and the Jewish People? It is arguably the case that according to Rambam, while the ideal is obviously the full achievement of both Individual and National transformation, each is a mitzvah unto itself. It is possible, within the covenantal relationship for a person to be engaged on one side of that striving but not the other, fulfilling at least one mitzvah in its fullness. By contrast, arguably, the *Halakhot Gedolot* is contending that while there is partial fulfillment of the mitzvah in putting on one *bayit* without the other, doing so is a failure in the fulfillment of the entirety of the single mitzvah. According to him, the unitary character of the mitzvah of Tefillin requires in its fullness an engagement in both the striving for Individual and National Redemption. (This is the answer to question 13: What is the import of the rabbinic debate as to whether the mitzvah of Tefillin should be counted as a single divine commandment or as two separate commandments (one for the application of each Bayit) in the listing of 613?)

IV. Conclusion

The complexity and richness of the mitzvah of Tefillin is itself a reflection of the complexity and richness of the covenantal relation between the Jewish People and God. Tefillin serves as an "*ot*," a symbolic embodiment of the central ideas of the covenant and, thereby, as a cognitive spur to its understanding; and as a "*zikaron*," an affirmation through behavioral enactment of the events through which God and the Jewish People originally entered into that covenant.

Wearing the Tefillin on the body each morning is a way of starting the day with the fulfillment of one, or two, mitzvot (Divine commandments). But it is also much more than that. It is a way of starting the day with consciousness of the mission with which God invested the Jewish People through the covenantal relationship. It is a way of starting the day with an awareness that in all we do, as individuals and as a nation, we must seek to invest reflections of God's holiness in our inner and outer lives, in our spiritual and our material presentations of ourselves within God's world.

JEFFREY S. FOX

"*The Jewish People are My Family*–A Kavvanah *for the* B'rakhah *of* Retseih"

I HAD THE GREAT PRIVILEGE of being a student in Rabbi Weiss' *shiurim* for four years as a member of the pioneering class in the YCT Rabbinical School. At the same time, I was serving as a rabbinic intern at the HIR - The Bayit. The Torah that he taught was deep and meaningful and was able to reach advanced students in yeshiva as well as beginners at the Free Service on Rosh haShana. It is also an honor to learn from him as the Rosh Yeshiva of Yeshivat Maharat, where I benefit from *shiurim* that he has refined over decades.

I found some of his greatest insights were shared through the lens of the siddur, or the *machzor* in particular, or through the lens of prayer in general.[1] Those Torahs may have come in a classic *shiur*, or from the pulpit on Shabbat or *Chag*. Rabbi Weiss' approach to the power of prayer has informed the way that I daven on a regular basis. I would like to take this opportunity to thank my Rebbe and mentor for all that he has given me personally and to Klal Yisrael more broadly.

In tribute to Rav Avi I would like to share an approach to a single tefilah, indeed to a single line of one *b'rakhah* of the Amidah. I hope that through a deeper understanding of the *b'rakhah* of *retseih* we can all learn to live up to his vision that the "Jewish People are my family."

The *b'rakhah* begins: רצה ה' אלקינו בעמך ישראל ובתפלתם - *Be desirous Adonai our God of Your people Israel and their prayers*. This article will seek to unpack this seemingly simple line and conclude with a beautiful approach developed by the Tsaddik from Warsaw, the Ga'on Rabbi Chaim Ya'akov Naftali Zilberberg (1850-1930).[2]

RABBI JEFFREY S. FOX is Rosh Yeshiva of Yeshivat Maharat. He was the first graduate of YCT Rabbinical School, and served as the Rabbi of Kehilat Kesher: The Community Synagogue of Tenafly and Englewood, for nearly seven years. Rabbi Fox lives in Riverdale with his wife, Beth Pepper, and their four sons.

One of the more challenging *b'rakhot* of the Amidah is the *b'rakhah* of *retseih*. The first section of this *b'rakhah* offers the hope that God receive with desire the prayers of the Jewish People. This is the seventeenth blessing of the weekday Amidah and comes on the heels of another *b'rakhah* that appears to address a similar theme.

The *b'rakhah* of *Sh'ma Koleinu* also expresses the hope that God will receive our prayers. What does the *b'rakhah* of *retseih* add that we did not already ask for in the *berakhah* of *Sh'ma Koleinu*? The simplest answer is that first we ask for God to hear and receive our prayers in *Sh'ma Koleinu*, then we move to a bigger request: we ask God to "be desirous [רצה]"of our prayers. Sometimes God may respond in the negative to our prayer, but when God desires to hear from us, the ability to say no is greatly limited.

The seventeenth *b'rakhah* of the weekday Amidah is referred to by Hazal simply as "*Avodah*" [service]." This title appears in three *mishnayot*[3] and in several passages in the Gemara.[4] The midrash gives us more color as to what the actual text of this *b'rakhah* may have been. In two places[5] we see a fragment of the *b'rakhah* Here we encounter the language: *Be desirous* [רצה], *God our Lord and dwell in Zion your city*. Similar language appears as well in a teshuvah of Rav Natronoi:[6]

וששאלתם: בשביל עבודה, היאך אנו אומרין אותה?	And you asked: regarding *avoda*, how should we recite it?
במתיבתא ובבית רבינו שבבבל ובכל מקום שיש בו חכמים, כך אומרין, "רצה י"י אלקינו ושכון בציון עירך מהרה ויעבדוך בניך בירושלים"	In the Yeshiva and in the house of our master in Bavel and in every place in which there are wise ones, this is what they say: "Be desirous God, our Lord, and dwell in Zion your city speedily, and your children will worship you in Jerusalem."

Rav Natronai is confident that this is the only text of the *b'rakhah* that is available. The text of the Midrashim (both the Midrash Vayikra Rabba and Pesikta d'Rav Kehana) seems to be echoed in the Teshuvah of Rav Natronai Gaon. However, by the time we arrived at the siddurim of Rav Sa'adia and Rav Amram Goan, the text became more similar to what we have today.

רצה ה' אלקינו בעמך ישראל ובתפלתם[7] עבודה לדביר בתיך

It seems that we have two different versions of this prayer, both of which begin with the word *retsei*[8] - רצה. The first version is a request of God to desire our prayers and bring *us* back to Jerusalem, while the second version is a request to bring *God* back to Jerusalem.[9] It appears that almost all current siddurim have the former. The first request reflects an anthropocentric approach to prayer, while the second reflects a theocentric approach to worship. Are we reciting these words to perfect ourselves or to perfect the divine realm? This is one of the foundational questions with which every person who takes their prayer life seriously must struggle.[10]

In addition, Rashi, in his commentary on the Bavli in two separate places,[11] makes a surprising claim about the age of this text. In both instances Rashi asserts that this language goes all the way back to the time of the Beit Hamikdash! While we have no witness to the text that is nearly that old, it does point to this prayer as one of the most ancient components of the Amidah.

Fleischer and Langer both emphasize that the word *retseih* appears in nearly every manuscript that is available today. The word *retseih* has significance both in its reference to sacrifices as well as in its own internal meaning.[12] Asking God to desire our prayers is a bold statement.

It is here that Rav Naftali Zilberberg, the Tsaddik of Warsaw, focuses his comment. The concept of Hashem being happy with the Jewish People that Rav Naftali picks up on is the central *kavvanah* of this tefilah.

He begins his commentary with the following parable:

למשל ראובן מבקש ממלך ב"ו בעד שמעון שיהי רצוי אצלו והמלך יודע שראובן עצמו מבזה ומזלזל את שמעון. מובן עד כמה נעשה ראובן אצל המלך לבוז וקלון . . . וכמעט שזה נחשב למורד במלכות שנראה שמחשיב מעלתו והבנתו על מעלת המלך בפרט אם אחר הבקשה הנ"ל עוד דרכו לזלזל את שמעון.

Imagine that Reuven asked from a flesh and blood king that Shimon be desired by the king while at the same time the king knows that Reuven mocks and demeans Shimon. It is understood how Reuven is made into a mockery and an embarrassment before the king. This almost seems like a rebellion against the kingdom because Reuven places his own thoughts on a higher level than the king's—especially if after the request he continues to mock and embarrass Shimon.

The message of this parable is apparent:

נמשל מובן כמה בושה וכלימה לאותם שזה דרכם כסל למו (תה' מט:יד) לבזות חלק גדול מכלל ישראל, זה מבזה בדרך כלל את כל בנ"י הדרים במדינת לטא או בגאליציען או בפרייסען או כל חסידים בדרך כלל או חסידים מרבי זה לחסידים מרבי אחר וכן בהיפוך.

The moral is obvious. How much of a terrible embarrassment is it to those who mock a large portion of the Jewish People. This one mocks all the Jews who live in Lita, or in Galicia or Prussia, or Chasidim in general, or the Chasidim of this or that Rebbe.

He goes on to outline which types of communities he is describing:

קיצור הדבר אלו מבזים את אלו ואלו מזלזלים את אלו וכאו"א מתפלל גם כן בכל יום ג' פעמים רצה ד' אלקינו בעמך ישראל, והרי זאת יודה כל אחד ואחד שכוונת תפילה זו על כל ישראל באין הבדל בין מדינה למדינה או בין חבורה לחבורה. . . .

In short—these mock those and these mock those, and none the less each and every one prays three times a day: "be desirous Adonai our God of Your people Israel." Behold, everyone will agree that the intention of this prayer refers to all of the Jewish People—without distinctions of geography or community. . . .

והרי יש שרגילים לבזות את תפילות חסידים בעבור שמאחרים אף באמת הרבה הרבה מהם שעושים עפ"י דין והתאחרותם רק אם עפ"י דין מותר להתאחר, והרבה הרבה שכוונתם לשמים לתועלת הלימוד וכדומה והרבה והרבה שוגגים גמורים.

For behold there are some that mock the prayers of the Chasidim that are made late in the day even though many of them [the chasidim] in fact follow the law and they only delay in circumstances when it is permissible to delay. And many of them have deep intentions for Heaven to raise up their learning. And many are simply unaware of the law.

. . .כן יש שרגילים לבזות תפילת המקידימים בטענות ותואנות שונות שאין התפילה בהתלהבות ואין הנקיון כראוי כ"כ.

And there are those who are used to mocking the ones who come early to tefilot because their prayers are not with great energy or they are not careful enough about cleanliness.

How embarrassed we must all be, says Rav Naftali:

עד כמה יש לנו להתבייש ולהכלם (מלבד העבודה החמורה והמרה של לשה"ר ושל בזיון ת"ח) מסתירה זו שיש עלינו מני' ובי', שתמיד אנו מבזים חלק גדול מכלל ישראל ואת תפלותיהם ותמיד אנו מתפללין שהש"י ירצה אותם ותפלותיהם , ויש ללמוד מזה מוסר נורא ואיום לשים רסן בפינו.

We must all be so embarrassed and ashamed from this internal contradiction. For we are always mocking a large portion of the Jewish People and their prayers; and we are always praying that Hashem should be desirous of their prayers. We should learn from this an awesome message and place a muzzle over our mouths.

This very simple message, that the Jewish People are ultimately one family is at the core of Rabbi Weiss' rabbinate and, according to Rav Naftali, is the underlying message of the *b'rakhah* of *retseih*.

He concludes his commentary with the following practical recommendation:

וכפי הנראה כוונו אכנה"ג שקודם אמירת ברכה זו נקבע בלבבנו לאהוב את כלל ישראל, יהי' מאיזהו מדינה ומאיזהו חבורה ושל כל מדינה ומדינה.	And it appears that the intention we are meant to have before this blessing according to the Men of the Great Assembly is to implant in our hearts love of the Jewish People regardless of city or group.
שהרי גם המדבר והמזלזל יודע בעצמו שיש בהם (הנדברים) גם מעלות רק בטבעו הרע להשפיל המעלות עדי ארץ ולהגי' החסרונות עד לרום, ובאמת חייבין לעשות בהיפוך להחשיב מעלות הזולת עד מרום אפי' הם קטנות והחסרונות לא נראה כלל.	For the one who mocks certainly knows that within the group of which he speaks there are lofty traits. Rather, it is in his evil nature to lower those traits to the ground and raise up all of their weaknesses to the heavens. And in truth we are required to do just the opposite—to focus on the lofty traits of the other and raise them up even though they may be minor, and the weaknesses we are meant not to see at all.

This *b'rakhah* contains within its opening line the powerful request that God be desirous of our prayers perhaps even despite our own behavior. According to Rav Naftali, the one thing that God will not ignore is hypocrisy. When we pray on behalf of the Jewish People it is unconscionable to then go on to mock large portions or communities with our family.

I would like to offer the concluding words of Rav Naftali as a challenge to all of us to live up to Rabbi Weiss' commitment to the Jewish People as our family:

שקודם אמירת ברכה נקבע בלבבנו לאהוב את כלל ישראל.

That prior to this blessing we implant in our hearts love of the Jewish People.

NOTES

1. Rabbi Weiss recently collected many of those *shiurim* into the magnificent *Holistic Prayer: A Guide to Jewish Spirituality* (New Milford, CT, and Jerusalem: Magid, 2013).
2. He was among the greatest *Dayanim* in Warsaw. He was the disciple of one of the disciples of Rabbi Akiva Eiger, as well as a disciple of Rabbi Yisrael Salanter and the Beit Ha'Levi. He wrote a short *mussar* work and commentary on the siddur called דרכי חיים. The book was printed in Poland the year he passed away. He was a prolific author who also wrote on Gemara, Shulkhan Aruch, Rambam and *Drashot* on the *parasha*.
3. Mishnah, *Rosh Hashanah* 4:5, in the context of the order of the *b'rakhot* of the Amidah for Rosh Hashanah, and then again in the Mishnah, *Tamid* 5:1 regarding

the tefillot of Yom Kippur, and in Mishnah, *Yoma* 7:1.

4. בבלי מסכת ברכות דף יא עמוד ב ודף כט עמוד ב, שבת דף כד עמוד א, מגילה דף יח עמוד א, סוטה דף לח עמוד ב.
5. ויקרא רבה רבה (מרגליות) פרשת צו פרשה ז, פסיקתא דרב כהנא (מנדלבוים) פיסקא כד שובה.
6. תשובות רב נטרונאי גאון ברודי (אופק) אורח חיים סימן לא.
7. The absence of the letter ה from the word עבודה is noteworthy. In the most recent siddur of the Masorati Movement in Israel, they took out the ה in an attempt to limit the overt reference to Temple worship.
8. It is important to note the following alternative text. Beginning from the siddur of Rav Sa'adia Gaon (page 42 in the Davidson, Assaf, Joel Hebrew and Judeo Arabic edition), we are alerted to a minhag whereby this phrase is only recited when there is an obligation to recite Birkat Cohaim. For an encyclopedic summary of this practice from Rav Sa'adia through the *Tur, Orah Haim* 120, see the second volume indices of the siddur of Rav Amram Goan recently published by Ner Israel Rabbinical College, addendum to ch. 62 (pages 669 through 679).
9. For a more lengthy analysis of the textual development of this *b'rakhah*, see the work of Dr. Ezra Fleischer in *Sinai* 60 "לנוסח ברכת עבודה" 5727 (1966/7), 274. For additional work reflecting the texts of the Cairo Geniza, see Yehezkel Luger, *The Weekday Amidah in the Cairo Genizah* [Hebr.] (Jerusalem: Orhot, 2001), 173-183.
10. Rabbi Weiss in the first chapter of *Holistic Prayer* develops this very dichotomy.
11. רש"י מסכת ברכות דף יא עמוד ב ד"ה ועבודה– The gemara in Berachot quoted the Mishna from Tamid 5:1. ועל עבודה ד"ה מסכת יומא דף סח עמוד ב.
12. Rabbi Weiss, in his *Holistic Prayer* (115), speaks of the power of the word רצה that "echoes the hope that we have made God's will our will, that the prayers heretofore recited were said with personal depth and meaning."

DANIEL ROSS GOODMAN

Tritsch-Tratsch Polka: A Cinematic Triptych in Honor of Rabbi Avi Weiss

Daniel Ross Goodman is a Ph.D. candidate in Modern Jewish Studies at the Jewish Theological Seminary (JTS) of America in New York. He received his rabbinic ordination from Yeshivat Chovevei Torah (YCT) Rabbinical School in 2016, where he was editor-in-chief of *Milin Havivin* for three years. He received the Whizin Prize in Jewish Ethics in 2014 and 2015, holds a law degree, and graduated as Valedictorian of the BMP Jewish Studies Program of Yeshiva University.

I. Moral Gravity and Spiritual Audacity: The Ethic of "Choosing Life" in Avraham's Akeidat Yitzhak and Alfonso Cuarón's Gravity

"Do what is right," Rabbi Weiss always taught us, "not what is popular." Rabbi Avi Weiss has lived by this principle of *azut dik'dusha* [spiritual audacity]. And he continues to act as an anchoring force of moral gravity. Rabbi Weiss's moral compass constantly directs us toward Judaism's central religious and ethical ideal: *uvaharta bahayim*, "choose life."

Rabbi Weiss's 5775 (2014) Shabbat Shuva *drashah* [address] was entitled "As the World Confronts Terror: Why the Yom Kippur Theme of Choosing Life is More Critical Than Ever." In this *drashah*, Rabbi Weiss discussed how the story of *Akeidat Yitzhak* [the binding of Isaac] is not, as certain Christological readings would have it, a story that idealizes martyrdom; rather, *Akedat Yitzhak* is a story that exemplifies the meaning of Deuteronomy 30:19's teaching to choose *life*. The binding of Isaac episode, Rabbi Weiss stated, is not about dying for God; the binding of Isaac episode teaches us what it means to *live* for God.

How do we know this? How can we be so sure of the seemingly counterintuitive notion that the *Akeidat Yitzhak* story teaches us what it means to choose *life*? Rabbi Weiss illustrated this *hiddush* [novel explanation] through a rabbinic teaching in *Midrash Tanhuma*. The midrash attempts to fill in some of the missing elements in the story of *Akedat Yitzhak*, an episode whose narrative is enshrouded in a penumbra of ambiguity and whose laconic dialogue wraps a veil of vagueness upon its characters. The *Tanhuma* attempts to pierce the veil of Abraham's unstated motives and unexpressed apprehensions by presenting us with an occurrence that Abraham may have experienced on the way to Mount Moriah:

> While Abraham and Isaac were traveling on the road to Mount Moriah, Satan appeared to Abraham in the guise of an old man and asked him where he was going. Abraham answered, "to pray." The old man asked, "Why then are you carrying wood, fire, and a knife?" Abraham answered, "We may spend a day or two there, and we will kill an animal, cook and eat it."
>
> "Old man," said Satan, "are you out of your mind? You are going to slay a son given to you at the age of one hundred! And tomorrow, when you do, He will tell you that you are a murderer, guilty of shedding your son's blood." Abraham said, "Still, I would obey Him." And Abraham turned away from Satan.[1]

I was not present when Rabbi Weiss delivered this *drashah* at the Hebrew Institute of Riverdale on September 27, 2014 (I was home—which is in western Massachusetts—during that Rosh Hashanah and the subsequent Shabbat), but I was present when Rabbi Weiss delivered an abridged version of this *drashah* at YCT on Sept. 29, 2014 to a full Beit Midrash at YCT. When Rabbi Weiss read the line, "and then the man said to Abraham, '*zaken* [old man]! Why are you suddenly willing to throw away the son that God has promised you, the son of your 100th year?!'", he looked up from the podium, glanced to his left, and made eye contact with me. "Danny," he asked, "why is this 'old man' calling Abraham a *zaken* [old man]?" Somewhat surprised that Rabbi Weiss would cold-call me and put me on the spot—and knowing that he must be asking *me*, and not another Daniel (even though there were five other Daniels at Chovevei at that time), because he was looking at me (and because he was calling me "Danny," even though only two or three other people in the world actually call me "Danny"), all I could muster up was, "Well . . . Avraham was pretty old, too."

"True," said Rabbi Weiss. "But why was *this* zaken calling *Avraham* a zaken?"

Rabbi Weiss paused. "The zaken who was calling *Avraham* a zaken," explained Rabbi Weiss, "was none other than Avraham himself." This 'zaken' that Avraham encountered along the road, Rabbi Weiss explained, was not a real, living, breathing being; rather, this zaken was Avraham's own consciousness. Avraham was speaking to himself. And throughout his three-day journey to Mount Moriah, Avraham was wrestling with himself. He was asking himself, 'can it be . . . can it *really* be . . . that God is asking me to do *this*? To kill my son? To kill a human being? To kill the son, the human being, that God promised me? Can I put an innocent human being to death, when I know that, more than anything else, the God that I stand for, live for, and teach others to believe in, is the God of *life*?'

In a knight's move of midrashic audacity, and *biz'khut* Rabbi Avraham Weiss, I offer the following *midrash* [interpretation] of Alfonso Cuarón's 2013 film *Gravity* as an artistic illumination of the meaning of "choosing life" in the context of Avraham Avinu's *Akeidat Yitzhak*.

• • •

"The heavens are the heavens of God, and the earth has been given to human beings."[2] If ever a literal interpretation of this verse from Psalms has been rendered on film, it is presented in Alfonso Cuarón's riveting *Gravity*.

The indefatigable human will to live, even in hostile environments, has been a persistent theme in Cuarón's work. *Pan's Labyrinth* (2006), a film that

Cuarón produced, dramatized a young girl's struggle to create an inner life for herself while her adult protectors were trying to survive in Franco's repressive Spain. In *Children of Men* (2006), perhaps Cuarón's best effort until *Gravity*, Theo's (Clive Owen) determination in guiding a pregnant woman to safety in a future dystopian world in which women have become infertile served as a cinematic demonstration of what it means to "choose life" (Deut. 30:19). And in *Gravity*, Cuarón goes one step further by exploring the fierce human drive to live in even the most extreme circumstances: outer space.

"Life in space is impossible." These are the film's opening words, and they are written in white font on the pitch-black background of outer space. This tagline immediately frames the type of space movie *Gravity* will be; it will not be a *2001: A Space Odyssey*, wherein human life in space is as harmonious and peaceful as a Strauss waltz. But neither will it depict space as a place of absolute horror in the vein of *Alien*. Though it is a film very much in dialogue with Kubrick's and Scott's classic films—several shots visually reference *2001*, and the motif of the masculine space-cadet heroine appears to be lifted directly from *Alien*—Cuarón's film is not only visually innovative but thematically groundbreaking as well. Rather than recycling *2001*'s or *Alien*'s conceptions of space, *Gravity* depicts space as the biblical Temple in Jerusalem: a place of both beauty and danger.[3] The sights are spectacular, but the slightest human error or natural impediment can lead to catastrophe. In short, this tagline, and the film in general, is a literal explanation of Psalms 115:16; both *Gravity* and Psalms postulate that human beings are simply meant to exist on planet earth, not in outer space. *Gravity* and Psalms 115:16 both imply that the human effort to conquer the heavens is a foolhardy one that, like the construction of the Tower of Babel, will inevitably result in disaster.

In *Gravity*, however, the disaster that imperils the human effort to conquer the heavens originates from the earth, not from space or from some other heavenly realm. While medical doctor Ryan Stone (Sandra Bullock) and astronaut Matt Kowalski (George Clooney) are conducting routine repairs on the Hubble Space Telescope, the Russians shoot down one of their own satellites. Debris from the shattered satellite is propelled into a violent collision course with Stone and Kowalski's shuttle. When the debris collides with the shuttle, Kowalski and Stone are hurtled away from the destroyed shuttle and compelled to embark upon a frantic mission that necessitates the employment of all of their ingenuity and inner strength in order to save their own lives. How they ultimately do so has been the subject of much debate (astrophysicist Neil deGrasse Tyson has poked holes in the scientific accuracy and physical efficacy of the techniques they employ to reach the International

Space Station), but what is significant in *Gravity* is its demonstration of the inner resources human beings possess that propel us to fight for life even in the most desperate of circumstances. If "Judaism and Christianity insist that death must be overcome,"[4] *Gravity* illustrates that the human capacity to overcome death exists even in the harshest regions of outer space.

These regions are displayed in breathtaking splendor by the renowned cinematographer Emmanuel Lubezki, and the moving computer-enhanced photographs of planet earth engender the kind of awe and wonder that the best science fiction films are meant to deliver. The film was originally released in 3D, but the 3D glasses only slightly enhanced the visual pleasure of those already magnificent shots; the three-dimensional photography only truly factored into the viewing experience during the scenes in which space junk seemed to be hurtling directly at us viewers.

The cast of the film, like the space shuttle's crew, is sparse but highly effective. Kowalski is a standard Clooney prototype—suave and über-confident, aware of his powers of attraction upon the opposite sex ("I know I'm devastatingly good looking but you gotta stop staring at me," he deadpans), and endowed with a preternatural degree of sang-froid. As the heard-but-not-seen voice of Houston's mission command, Ed Harris mostly reprises his role as NASA flight director Eugene Kranz in *Apollo 13* (1995) and channels elements of his John Glenn from *The Right Stuff* (1983) in yet another space role; some would add his role as Christof in *The Truman Show* (1998) to this list, though this would be somewhat of a stretch. And in a carefully wrought performance for which she justly garnered an Oscar nomination, Sandra Bullock singlehandedly carries the entire crisp ninety-minute affair. She enables the audience to identify with her extreme anxiety without badgering viewers over the heads with melodramatic hyperventilating—though, in one of the few flaws of an otherwise perfect movie, she does cross this threadbare-thin line at certain points; granted, in what is asked of her in this role, it is a line almost impossible not to cross.

Gravity also suggests that space is like a foxhole: there are no atheists in either place. Or, more precisely, even if there are atheists in space, in certain circumstances, they will still experience a desire to pray. When Stone thinks she's about to die, she wants to pray, but doesn't know how. "No one ever taught me how to pray," she wistfully remarks. In the Russian space shuttle, she sees an icon of Jesus, and in the Chinese shuttle, she sees a figurine of Buddha. Cuarón's camera lingers on these images for a few moments to ensure we don't miss them, as if to say that if Stone is to return to earth, she must believe in *some*thing, whether it is Jesus, Buddha, or her own untapped inner strength—if not the transcendent God without, then perhaps the immanent God within.

In fact, that Stone's discovery of her own inner resources occurs in nearby proximity to the close-ups of these religious icons suggests that she may have, in her own way, discovered God. Like Rabbi Irving Greenberg's interpretation of the Torah as narrative, not history,[5] the theologian Rabbi Neil Gillman reads the Bible's account of the revelation at Sinai not as an historically accurate description of an actual event, but as an attempt to put an ineffable, indescribable moment into words.[6] 'If the ancient Hebrews did not literally hear God at Sinai as the Bible describes,' I asked Rabbi Gillman, 'then what exactly was revealed to them? Do you think they invented God?' A revelation *did* occur, he responded—*some*thing happened in the Sinai desert. But *what* exactly happened, he said, we do not know, and perhaps never will know. During the Hebrews' journey through the unknown, unforgiving Sinai desert, he explained, they culled all of their collective physical, spiritual, and psychological resources in order to survive. And during this process, they discovered strengths about themselves and unknown inner capacities that they never previously imagined they possessed. This, Rabbi Gillman explained, was their revelation of God. Their discovery of their own inner strength *was* their discovery of God: "They did not *invent* God; they *discovered* God, and *invented* the *metaphors*."[7]

In the process of discovering their collective inner strength during the Sinai wilderness, the ancient Hebrews discovered a transcendent God. In the process of accessing inner powers she never imagined she had possessed,[8] Ryan Stone discovers an immanent God in outer space. The metaphor that the Hebrews invented for this discovery of God was the name YHVH (or "Yahweh"); Ryan Stone's invented metaphor for this discovery may be the word "myself." It is this discovery that gives her the further strength to confront her personal Hamletesque quandary:

> I get it, it's nice up here. You could just shut down all the systems, turn down all the lights, just close your eyes and tune out everyone. There's nobody up here that can hurt you. It's safe. What's the point of going on? What's the point of living? . . . It's still a matter of what you do now. If you decide to go then you just gotta get on with it. Sit back, enjoy the ride, you gotta plant both your feet on the ground and start living life. Hey, Ryan, it's time to go home.

How *Gravity* portrays Ryan's manner of addressing her Hamlet dilemma is something that must be seen to be believed—or, perhaps more precisely, it is something that must be believed in order to be seen.

As in *Gravity*, so in the *Akeidah*: just as Stone's conversation with Clooney, we eventually learn, is really a conversation with herself—Clooney is a personification of her own paralyzed consciousness—the Midrash Tanhuma's *zaken* [old man] is a personification of Avraham's perambulating consciousness. Just as, after a harrowing ordeal and a near-death experience, Stone eventually chooses life, so too, after a harrowing three-day journey and the near-death of Isaac, Avraham eventually chooses life as well.

I wish to conclude with the following *drash*. It may be a bit audacious, but if I have learned anything from Rabbi Weiss, it is that if you believe you are right, you most not concern yourself with popularity. And the following *drash*, I believe—if Rabbi Weiss's interpretation of the *Tanhuma* is truthful—is, if not right, then true: Avraham passed the test of the Akeidah *not* because he was willing to *kill* Isaac, but because, ultimately, he was willing to let Isaac *live*. When Avraham heard the voice of the angel telling him to desist from killing Isaac, he could have reasoned, 'God Himself told me to kill my son, and now an angel is telling me *not* to kill him? How can I obey the voice of the angel instead of the command of God? In a conflict between the command of the master and the command of the disciple, would one heed the command of the disciple?' But Avraham knew that the angel was correct—*Avraham knew that the angel was completely correct to such an extent that the angel's command could even override the command of God.* And how did Avraham know this? Because, as the rabbis (and Shakespeare) teach, "this to thine own self be true": Abraham trusted his own inner moral and ethical intuitions, and stayed true to himself. (See *Midrash Tanhuma* [*Vayigash* 11] and *Avot deRabbi Natan* 33:1 on Psalms 15:7, narrating the myth that Avraham's two kidneys taught him Torah—a midrash which poignantly teaches that Avraham's own ethical intuitions—and perhaps ours as well—are religiously significant, and deserve to be heard.) Avraham knew that God would never, in the end, actually desire him to kill an innocent human being. He knew that the God of life, above all else, desires human beings upon whom He has bestowed the gift of life to continue to choose life.

Indeed, in the ancient world, human sacrifice was not uncommon, and when one believed that the gods had commanded one to sacrifice a human being—even if the human happened to be one's own child—one unequivocally obeyed the command of the gods. When the Greek warrior Agamemnon believed that the gods (Artemis, specifically) demanded that he sacrifice his own daughter (as recounted in Aeschylus's play *Agamemnon*) in order to calm the winds so that the Greek fleet could safely sail to Troy, Agamemnon obeyed without question. This was not considered a "trial" on Agamemnon's part; in the ancient world, sacrificing a child to appease the gods was de rigueur. Likewise, when God commanded Avraham to sacrifice his son Isaac, the "trial" was not whether Avraham would obey *God*; the trial was whether Avraham would obey the *angel*—the angel that told Avraham *not* to heed the original command of God. Avraham passed this trial not when he agreed to sacrifice Isaac, but when he agreed to let Isaac *live*.

And perhaps, in the spirit of the *Tanhuma*—and in the audacious, but morally grand spirit of *Gravity* and Rabbi Weiss—even the angel's command to 'desist from slaughtering your son' was in fact none other than an emanation from Avraham's own mind. Not only the *zaken* [old man], but even the angel, was a projection of Avraham's own consciousness. 'Desist,' Avraham said to himself. 'Do not lift your hand upon this lad,' the angelic aspect of Avraham's consciousness said. 'Yes, you—Abraham, you silly old man you—yes, you may have thought that you have heard the voice of God commanding you to kill your innocent son,' said Avraham's angel, said Avraham's inner Gabriel. 'But did you *really*? Did you *really* hear this voice? Are you *sure*? Really, *really*, absolutely, one-hundred-and-fifty percent sure?' said the angelic Voice in his head. 'Perhaps God said "*ha'aleihu*" (bring him up), not "*shah'teihu*" (slaughter him)? And you *have* "brought him up," have you not?' Avraham carefully pondered the words of his inner angel, pored over his soul, checked his ethico-religious moral pulse, and concluded: 'No. I cannot do it. I *will* not do it. I cannot, will not, shall not, kill my son, my beloved son, my innocent son. I may have thought that I heard God tell me to do this, but I cannot believe that this is what I accurately heard, nor can I truly believe that this is what this God truly desires. No—I will not, cannot, shall not do this deed. *Ad kahn*. Some pagans may venerate Hades, other polytheists worship gods of the underworld, and the Egyptians may have constructed a cult of death, but my God is not like their gods—their gods are gods of death; my God is the God of life. I cannot, will not, shall not kill my son—I shall not do this deed—no. I shall let him live. And I shall pass this teaching on to him, to his children, to his children's children, and to the great nation which God has promised will issue from his offspring: that, more than anything else, the God of life created us human beings in His image so that we may imitate the God of life by creating children, beauty, and wisdom—and by choosing life. And, at the end of his life, when Moses's thoughts could have easily turned to death, this people's great teacher will teach his people the teaching that will become the predominant imperative of their entire civilization: "choose life, so that you and your children shall live."'

NOTES

1. *Midrash Tanhuma-Yelammedenu*, *Va-Yera* 22; also found in *b. Sanhedrin* 89b, *Genesis Rabbah* 56:4; *Midrash va-Yosha*; and *Pesikta Rabbati* 40:67-69. Translation from Howard Schwartz, *Tree of Souls: The Mythology of Judaism* (New York: Oxford Univ. Press, 2007), 340.
2. Psalms 115:16, my translation.
3. See Moshe Simon-Shushan, *Stories of the Law: Narrative Discourse and the Construction of Authority in the Mishnah* (New York: Oxford, 2012), 216-19. The Temple was a place of order and purity, but chaos and death could occasionally ensue as a result of human misdeeds and ritual misprisions; God smote Nadab and Abihu for improper behavior in the sanctuary (Leviticus 10:1-7), Uzzah died for touching the Ark whilst attempting to prevent it from falling (II Samuel 6:6-7), and a priest died for attempting to reveal the Ark's location (Mishnah, *Shekalim* 6:1-2); ibid.
4. Irving Greenberg, "On the Road to a New Encounter between Judaism and Christianity," in *For the Sake of Heaven and Earth* (Philadelphia: Jewish Publication Society, 2004), 18. In a review felicitously titled "Between Heaven and Earth," A.O. Scott unintentionally adumbrated *Gravity*'s Judeo-Christian motif of "choosing life" in noting that the film, for all of its "pictorial grandeur," is ultimately "about the longing to be pulled back down onto the crowded, watery sphere where life is tedious, complicated, sad and possible." A.O. Scott, "Between Earth and Heaven," *New York Times*, 10/3/2013, accessed on Dec. 4, 2013 available at http://www.nytimes.com/2013/10/04/movies/gravity-stars-sandra-bullock-and-george-clooney.html?_r=0&pagewanted=1
5. Eighth lecture in the course series "Shaping a Religious Response: The Rabbinic Engagement with a World in Transformation," delivered at Yeshivat Chovevei Torah Rabbinical School, Dec. 4, 2013. According to Rabbi Greenberg, the Bible is not meant to be interpreted as a simple collection of facts; rather, it is meant to be read as a narrative, because its selection of specific facts creates a structured story. This story is meant to serve as a normative guide for persons attempting to find meaning in life and their place in the world.
6. Neil Gillman, *Sacred Fragments: Recovering Theology for the Modern Jew* (Philadelphia: Jewish Publication Society, 1990).
7. Personal communication. This quote is taken from memory, but I trust that my memory of this quote is accurate; Rabbi Gillman is fond of this observation, and has repeated it in other settings.
8. Spoiler Alert: one of these powers is a keen imaginative capacity. Stone's imaginative capacity allows her to conjure an image of Kowalski. Similar to the rabbinic explanation (*b. Sotah* 36b; *Genesis Rabbah* 86:7; *Midrash Tanhuma* 8-9) of how Joseph was able to resist the advances of Potiphar's wife in Genesis 39:7-23—a "likeness of his father [Jacob] appeared to Joseph" warning him of the consequences of submitting to temptation—a talking, breathing "likeness" of Kowalski provides Stone with the mental fortitude she needs to persevere. Cuarón's use of this filmic device allows this intriguing rabbinic narrative to be understood on a cinematic plane.

II. Is This All There Is? *Or is there . . . a* Magic in the Moonlight *(2014)*

Does God exist? Does life have any meaning? Does the universe have a purpose? Who among us has not brooded upon these baffling inscrutabilities? Woody Allen certainly has, and his *Magic in the Moonlight* (2014) is his most theological, philosophical, and autobiographical movie yet.

Lord knows Woody Allen has put himself on screen before, but even though he doesn't actually appear in *Magic in the Moonlight*, his presence is so palpable that you could swear he was in it—which, in fact, is this film's one true act of prestidigitation. This is a movie about magic, but Allen's screenplay employs no legerdemain; he reveals his conscience, exposes his deepest existential anxieties, and even bares his soul. Never before has Woody Allen brought forth a film as blatantly autobiographical as *Magic in the Moonlight*. Not that this is a bad thing—John Updike was a notoriously autobiographical writer, usually to great literary effect—it is just that in Allen's latest feature (his forty-fourth, by my count, which doesn't include his made-for-TV movies), the characters sometimes seem more like his mouthpieces than actual cinematic personas.

But oh, what mouthpieces! Where else in modern movies do we hear such monologues? Where else in contemporary cinema can we hear similar disquisitions and deliberations about the existence of God, the meaning of life, and the purpose of the universe? Critics continue to castigate Woody Allen for his alleged cinematic crimes—recycling old ideas, reshuffling used concepts, relying on built-in audience goodwill even though "he has nothing new to say"—but are these really crimes at all? After all, from Monet's water lilies to Cézanne's Mount Sainte-Victoire to Rothko's multiforms, the greatest artists have consistently circled back to familiar themes—but when they do so, they always paint the same scene in a slightly different light, with a slightly different shade of color, and with a slightly but significantly altered perspective.

As in art, so in film: Hitchcock gave us many tremendous tales of mystery and suspense, Tarantino continues to give us superb slugfest spectacles, and Allen continues to give us excellent existential philosophical-comedies, so why do we continue to complain? Is it because of—in contrast to, say, Terrence Malick—the sheer amount of films he has now directed? I suppose we'd also tire of gourmet cuisine if we ate Daniel Boulud's cooking every night for dinner. And if the repetition is the source of our griping, the riposte may come from religion itself: the liturgical masters of the great religious traditions knew that certain messages needed to be repeated day after day, month after month, and year after year in order for people to properly internalize the values that a religious text seeks to convey. For instance, the composers of Jewish liturgy believed that the central Jewish teaching is its monotheistic message; all other Jewish teachings, they knew, would naturally flow from an acceptance of the monotheistic creed. Thus, they took a verse from the Torah (Deuteronomy 6:4)—"Hear O Israel, the Lord Our God, the Lord is One"—and placed it in the prayer book. They mandated that it be said once during the morning prayer-service, once during the evening prayer-service, and once again before going to bed, thereby ensuring that Jews would never forget its message of monotheism and the ethical values embedded therein. And, by inserting the phrase "Blessed art thou, God, reviver of the dead" into the thrice-daily prayer of the Amidah, they further ensured that the eternal Jewish message of hope—symbolized by the resurrection creed—would never be forgotten as well. The Jewish ecclesiastical authorities surely understood the psychology behind the adage, "the three-fold cord is not quickly broken" (Ecclesiastes 4:12).

All of this is not to say that Woody Allen is the second coming of a great Jewish liturgical composer; it is not even to suggest that he's as great of an artist as Monet or Cézanne (notwithstanding Colin Firth's—Allen's *Magic in the Moonlight* mouthpiece—description of himself a great artist). But it is to suggest that the secret of great art, similar to the secret of establishing time-tested religious principles, lies in repetition. We should not be so hasty to dismiss "yet another" Woody Allen film with "yet more armchair philosophizing" about the meaning of life.

However—and here is where *Magic in the Moonlight* distinguishes itself from all prior Allen films—*Magic in the Moonlight* is no mere "more armchair philosophizing." Yes, Woody Allen has pondered existential issues in many a film past, but never before has he confronted God so openly. Never before has he thought up a film as theologically minded as *Magic in the Moonlight*.

The film's plot may be simple, but its messages are complex. Set in the artistically fertile interwar era of 1920s Europe—a unique historical epoch memorably mined by Bob Fosse in *All That Jazz* (1978)—Stanley Crawford (Colin Firth), a renowned magician whose off-stage specialty is exposing psychics, magicians, and spiritualists as the frauds he knows them to be, is invited to the south of France in order to debunk a spiritualist (Sophie Baker, played by Emma Stone) who has an extremely wealthy American family in her sway. A sober man of science with a cynical disposition, Stanley is naturally skeptical of Sophie's spiritualist "sensations," but the more time he spends with her, the more he is astounded by her seemingly supernatural skills. He eventually becomes so taken with her talents that he starts to question the very foundations—science, rationalism, and materialism—upon which he has carefully constructed the edifice of his conscience.

Firth's and Stone's chemistry is surprisingly delightful, and their romps recall the great cinematic screwball comedy pairings of yesteryear: Clark Gable and Claudette Colbert in Frank Capra's *It Happened One Night* (1934), and, in particular, Cary Grant and Katherine Hepburn in Howard Hawks' *Bringing Up Baby* (1938), another film featuring a sober man of science whose seriousness is mellowed by a magical woman.

One film, though, stands out as the motivic predecessor of *Magic in the Moonlight*: Adrian Lyne's *Lolita* (1997). Like Lyne's controversial adaptation of Nabokov's controversial novel, *Magic in the Moonlight* also showcases the disconcertingly seedy specter of an older, rational, cynical, intellectual European man becoming infatuated with a younger, wide-eyed, precocious, redheaded American girl. When Stanley and Sophie first form an emotional bond during a road-trip to Provence, we recall that in *Lolita*, Nabokov also used the motif of the road-trip to famous (or infamous) literary effect. And when Sophie cuddles up close to Stanley during one unsettling scene, we notice that Stanley looks like, is dressed like, and even sounds like Jeremy Irons' Humbert Humbert. Sophie is even photographed in the same voyeuristic, "male gaze" manner in which Dominique Swain was photographed in *Lolita*. Is Mr. Allen, who famously said that "the heart wants what it wants," trying to tell us something about the nature of (older) male love? Is there something to be made out of the eerie phonetic similarities between 'Stanley' and 'Woody,' 'Olivia' (Stanley's middle-age fiancée) and 'Mia,' and 'Sophie' and 'Soon-Yi'? Is this film Mr. Allen's mea culpa—or his apologia—or both? Like the unanswered theological questions posed in *Magic in the Moonlight*, these unanswered biographical questions lie in fallow fields, beckoning seekers and cinephiles to harvest these fallen sheaves.

Mr. Allen's typically eclectic musical choices in *Magic in the Moonlight*—ranging from big-band jazz to Ravel's "Boléro" to Beethoven's Ninth Symphony—make the movie seem like a lightweight summer trifle. Not that the Ninth is light—its familiar molto vivace movement is especially ominous when used in film; its striking second movement immediately evokes the dark, dystopian denseness of Stanley Kubrick's *A Clockwork Orange* (1971). And the film's rococo backdrops and lush cinematography also lend it a feathery feel. One particular shot, a cinematographic composition of Stanley speaking with Sophie as she sits on a swing in a luxurious garden setting, is an almost exact filmic carbon copy of Jean Honoré Fragonard's rococo masterpiece "The Swing" (1767; oil on canvas; The Wallace Collection, London).

But while the film affects a light appearance, the questions its characters ponder are some of the heaviest dilemmas known to man: Is this all there is? Or is there something more—something beyond what the mere eye can see? Is life "nasty, brutish, and short," as the Hobbes-spouting Stanley likes to state, or is it filled with a mysterious, mystical magic, as the whimsical, waifish Sophie (who is Audrey Hepburn-esque in her diaphanousness) is want to believe? These are only several of the intractable questions that Stanley is compelled to confront, and his reassessment of everything he thought he stood for may have viewers questioning many of their assumptions about God, life, and the universe, or—because it is a non-didactic, nuanced, subtle film with no unitary message—it may not. Like the religious-truth claims of faith, the multiple messages in *Magic in the Moonlight* are conveyed but can never be scientifically proven; it is left up to us to decide whether to take the proverbial leap of faith into the *mysterium tremendum* and accept them, or to rationalistically remain on materialistic terra firma and reject them.

One of the most salient symbols in *Magic in the Moonlight* is the astronomic observatory. While Stanley and Sophie are driving back from Provence, their car breaks down, and they take shelter in a nearby observatory. It is a place that Stanley used to frequent as a child, he explains to Sophie. When Stanley opens the roof of the observatory so that they'll be able to see the starry night sky, the observatory's magisterial telescope clearly points to the resplendent silver moon crescent.

Stanley, the self-described "sober man of science," flatters himself with this false appellation, for unlike the great astronomers, he is startlingly close-minded in his doctrinaire, unchanging and inflexible worldview. Only when he is with Sophie does he first begin to open the closed roof of the "observatory"—the closed, settled viewpoint of his own mind—to begin to explore what may lie beyond.

In fact, the irony represented by Stanley's affinity for astronomy is illuming: Stanley regards the open-minded religious dolts—the believers in "delusions" who place their chimerical wishes in faith's fraudulent creeds and religions' false hopes—as erring souls. And he perceives the close-minded men of science—those for whom concepts like "belief," "faith," and "spirituality" are irrelevant in a world of empiricism, observation, and experimentation—as the only coterie of humankind in possession of truth. Yet it was the original "sober men"—*and* women—of science, the great explorers, astronomers, and scientists of years yore who, in their *open*-mindedness—in their willingness to entertain the possibility that there *must* be something more than meets the earthly eye, in their belief that there *must* be something more than this planet, and in their flexibility to integrate new scientific revelations into their old worldviews—opened the knowledge-base of humanity to the wonders of the universe. By pointing the telescope into the sky, the cosmologically curious Copernicus, Kepler, Galileo and Giordano Bruno challenged the close-minded men of medieval religion—the men who believed that this world was fixed and immovable, and that the center of the solar system was our planet—and opened our minds to the awe-inspiring spectacles of this magisterial universe. And it is the cosmologists, astrophysicists, and scientists—those with genuinely open-minded spirits—who continue to push the boundaries of our consciousness by insisting that there is more out there that we do not know, that there are more wonders waiting to be discovered, and that there are more mysteries waiting to be solved. The "observatory," as Stanley subtly indicates, must remain open if we deign to discover the manifold delights of our magnificent material domain.

III. Inside Llewyn Davis

The Coen brothers are indubitably the most versatile, skillful, and interesting filmmakers in contemporary American cinema. Witness their last five films: *No Country for Old Men* (2007), a flawless,[1] chilling twenty-first century version of *The Night of the Hunter* (1955) which netted the Coen brothers a Best Picture Oscar; the underrated ensemble comedy *Burn After Reading* (2008), a film that features what is arguably Brad Pitt's finest comedic performance since *Twelve Monkeys* (1995); the dark comedy *A Serious Man* (2009), a twenty-first century take on The Book of Job which some critics deemed to be their best film to date—this amongst a filmography that already boasts *Fargo* (1996), *The Big Lebowski* (1998), *Barton Fink* (1991), and *The Hudsucker Proxy* (1994); a virtuosic revival of the Western, *True Grit* (2010); and now, an unclassifiable, confounding tragedy, *Inside Llewyn Davis* (2013), a film that has the feel of a Kafka story ("The Trial," specifically) transmuted to celluloid.

Inside Llewyn Davis is a leisurely paced tale of the trials and sorrows of a young singer (Oscar Issac) aspiring to carve out a niche for himself in the early 1960's pre-Dylan Greenwich Village folk scene. The film's subdued, unaffected tone, its drawing-room and kitchen-sink scenes, and its adagietto tempo hearken back to the profoundly personal films of the 1970's auteurs, recalling the time when Scorsese, Coppola, Altman, and pre-*Star Wars* George Lucas conveyed personal messages to the film-going public. Except, in *Inside Llewyn Davis*, the Coen brothers have not only made a personal film—they have "done" the personal film before, most recently in *A Serious Man*—but they have gone for something much, much deeper. Like Herman Melville's *Moby-Dick*, *Inside Llewyn Davis* is reaching for something very big—a sweeping, existential interpretation of the human condition, perhaps—and the success (if such a term can be used for such a film) of this movie rises and falls with the perception of whether they have attained this result.

The Coen brothers' tragic take on the music movie is a subversive corrective to films like *Walk the Line* (2005), *Coal Miner's Daughter* (1980), and other musician biopics in which the path from a hardscrabble existence to musical success seems predetermined. *Inside Llewyn Davis* reminds us that for every Loretta Lynn and Jonny Cash, there are hundreds of Llewyn Davises. The path to success in the entertainment industry is strewn with the sad tales of those who did not succeed. Llewyn Davis, a character based upon Dave Van Ronk, is one of those figures.

Inside Llewyn Davis holds out the promise of being a unique viewing experience, and it most certainly is. However, this does not mean it offers a pleasing viewing experience. In fact, my initial reaction to the film after leaving the theater was one of visceral dislike; I had never reacted so negatively to any Coen brothers' movie before. And I have seen—and loved—virtually all of their films. What, I wondered, was so unlikable about this particular Coen brothers film?

Some of its unlikability inhered in Oscar Isaac's remarkably pathos-free performance as Llewyn Davis. The character is so devoid of emotion that he seems virtually inhuman. Spending time in the theater with a character as congenitally incapable of caring as Isaac's Davis provokes a reciprocal reaction that makes it difficult to become emotionally invested in the character.

The other reason this film is so unlikable is because it lacks the comedic elements that we have come to expect and enjoy in Coen brothers films. Aside from the hackneyed screwball subplot that involves chasing a runaway cat (a device the Coen brothers previously used in *The Ladykillers* [2004], and one that is also used in Noah Baumbach's *The Squid and the Whale* [2005]), John Goodman provides some of the only comic relief, but mostly as a dialogic symbol of "John Goodman, comic character actor in Coen brothers films." He's not particularly funny in this role, but his mere presence in another Coen Brothers film conjures his past performances in Coen brothers films from *Raising Arizona* (1987) onwards, and gives the viewer a kernel of hope that this movie will be like many of the others. It is not.

But mostly, this film is so unlikable because it paints a picture of a world that we would rather not look at; for those of us who have suffered disappointment, heartbreak, and failure—and what human being has not?—it is a picture that may be all too recognizable. Like Kafka's frightening parables about a careless, heartless world, *Inside Llewyn Davis* is an unnerving look at a world with an existential void at its core. It is a film that adopts a fundamentally tragic view of life—but so do many of the Coen brothers' other works, most notably *No Country for Old Men* and *Fargo*. Where *Inside Llewyn Davis* departs from these works is that it is, on the surface, irredeemably tragic—there is no foreseeable saving grace in the world of Llewyn Davis. It is not only a tragic world, but a Sisyphean one—a cold world without a shred of hope, a lonely world in which we are doomed to a never-ending cycle of disappointment, despair, and defeat. In short, it is the world of Nietzsche's madman: it is a world without God.

The great ethico-theological idea that the Hebrew Bible introduced to the world was the idea of a moral God who is involved in the world. As Nahum Sarna observed regarding the biblical monotheistic conception of God,

> The God of the Bible is not a remote deity, inactive and ineffective. Having created the world, He did not remove himself from humanity and leave man to his own devices. On the contrary, He is very much concerned with the world He created and is directly interested in human behavior.[2]

Abraham, the Jewish sages teach, was the first human being to conceive of a personal God: "From the day that God created the world, no one addressed God as 'master' until Abraham addressed God as "Adon*ai*" [*my* master]. Abraham saw himself not at the mercy of uncaring gods but as standing in a relationship with a caring, personal God."[3] Calling God "Adonai," my master, conveys the speaker's belief that God has a personal relationship with each individual. More than steering the world from polytheism to monotheism, Abraham and the monotheistic religions that claim him as their patriarch taught the world that the universe is not a chaotic, cold, hostile arena where people are at the mercy of mercurial gods; instead, the monotheistic faiths portrayed the universe as an intelligible (if not altogether orderly) domain overseen by a personal, loving God.

Since the time of Spinoza, the notion of a personal God presiding over an orderly universe has received many blows. These blows first came from philosophy and science, then from literature and psychology, and finally from the behavior of humanity itself. Now, the Coen brothers have demonstrated that film is a medium capable of depicting the consequence of what it means to believe that we live in a world without God.

Llewyn Davis is an unconnected, unmoored, rootless folk singer adrift in an impersonal, uncaring cosmos. Peering down from his squalid Bohemian Greenwich Village pied-à-terre, he condescends towards those upwardly mobile, middle-class aspiring persons who do not create and "just exist," but Llewyn barely manages to exist himself. And what kind of existence is his lot? Llewyn exists without a sense of a deeply rooted, venerable past, without a stable community of family and friends in the present, and without an inkling of a hopeful, redemptive future. He is an exemplar of the dreadful Durkheiminan anomie that preys upon individuals who lack the warmth and shared values of a supportive religious community.[4]

One who reaches for too much ends up grasping nothing at all: "*tafasta merubah lo tafasta, tafasta muat tafasta*", the Talmud states (*b. Yoma* 80a; *b. Hagigah* 17a). Immediately after viewing the film, I felt as if the Coen brothers had reached for too much, and had come up empty. But this is not the type of film that deserves a knee-jerk reaction. If one attempts to rapidly consume and digest it like a fast-food entrée, it will not be appreciated. Instead, it should be slowly digested like a complex carbohydrate and processed only after a few days—or even after a few weeks.

"You'll have to explain this one to me," a friend I bumped into at the theater said to me after the movie. I'm still not sure I can, but what can be said is that the highly allusive *Inside Llewyn Davis*, in addition to resembling a cinematic version of a Kafka parable, also bears strong resonances of Dante's deeply symbolic *Divine Comedy*. Just as each individual and each episode in *The Divine Comedy* is profoundly symbolic, each individual and each episode in *Inside Llewyn Davis* also carries symbolic weight. For instance, what Llewyn causes his sister to do with his records and memorabilia is analogous to being sprinkled with the waters of the mythological river Lethe in *The Divine Comedy*.

In the Coen brothers' Dante-esque film, no creature is more symbolic than "Ulysses" the cat. In many respects, the wandering cat is a feline proxy of Llewyn, and is appropriately named Ulysses.[5] For just as Ulysses was a wanderer, adrift midway through life's journey, so too is Llewyn. Just as Ulysses lacks a true home and community for much of his journey, so too does Llewyn.[6] And just as Ulysses is a crucial figure in Dante's *Divine Comedy* (particularly in the latter cantos of *Paradiso*) who symbolizes the possibility of redemption—his eventual returning to his home is a microcosmic symbol of the world's eventual restoration to its pure, pre-sin state on a macrocosmic plane—the dual returns of Llewyn and Ulysses the cat to their respective abodes adumbrates the Coen brothers' interest in the redemptive possibility of return and restoration. (The motif of return is operative in *Raising Arizona*, *Fargo*, *The Big Lebowski*, and *No Country for Old Men* as well.) Thus, naming the cat Ulysses (who, like the original Ulysses, undertakes an "incredible journey" of its own) serves to evoke the surprising possibility of return and redemption amidst our seemingly hopeless journeys through a cosmos that is, on the surface level, Sisyphean. Furthermore, *Inside Llewyn Davis*'s ambiguous ending conjures the similarly strange ending of Joyce's *Finnegan's Wake* (the nearly impenetrable novel by the author of the modern *Ulysses*): both end where they begin; for both Llewyn and Finn, their nadirs effectuate their eternal Eliadian returns—their ends bring about their recurrent rebirths.

Indeed, almost more than it is a Kafkaesque parable of life in an absurd universe, *Inside Llewyn Davis* is a Dante-esque tale of a journey through a hellish environment which culminates in—or at least holds out the hope of—eventual redemption.

NOTES

1. The great artists paint the same picture over and over and over again—Monet and his water lilies, Twombley and his Ledas, Cezanne and his vistas of Mont Sainte-Victoire—until they get it just right; up until *No Country for Old Men*, the Coen brothers had been making movies that were preoccupied with the same concerns—the ambiguity of morality; anomie; existential loneliness—and that featured common motifs—restoration and return; odysseys; folk music; desolate, heartless landscapes; empty roads; terrifying bounty hunters; dimwitted criminals committing bungled crimes—and their experimentations with this form reached its apotheosis in *No Country for Old Men*, in which all of their themes and motifs harmonized to form a filmic masterpiece. (In fact, their usage of the Four Tops song "It's the Same Old Song" in the closing credits of their first feature, *Blood Simple* (1985), contains a line that characterizes nearly all of their subsequent films: "It's the same, same old song / But with a different meaning.")
2. Nahum M. Sarna, *Understanding Genesis: The World of the Bible in the Light of History* (New York: Schocken, 1970), 52. See also ibid., 52-58, and Jonathan Sacks, "Noach: True Morality," *Covenant & Conversation*, 2012 (positing that the concept of revelation implies objective, universal morality), available at http://www.aish. com/tp/i/sacks/174092141.html
3. Eliakim Koenigsberg (citing Rabbi Shimon Schwab), "Parshas Lech Lecha—My G-d," *Parsha Bytes*, Oct. 10, 2013, accessed Dec. 31, 2013 http://www.yutorah.org/lectures/lecture.cfm/798650/Rabbi_Eliakim_Koenigsberg/Parsha_Bytes_-_Parshas_Lech_Lecha_-_My_G-d

4. Émile Durkheim, *The Division of Labor in Society* (1893); idem, *Suicide* (1897).
5. The name "Ulysses" is itself a trope that occasionally recurs in Coen brothers' films; it is the name of the character played by George Clooney in *O Brother, Where Art Thou?* (2000)—a film that exemplifies the Coen brothers' long-gestating interest in *The Odyssey*.
6. Other parallels between Llewyn and Ulysses become illumined upon close watching: Llewyn felt that only his departed singing partner was his musical equal, similar to how Odysseus felt that only "ghosts"—the absent Agamemnon, Achilles, and Ajax—were his "equals." See Harold Bloom, *Genius: A Mosaic of One Hundred Exemplary Creative Minds* (New York: Warner Books, 2002), 508. Additionally, Llewyn is accused by Jean (Carey Mulligan) of turning everything he touches into human waste; he can be said to be possessed by some kind of curse. If Llewyn is thought of as an Odysseus, it is interesting to observe that the name "Odysseus" (or "Ulysses" in Latin) refers to one who "inflicts his curse upon others, or someone who himself is victimized by a curse." (Ibid., 505)

CHAYA ROSENFELD GORSETMAN

Educating in the Divine Image

THE TERM OPEN ORTHODOXY originated with Rabbi Avi Weiss to distinguish between the more right wing communities of Orthodoxy. In an essay on Open Orthodoxy in *Judaism* (Fall 1997), Rabbi Weiss posits: "It is open in that our ideology acknowledges, considers and takes into account in varying ways a wide spectrum of voices. It is Orthodox in that our commitment to Halakha is fervent and demanding." He further asserts that "for the Open Orthodox Jew, true and profound religio-legal creativity and spiritual striving emerges from the tension between the poles of strict halakhic adherence and open ideological pursuits. They appear to be opposites when in fact they are one." (p. 34)

For Rabbi Weiss, Open Orthodoxy must (and can) find expression in many different aspects of human existence. From my prospective, one of the most essential places to actualize Open Orthodoxy is in Jewish schools. In particular, Open Orthodoxy can best be introduced in modern Orthodox schools by addressing gender in an intentional and thoughtful manner to include the "wide spectrum of voices." It is in the spirit that every person is created in the divine image that I offer a section from a book that my co-author Elana Sztokman and I wrote regarding gender issues in modern Orthodox day schools.[1]

The core Jewish ethos is not gender-dependent but rather based on a vision of both women and men created in the Divine image. Jewish practices,

---

DR. CHAYA GORSETMAN is a Clinical Associate Professor of Education, Co Chair of the Education Department at Stern College for Women of Yeshiva University. She specializes in supervision of student teachers and curriculum studies. Her research has focused on how gender is expressed in Orthodox Jewish day schools and as such served as the director and co-author of the JOFA Gender and Orthodoxy Curriculum Project, *Bereshit: A New Beginning—A Differentiated Approach to Learning and Teaching*. She is the co-author of *Educating in the Divine Image: Gender Issues in Orthodox Jewish Day Schools*, winner of the 2013 National Jewish Book Award.

values, rituals, and texts can be transmitted to both girls and boys in ways that do not keep people boxed into strict gender expectations but rather free them to embrace the full range of Jewish religious life. Shabbat, for example, can be presented as belonging to males and females equally, as partners in the endeavor of sanctifying God and Torah. Both men and women can be shown cleaning the house, and both girls and boys can pray. Whatever activities are believed to be the most important reflections of the biblical commandments to keep Shabbat can be owned equally by all members of the community, and that inclusivity can undoubtedly be reflected in educational messages—but it takes some forethought.

Educating for a compassionate, inclusive practice, one in which all members of the community are seen as equal partners in reflecting the divine image, requires work. Awareness about the ways in which gender socialization create community can have a profound impact on the way in which both children and adults construct Jewish society.

Educating for a more humane vision of gender requires some deeper understandings about education and a willingness to address how gender messages are transmitted. Indeed, education happens all the time. Education is not merely the formal school curriculum that fills tests and for which grades are given. People, especially young people, receive messages constantly in sometimes subtle and unintended ways. We absorb life lessons through the myriad of interactions and exchanges that form our days. Adults teach children lessons in the ways we interact with them, the way we speak to them, and the way we behave and speak amongst ourselves. Education is in the walls, in the air, at the dining room table, on our bodies and in our facial expressions. It happens in the home, on the street, in the park, and sometimes even in classrooms. Messages are transmitted knowingly and unknowingly, intentionally and unintentionally—in fact, sometimes the most unintended messages are the most powerfully internalized. This is especially true about gender. "The social construction of gender is an active and ongoing process," writes Barrie Thorne.[2] "Gender categories, gender identities, gender divisions, gender-based groups, gender meanings—all are produced, actively and collaboratively, in everyday life." The cultures of gender are made and absorbed by children and adults alike, as they navigate their way through their life-long searches for connection, for meaning, and for approval. As Hervé Varenne and Ray McDermott write, "The human world is made up of the remnants of everyone else's activities. It is an artifact or, in words we like to use, a *cultural fact*. . . . It is always made and always about to be remade."[3] Becoming aware of the ubiquitous processes of education in socializing for gender is the crucial first step in creating a compassionate and inclusive religious practicing community.

Education and Gender in Jewish Observance

Socialization into gender has evolved as a central focus of religious Jewish life. In day schools, Jewish camps, synagogues, playgrounds, communal centers and living rooms, messages about what makes proper womanhood and manhood abound: about whose presence matters, whose voice is heard, who has leadership and power, and who is considered responsible or caring or intelligent or strong. In prayer, in ritual, in text, in language, in everyday practices and interactions, messages about gender abound. "Torah," writes Judith Plaskow, "'Jewish' sources, 'Jewish' teaching—puts itself forward as *Jewish* teaching but speaks in the voice of only half the Jewish people."[4]

In many respects this is an exhilarating time for Jewish women. Everywhere women are learning, thinking, practicing, taking ownership and challenging accepted practices in order to bring about greater equality and social justice in nearly every possible realm. They are writing Torah scrolls, pleading in the rabbinical courts, adopting and creating rituals, rediscovering ancient women's and girls' ceremonies, writing new prayers reflecting contemporary realities, teaching Talmud, offering halakhic opinions, entering leadership positions—in rabbinical leadership positions, and even quasi-rabbinical positions in the Orthodox world—writing books, plays, films and television shows and documentaries, and speaking out on behalf of women's rights in marriage, divorce, public life, family life, and synagogue. Even the Orthodox Rabbinical Council of America has acknowledged the significance of these changes. "The RCA reaffirms its commitment to women's Torah education and scholarship at the highest levels, and to the assumption of appropriate leadership roles within the Jewish community," the RCA wrote in a much-publicized statement in March 2010 about women's leadership roles.[5]

However, despite these changing realities, there are many other messages about gender being transmitted in day schools—especially Orthodox day schools—that are at odds with women's advancement. For example, while women have made great strides in advanced Jewish learning, often the most educated women are excluded from day schools. The women Talmud teachers, Blu Greenberg said, are virtually absent from day school staffs. "The first generation of female Talmud scholars has found that the institutions that educated them will not welcome them back."[6] Similarly, Rachel Furst writes of the time she was asked to describe a religious role model she had in school, and could not think of a single woman. This "posed a problem," she writes. "Though I craved a spiritual mentor, there was no one person whom I could cite as my religious role model." Even her attempts to lobby the school administration were of no avail. "Observing the special relationship my male classmates had with their Gemara teacher, who lived in the neighborhood and held weekly Shabbat-afternoon gatherings in his home, along with Friday night *tisches* and personal *schmoozes*, I lobbied the school administration for a parallel experience for the female members of our class."

Certainly there are signs of improvement since the 1980s when women's scholarship was habitually overlooked. The 2009 book edited by Jack Wertheimer, *Learning and Community: Jewish Supplementary Schools in the Twenty-First Century*,[7] is an example of a book that demonstrates a gender consciousness, with an equal number of male and female contributors. However, while some areas of Jewish life show responsiveness to calls for gender equity, other corners of Jewish life demonstrate entrenched inequality that seems not to have changed at all over thirty years. As recently as 2007, for example, a leading academic institute of Jewish education published a book following a conference on Jewish education that had not a single female contributor.[8] (It seems that there may not have been any women presenting at the conference either). For a very long time, it seems, the "default" Jewish person—especially the default religious person—has been male, and undoing these patterns can be an uphill battle. Thus, signs of change coexist with signs of stagnation.

It is important to note that while the exclusion of women from public life is most pronounced in the Orthodox community, the rest of the Jewish community is hardly immune. Jane Eisner, editor of *The Forward*, has been tracking discrimination against women in the Jewish community for several years. "Women lead only a sliver of the major Jewish nonprofits, and their overall earnings are dwarfed by their male counterparts," Eisner notes. "But the problem goes deeper: Too many public discussions, events and programs hosted by the Jewish community have few or no women participating."[9] According to *The Forward*'s gender salary survey, of national Jewish organizations, there is "communal stagnation in gender equality, as the number of women in leadership roles remains at the same low level, and the gap between male and female salaries has grown even larger."[10]

This message comes through loud and clear in every corner of Jewish life, from private to public, ritualistic to secular. A few recent examples from public life:

- The 2012 annual *Jerusalem Post* conference featured nineteen men and two women speakers.[11]

- A 2011 special invitation from the Jewish National Fund did not list one woman among the planners.

- A 2011 medical ethics conference sponsored by Yeshiva University advertised a program with twelve male speakers and two female speakers.

- A 2009 conference of the Van Leer Institute on the future of modern Orthodoxy featured dozens of men and only one woman speaker.

- The "Judaism" pages in *The Jerusalem Post* routinely print articles by men only.

- A 2011 lecture series of (the all-women) Stern College for Women was composed of almost exclusively men, and was advertised using images of men praying at the Western Wall.

The messages from these stories is that the Jewish "public" is a male public, that leaders, speakers and thinkers are mainly male, and that men's voices and ideas are more valued and valuable than women's. As Nessa Rapoport, commenting on an all-male panel at a Jewish lecture series, asks, "Why . . . have Jews proven themselves to be so singularly un-amenable to current ideas about gender? Why . . . were these Jewish offerings, when viewed through a gender lens, no different from the ads that might have appeared forty years earlier, in the heart of the fifties, when I was growing up and men's and women's roles were the most rigid and alienated from each other than they would ever be in this century?"[12]

There are undoubtedly other instances of panels and conferences in which there has been more balanced gender representation. The American Jewish Studies (AJS) annual conference, for example, can be seen as a model of gender balance in its programming.[13] Gender equity is undoubtedly a function of awareness and consciousness—in fact, AJS dedicates significant resources to promoting gender equity in its organizational culture and messages. It seems, then, that there is a growing gender consciousness in many areas of Jewish communal life, and persistent signs of stagnation in others. The current state of gender practice around the Jewish world has two competing trends: growing awareness in some corners and lack of awareness in others. Research and activism have clearly had some impact, but not nearly enough. And it is perhaps surprising that signs of resistance are seen not only in Orthodox synagogues but also in places such as a conference put on by *The Jerusalem Post* in the year 2012.

That said, the culture of retrograde gender messages is arguably most striking in the Orthodox community, especially in Israel. Rabbi Elyakim Levanon of the religious Zionist Elon Moreh community ruled in 2010 that women are banned from running for public office. Responding to a query by a woman requesting permission to run for her local council, he declared: "The first problem is giving women authority, and being a secretary means having authority. The second problem is mixing men and women. Secretary meetings are held at night and sometimes end very late. It is not proper to be in mixed company in such situations. . . . The husband presents the family's opinion. . . . This is the proper way to prevent a situation in which the woman votes one way and her husband votes another."[14] A few days later, Kiryat Arba Rabbi Dov Lior expressed support for Levanon and proclaimed that violent behavior in youth is a direct outgrowth of women leaving the house to earn money.

Jews in both Israel and North America are thus exposed to two competing messages pulling at their identities simultaneously: the advancement of women in society and Jewish life alongside retrograde messages about gender and tradition. Although the messages are more glaring in Orthodox settings, gender messages permeate Jewish culture and society worldwide, and young people with forming identities are given the task of navigating these messages and figuring out what it means to be a religious man or a religious woman. This process, which takes place at home, at school, on the street, and in Jewish institutions public and private, is complex and filled with tensions and pulls in different directions. It compels educators to think through the educational and ethical implications of gender messages.

The Jewish community needs to address the root of this problem: the source of the gender consciousness that forms these messages. An exploration of educational processes and the formation of cultures within Jewish schools is a key step towards making change and inviting women to be equally valued members of Jewish society.

Meanwhile, considering how much has changed in the domain of women's education in the past 15 years, it seems significant that day schools have, for the most part, not taken the time to address the gender issue. "Benign neglect seems to be the operational mode of day schools," Blu Greenberg writes.[15] The message is that when it comes to gender, the thinking is static; we continue to do what we did and nothing changes. Though some day schools have made changes such as allowing girls to read Megillah, most don't write about it nor do they advertise it. It is still hidden, almost incidental, a side issue perhaps for some fringe group in the school, instead of being a central element of the school practice, a source of pride that addresses a critical component of the mission for the entire school community.

The lack of attention to mixed gender messages in Orthodox day schools is apparent from school mission statements. In our examination of 15 mission statements from self-identified modern Orthodox day schools in the United States, we found that only one school articulates the centrality of their commitment toward gender equality in its mission statement: "Equality in women's Jewish learning as evidenced by coeducational classes, including Talmud, Halakhah, and Tanakh. This allows the natural integration of genders in Torah study, at all grade levels, within the parameters of halakhah." Ten of the schools mention that they are coed without any mention of how they intend to address issues of gender, but it is clear that coeducation is defining of identity. By contrast, for example, all schools speak about the centrality of Israel and dedicate a paragraph in powerful language to the significance of the philosophy of the school, which illustrates that while Israel is a central value that has been discussed and articulated, gender equity is not. Three schools write about the "self-actualization" of every student, although they do not state how they will actualize this belief within the curriculum or school practices—that is, what they will do to show that girls are able to self-actualize along with boys.

The disparity and conflict between messages of inclusion and messages of gender segregation have significant impacts on the developing identities of young children, and may find expression in unanticipated internal conflicts and cognitive dissonance among adults. As Eileen M. Trauth points out, when parents and educators transmit messages about gender that conflict with real life, children seek out a variety of strategies to resolve or reduce the emotional and cognitive dissonance caused by role conflict.[16]

One set of impacts relates to female ambition and self-awareness. A day school student may have a mother working as a lawyer, physician, college professor, businessperson, or head of school, while leadership roles in religious practice and communal life remain all male. The message is that outside of the religious realm, girls can advance, but inside the religion, they can only go so far. This places girls' ambition and drive for activity in a difficult bind. As Nessa Rapoport writes, "I suspect that somewhere in most Jewish hearts and minds…lies an idea. And the idea is that only one kind of person *really* knows, and that person is a male person. Secretly, probably, a rabbi. With a beard."[17] Girls' needs and desires to be active participants in religious life rather than spectators create a heightened conflict. To quote veteran educator Esther Krauss, "our brightest girls will surely turn their backs on us intellectually if we persist in restricting their Jewish intellectual horizons."[18] On the other hand, some girls educated for passivity may respond with passivity. "Girls are required to attend tefillah, but the prevailing attitude is that '*davening* is for boys,'" Blu Greenberg wrote. "Boys are taught early on that a community of prayer exists and that they are expected to be part of it. In contrast, girls remain passive and unconnected, eyes glazing over at the morning minyan [prayer group]".[19] The instituted passivity will undoubtedly have long-term consequences for girls' self-awareness and connection to self.

Although there has not yet been a comprehensive study of the impact of conflicting gender messages on graduates of the day school system, anecdotal evidence suggests confusion and obliviousness. Take, for example, my exchange with a student leader in an institution of higher learning for women, one of the cornerstone institutions of modern Orthodoxy for women. The newly elected treasurer of the "Torah Action Committee" took on an initiative to distribute posters on Friday reminding people to keep Shabbat. She hung up two posters: one with pictures of men dancing and one of Uncle Sam—that is, no images of women, despite the fact that this is an all-women's college. When I asked her about the purpose of these posters, she replied that she "wants to make people spiritual." Yet, in the search for images of spirituality, it did not occur to her to find a photo of the women in the Beit Midrash learning Torah, or women praying. "I never thought of it," she replied. So while women may be making serious advancements in study and leadership and while women are taking active roles in schools and in management, this is not necessarily accompanied by an awareness of gender issues and gender messages. An appreciation of the idea that both men and women are equal participants in religious life is not an idea being systematically internalized by graduates of the day school system. Even active young women like this particular student do not have within their consciousness images of women leading public religious life. Even women in leadership are not necessarily mindful of the importance of inclusivity and partnership in Jewish life. The message that active, engaged religious practice can and should be equally owned by all members of the Jewish community is not being effectively transmitted. And as Sylvia Barack Fishman notes, "the importance of intensive Jewish education in helping women to achieve feminist goals within the religious sphere . . . can hardly be overestimated."[20]

A Different Vision of Education: Gender and the Divine Image

Gender awareness is about more than merely women's advancement. It is about creating a community of Jewish observance and practice that is built on the values of compassion, inclusivity, and care. Socializing for a religious practice that is equally attentive to the experiences and perspective of all members of the community is mandated by a vision of equality, justice, and the healthy identity development of all communal members. On the most profound spiritual level, we are talking about fostering the divine spirit in all Jews, about teaching people to see the divine image in others. As Rabbi Irving Greenberg suggests, the position of women in Orthodox Judaism today "does not allow women to realize their potential as *tzelem elohim* [divine image]. Women are asked to sacrifice their uniqueness and individual worthiness as Jews for the good of the community."[21] The view of both women and men as equally bestowed with the divine image creates new possibilities for educating about gender. It is about the social, emotional and spiritual value of complete engagement for men and women, boys and girls.

The problem we are addressing, then, is not a halakhic issue but an educational and sociological one. Many scholars and activists have been exploring the issue of gender in *halakhah* for some time. "Many people . . . would regard the status of women in Jewish tradition as the greatest challenge to Torah Judaism," writes Tamar Ross. "But . . . most Orthodox Jews today still see the problem as mainly a halakhic one; that is, in terms of the challenges posed to Orthodoxy on a practical level by the new role of women in the Western world. . . . I believe, however, that this way of phrasing the challenge raised by the women's revolution is shortsighted and mistaken. . . . Orthodox leaders have not yet spelled out for themselves the broader implications of the women's revolution."[22] Although much of the gender discussion in Jewish life focuses on *halakhah* and ritual, the discussion of education, which has the most long-term and broad-reaching implications, has not taken place in earnest.

Changing attitudes and raising awareness form the first step in making small changes in the school environment. This is about encouraging schools and educators to be responsive to social changes and understandings in order enhance and enrich the lives of both children and the adults who work with them.

In my college classes with student teachers, for example, I often discuss the unquestioned practice in many Jewish schools for the teachers to appoint an "*Ima [mother] Shabbat*" and "*Abba [father] Shabbat*" in which the girl lights the candles and the boy says Kiddush (in some cases, the girl is also responsible for bringing a cake for the class and the boy is responsible for bringing a bottle of grape juice). If all children are meant to fully practice Judaism, learning all the blessings and mastering all the traditions, what happens when each gender only learns half of the tradition? I regularly find that when these questions are raised, the student-teachers are always surprised that they had never considered these issues before, and had never been exposed to this kind of thinking. Raising awareness with student-teachers often leads to other conversations regarding gender and changes in not only their attitudes, but also in their practice. Many student-teachers later reported that they reconsidered this model of *Kabbalat Shabbat* and adopted alternative practices, such as allowing the children to recite the blessing together. Moreover, following these conversations, student-teachers often comment that they become more conscious of books that they read to children and pictures they display in the classroom.

Parents and educators should be taking a reflective look at their own practices and texts and asking the sometimes difficult questions. Does the existing curriculum have different expectations of girls and boys in terms of academics, religion, or general behavior? Do books and school assemblies and wall décor present unequal images of women and men? How are boys and girls experiencing religious life or school differently? What are the implications of those differences? As Gail Twersky Reimer argues, "a close reading of the text enables us to suggest to students that the exclusion of women . . . has its source in human interpretation rather than in Divine word. A classroom that promotes this kind of close reading makes room for young women to acknowledge the pain of hearing themselves excluded, but also makes it possible for them to move beyond that pain and recover the word of God for themselves".[23]

Educators, parents and lay leaders need to be supported in the process of raising awareness and consciousness about how girls and boys are experiencing school life and religious life. Schools should be prioritizing gender awareness in order to promote the health of the students and of the Jewish community at large. Schools would be wise to form committees of teachers and parents, men and women, and examine parts of the curriculum and ask the potent questions about gender. What are the messages in the curriculum that exclude girls? What can we infuse into the curriculum to make it more inclusive? How are plays written? Are both boys and girls participating in ways that reflect the reality they experience outside of school?

When gender awareness is raised and the school acknowledges that it is important business to look at gender in a systematic way, teachers will begin to make the changes necessary to best introduce and promulgate the Open Orthodox philosophy of Rabbi Weiss. "The issue," writes Devora Steinmetz, "is not how to teach children to be feminist, but how to educate our children for integrity, responsibility, and commitment, so that they can address the challenges of feminism as well as other difficult challenges, conflicts and problems that they will encounter. . . . I think that educating for these core dispositions is what we, as Jewish feminists and as people of truth, should be concerned with."[24] It is about adjusting a cultural lens to think of all students as equal learners and equal participants in spiritual life: about seeing the Divine image—*tzelem elokim*—in all students.

Over the past years, since Rabbi Weiss has introduced and expanded upon the concept of Open Orthodoxy to try new ways of engaging other Jews, he has come under immense attack by various segments of the Orthodox community. No doubt such is the fate of innovators or those who choose to dispute conventional wisdom in favor of seeking better solutions to contemporary challenges. Assuredly, by himself, Rabbi Weiss cannot be expected to find the best theological and halakhic solution to each social challenge. However, in part because of his love of Klal Yisrael and in part because of his courage, he has already succeeded in raising the sensibilities and sensitivities of whole segments of the broader Jewish community. It is now up to the rest of us to demonstrate how his enabling philosophies can be applied to the myriad endeavors of Jews everywhere and stir Jewish learning, Jewish compassion and Jewish observance.

NOTES

1. Chaya Rosenfeld Gorsetman and Elana Maryles Sztokman, *Educating in the Divine Image: Gender Issues in Orthodox Jewish Day Schools* (Brandeis: 2013).
2. Barrie Thorne, *Gender Play: Girls and Boys in School* (New Brunswick, NJ: Rutgers University Press, 1993), 4.
3. Hervé Varenne and Ray McDermott, *Successful Failure: The Schools America Builds* (Westview Press: 1998), 3-4.
4. Judith Plaskow, "Setting the problem, Laying the ground", in Marvin M. Ellison and Kelly Brown Douglas, ed.s, *Sexuality and the Sacred: Sources for Theological Reflection* (Kentucky: Westminster Press, 1994, 2010), 19.
5. http://www.rabbis.org/news/article.cfm?id=105534 accessed November 10, 2010
6. Blu Greenberg, "The challenges ahead", *JOFA Journal* 3:2 (2002), 2.

7. Jack Wertheimer, *Learning and Community: Jewish Supplementary Schools in the Twenty-First Century* (UPNE: UPNE).
8. Zvi Grumet, ed., *Jewish Education in Transition: Proceedings of the First International Conference on Jewish Education* (Ben Yehuda Press: 2007).
9. Jane Eisner, "Where Are The Jewish Women?" *Huffington Post*, 01/25/2012 http://www.huffingtonpost.com/jane-eisner/where-are-the-jewish-women_b_1229235.html
10. Jane Eisner, Maia Efrem, "Gender Equality Elusive in Salary Survey," *Forward Association, Inc.*, Dec. 9, 2011, http://www.bjpa.org/Publications/details.cfm?PublicationID=13452
11. http://www.jpost.com/LandedPages/Speakers.aspx
12. Nessa Rapoport, "Dreams of paradise: Learning in God's image," in Janna Kaplan and Shulamith Reinharz, ed.s, *Gender Issues in Jewish Day Schools* (The Women's Studies Program; Waltham, MA: Brandeis Univ. Press, 1997), 17.
13. See, e.g., the program of the 2011 AJS conference, with an equal number and male and female presenters. http://www.ajsnet.org/2011prog/AJSprogram2011-draft-111811.pdf
14. Elana Sztokman, "How Modern Orthodoxy Is Losing Touch With Modernity," *The Forward*, May 27, 2010, http://blogs.forward.com/sisterhood-blog/128396/#ixzz1V0stKPlI, accessed July 1, 2011
15. Blu Greenberg, "Gender: A Challenge and an Opportunity," *Jewish Educational Leadership* 6:3 (2008), 24.
16. L. Kvasny, K.D. Joshi, and E.M. Trauth, E.M, "The Influence of Self-Efficacy, Gender Stereotypes and the Importance of IT Skills on College Students' Intentions to Pursue IT Careers," *iConference* 2011 (Seattle, WA).
17. Nessa Rapoport "Dreams of paradise: Learning in God's image," *Gender Issues in Jewish Day Schools*, Janna Kaplan and Shulamit Reinharz, ed.s (The Women's Studies Program; Waltham, MA: Brandeis Univ. Press, 1997), 17.
18. Esther Krauss, "Educating the Jewish woman of the twenty-first century: A modest proposal," *Ten Daat* 3:3 (1989),12-15.
19. Blu Greenberg, "The challenges ahead," *JOFA Journal* 2002 (3:2), 1.
20. Sylvia Barack Fishman, *A Breath of Life: Feminism in the American Jewish Community* (Hanover and London: Brandeis University Press, 1995), 181.
21. Quoted by Idana Goldberg, "Orthodoxy and feminism," in Rabbi Elyse Goldstein, ed., *New Jewish Feminism: Probing the Past, Forging the Future* (Woodstock, VT: Jewish Lights, 2008), 289.
22. Tamar Ross, *Expanding the Palace of Torah: Orthodoxy and Feminism* (Waltham, MA: Brandeis University Press, 2004), xiv.
23. Gail Twersky Reimer, "Suggestions for the study of Shavuot and Sinai," in Janna Kaplan and Shulamit Reinharz, ed.s, *Gender Issues in Jewish Day Schools* (The Women's Studies Program; Waltham, MA: Brandeis Univ. Press, 1997), 42.
24. Devora Steinmetz, "What we should educate for," *JOFA Journal* 3:2 (2002), 1.

JEFFREY S. GUROCK

Checking Up on America's "Tentative Orthodox" Jews

WRITING CONTEMPORARY HISTORY—telling the story of events, issues, processes or personalities of the recent past—is always a dicey proposition. Unlike examinations of long-ago circumstances, where new evidence rarely comes to light and only interpretations vary, when considering up-to-date activities, the facts on the ground often change and conspire to render your treatment outdated. Such I fear may well be the fate of the epilogue to my book, *Orthodox Jews in America*. Modern Orthodox rabbis, trained at Yeshiva Chovevei Torah (YCT) under the guidance and inspiration of Rabbi Avi Weiss, are among those who are making my concluding remarks worthy of revisiting.

At the close of my study of 350 years of the challenges that Orthodoxy has faced in an increasingly open, free society, I took my readers on a virtual tour of Jewish communities that I knew of, or had visited as a scholar-in-residence, primarily to explore how Orthodox rabbis and their synagogues were doing on the hustings—away from the New York epicenter—among those whom I called the "Tentative Orthodox."[1] These are the Jews whom others have mislabeled—and I have been guilty too—as "non-observant Orthodox."[2] These individuals and families harbor no doctrinal difficulties with what the tradition teaches, but for a variety of social, cultural and, above all, economic reasons, are unable to follow punctiliously the demands of the halakhah. At the same time, through word and deed, they distance themselves from liberal Jewish practice and institutional life. Many of them have difficulties finding comfort zones in Reform or Conservative precincts. The classic case, for me, is the Jew who carefully observes Sabbath traditions in his or her home, but to support a family may labor on the Sabbath day in a shop, store or factory in clear violation of the cardinal principle of no work on the day of rest. The problem with such a value-laden designation is the reality that no one is completely non-observant of the mitzvot. Nor, for that matter, is anyone even

JEFFREY S. GUROCK is the Libby M. Klaperman Professor of American Jewish History at Yeshiva University.

capable of fulfilling all of the commandments. Perhaps, Rabbi Weiss' influence—his acceptance of, and tolerance towards, all Jews—has rubbed off on my scholarship.[3] In any event, I showed that that type of congregant has not disappeared, even in an era of Orthodox triumphalism.

The three case studies that follow—up to date as of the fall of 2015—evidence that this constituency still exists and in each instance predominates in its locale along with its welter of religious and social proclivities. What has changed—to some extent—are the efforts synagogue leaders have made to gain or to retain these worshippers' allegiances. Readers also will see in this tale of three towns, the communal and particularly the personal challenges—including in two cases, the ultimate impermanence of their own presence in small city pulpits—that rabbis face in leading Jews to affirm their commitments to the Torah.

One simulated peregrination—back in 2005—took me on a trip to Portland, Maine, where I encountered an Orthodox presence in decline and a rabbi and his wife who were largely bereft of any deeply committed laity. The tip-off that all was not well in town was noticeable the evening of Tisha B'Av when the rabbi struggled to gather a minyan the night that the Book of Lamentations was read. He produced the quorum at night, but not the next morning, when only eight worshippers appeared. My greatest concern was that I might have the same paltry number of listeners at my late-afternoon lecture. But the rabbi reassured me that there would be a respectable turnout since the Jews in town liked to hear outside speakers. He also reassured me that the audience would be attentive since probably he, his rebbetzin, and I would be the only ones in the sanctuary who would be fasting on that day of Jewish national mourning.

Surveying the larger communal scene, there seemed that there was no potential for the growth of Orthodox life. Kosher meat was available in supermarkets for home dining, but the only public kosher establishment was the local old-age home. As far as attracting the grandchildren or great-grandchildren of those who built this once immigrant congregation back to their 100 year-old synagogue, those who affiliated with synagogue life were more than comfortable in Portland's more vibrant Reform temple. The liberal congregation had plenty of room in its sanctuary for them as well as for Jewish newcomers to the city. How is that outpost synagogue doing a decade later? And has it reached any more Jews?

I have not been back to southeastern Maine, but reports have it that during the tenure of YCT ordainee Rabbi Akiva Herzfeld, Orthodoxy made modest gains and showed signs of persistence, even if challenges to substantial growth remained. The extent to which an Orthodox presence both survived and advanced is due to the loyalty of some long-standing members—the residual folks that the rabbi encountered when he first ventured up north to their ancestral religious home—but also to a novel approach to religious life that stands fundamentally in line with the mission of Herzfeld's alma mater and the teachings of Rabbi Weiss. However, these dual motivations—filiopietism and rabbinic creativity—have not always acted in concert with each other.

Under Herzfeld, Shaarey Tphiloh's "philosophy . . . embrace[d] an Orthodoxy that is modern, open and inclusive." In that spirit, it propounded that "the modern world should inform . . . religious experience." Its openness emphasized responsibility for service to the Jewish people worldwide, especially in the State of Israel, as well as concern for the local Portland community and the needs of the "larger American community." And 'inclusiveness" meant not only welcoming into synagogue life Jews of all religious persuasions but also partnership with other Jewish movements and even "joint aid programs" with "local churches." One of Herzfeld's proudest accomplishments was the construction of a community-wide ritualarium, Mikvat Shalom, which serves—and is supported by—elements of all Jewish movements. Prior to his tenure, Shaarey Tphiloh had an under-funded and under-used mikvah which was frequented mostly by Chabad emissaries in town. Though some naysayers within and without his shul questioned letting Conservative and Reform rabbis use the now-upgraded facility, Herzfeld persevered in being blind to denominational labels when it comes to advocacy for greater observance of a cardinal mitzvah.

Bringing people in also translated itself into Shaarey Tphiloh positioning itself as a "home for the young and elderly, the able bodied and the mentally and physically challenged." Following in the footsteps of YCT's flagship, well-nigh sponsoring synagogue—the Hebrew Institute of Riverdale (HIR)—Shaarey Tphiloh "redesigned [its] main sanctuary to make it fully wheelchair accessible."

The Portland synagogue also emulated HIR programmatically when it announced that it would celebrate Martin Luther King Day "in honor of the man who has provided the world with guidance on how to accord respect to each human being. "And like the Rabbi Weiss' activist congregational mode, under Herzfeld, the synagogue became "not only a place in which we gather to pray," but also a place to "gather to talk and harbor ideas so that we can take action in the world."[4]

As an Open Orthodox rabbi, Herzfeld showed an affinity for the elasticity of the halakhah. In one notable instance, it was precisely this comfort with expanding the reach of Jewish tradition that garnered him national recognition but also led to questioning of his fidelity to Orthodoxy's straight and narrow in some quarters.

In December 2011, Herzfeld made his unconventional decision to invite Reform rabbi Alice Goldfinger to lead a portion of Friday evening services. As Goldfinger later told the *Forward*, after having sustained a traumatic brain injury from a fall on the ice in December 2009, she was unable to "work as a rabbi again" and her "former congregation didn't know what to do with her two children (she is a single mom), so they didn't do anything." Living about 15 miles from the temple—and perhaps, estranged from the congregation that she had loyally served for ten years—Goldfinger, at Herzfeld's behest, crossed over into Shaary Tephiloh's gates to observe the yahrzeit of her mother. Herzfeld would later say that she had been "very supportive of me" and "we had worked together as a community," as he extended to her the honor of reciting and singing the Kabbalat Shabbat liturgy before she would say the Kaddish. Very often, men observing that anniversary are invited to lead services in memory and in honor of their departed relatives. But here, effectively, a woman was serving as a cantor, which to the vast majority of Orthodox minds was an abridgement of Orthodox understanding of Jewish law.[5]

Deeply moved, she not only prevailed upon her children who were decidedly non-traditional to attend the service, but also was joined by some of her erstwhile congregants to what she called "*our* 108 year-old Orthodox congregation, led by *our* Orthodox rabbi." Apparently, while her temporary new rabbi Akiva Herzfeld sided intellectually with the majority rule about women cantors, he felt a transcendent personal, human side to the religious call. As Goldfinger finished the story: "After the service Rabbi Herzfeld said: 'I want you to know that I do not believe women should lead worship with men present, but one of us had to be uncomfortable. Why should it be you and not me?'"[6]

Several years later, Herzfeld would explain that the issue for him was behavioral and not halakhic: "I did not grow up with a woman leading services and it was not something that I was used to, and even if there was halakhic justification to allow it, the culture of the shul and the people who attend the shul on a regular basis who grew up Orthodox had never seen it. It would cause discomfort. Any change brings discomfort."[7]

Goldfinger, who promised her blog readers that this "making of history" would be, for her, a once in a lifetime event would, however, not forget that while "he can't repair my broken brain . . . Rabbi Herzfeld brought healing to my broken heart." And she paid tribute to her colleague by nominating him for a *Forward*-generated list of "America's Most Inspiring Rabbis." When this account was published, it went viral as "the most read profile of [the] entire Inspiring Rabbi series."[8]

Predictably, when the *Forward* story found its way into the Orthodox bloggers' world, Herzfeld absorbed his share of flack. One critic opined "this would have been a beautiful story except all he did was compromise his 'orthodoxy' for her comfort, which is clearly not an orthodox act." Another respondent who also saw some positive qualities in Herzfeld's decision but was ultimately unmoved said: "what a sad story, his motives and compassion are truly inspirational and to be lauded, his willingness to sacrifice his (halakhic) principles on the altar of modern liberalism, truly shameful." But the Portland rabbi also found support on the web. One backer addressed the calculus of strict construction of Jewish law versus humane activity. He wrote: "I think Hashem [God] would be very proud of, regardless of whether it was technically proper under Jewish law." And still another respondent—who seemingly shared the Maine rabbi's point of view—questioned whether in fact Herzfeld had crossed an unassailable religious line, as he suggested that "Kabbalat Shabbat is only the material before *Barchu* [the call to prayer that begins the evening service] he let her lead that, which is not a basic halakhic problem according to many *poskim* [decisors of Jewish law]."[9]

Back home in Portland, Herzfeld's determined outreach received mixed reviews. One congregant reportedly told Goldfinger: "That was great! Why don't we do that more often?" Others were not so certain that they approved. Herzfeld has said that he intuited "some push-back;" even though it "does not always come in a frontward manner, sometimes you get pushed from behind" by those who could not relate to change. Herzfeld was sure to note that there was no correlation between personal levels of observance and resistance to change. In his community, as always, the majority of those who defined themselves as Orthodox were wont to drive to services, and since there was no eruv in town, carrying *taleisim* to shul was standard fare.

So how successful was Herzfeld within a congregation consisting of essentially Tentative Orthodox Jews? When he began in Portland on a once a month basis in 2007—while still a student at YCT—he encountered a congregation of "eight or nine older men in their eighties and nineties and a few ladies." Six year later, he ministered to a membership of approximately 65 families, forty to fifty of whom regularly attend Sabbath morning services, "including children;" a positive sign for the future.[10] As another marker, in recent years Tisha B'Av has been commemorated with a minyan during both evening and daytime prayer services; albeit that "progress" carried with it an interesting caveat in 2013. In July of that year, the numbers at Shaarey Tphiloh ironically increased due to the reticence of some congregants to participate in a community-wide service where a woman would be reading the Book of Lamentations. In other words, here Herzfeld's Tentative Orthodox Jews demonstrated their fidelity to their definition to tradition through distancing themselves from liberal Jewish practice, even if it is unlikely that they fasted and abstained from other normal activities. Meanwhile, given the paucity of strictly-kosher eaters in town, there is no movement afoot to open a kosher restaurant. The best place for the several Jewish families who live close to the synagogue and the Herzfeld's home was to garner an open invitation to the rabbi and his wife's for a Sabbath meal. The presence of these neighbors also facilitated play-dates with the Herzfeld youngsters that made for a happier social life than the one Rabbi Herzfeld first encountered when he came to Portland.

However, as of the fall of 2014, Herzfeld was not longer at the helm of the synagogue. (Readers may already have intuited the direction this story was taking since much of my account was written in the past tense.) In an email to me in May, 2014, he explained that his family was scheduled to move to Israel in the fall because "we have four children, six and under," and "they will have broader opportunities for educational learning and youth activities in Israel than are available in the U.S." For Herzfeld, "Maine is beautiful and amazing but this seemed like the best time for the children to go to Israel." Herzfeld was gratified that "people here have supported us in our decision to make aliyah." Yet his departure left his worshippers bereft. A year later, Shaarey Tphiloh—as of July, 2015—had not found a successor. YCT has sent students periodically as temporary rabbis. And the school "will help them for the [High] holidays and [then] see what happens next.[11]

Meanwhile, over the past several years, I have kept closer tabs on the complexities of Tentative Orthodoxy in Charleston, South Carolina and its relationship to more observant fellow Jews in the Palmetto City. My connection with that community dates back to 2004 when its long-existing Orthodox congregation Beth Israel-Brith Sholom (BSBI) commissioned me to write its history as it commemorated its 150th anniversary. My affection for that quaint and historic Southern town was intensified in the spring semester of 2012 when my wife and I sojourned there while I taught at its College of Charleston. My take on that constituency in *Orthodoxy in Charleston*—which I summarized in my larger work's "road trip"—was that while since the 1970's, the membership rolls had declined appreciably, with the local Conservative congregation being the prime beneficiary, nonetheless the main downtown synagogue venue continued to attract "close to six hundred" worshippers during the prime times of the Jewish year, "the first day of Rosh ha-Shanah and Yom Kippur right before Yizkor." Those who were drawn to their ancestral religious home do so in large part because this is the holy place that generations of their relatives had attended. However, to get to the sanctuary, 90% of members drive their cars. As quintessential Tentative Orthodox Jews, many also park their vehicles out of sight of the shul's front door.[12]

BSBI did have its more observant Orthodox families—starting with the 10% who walked to shul on holy days. For a long time—since the 1970's—many of these Jews prayed in a satellite venue called Minyan House situated several miles away over the Ashley River. And more recently, a third appendage of committed congregants established their own minyan within Charleston's Jewish Community Center (JCC), also across the Ashley River. The several segments of BSBI were formally linked through membership and the appearance of the "circuit-riding rabbi" who devotedly served the spreading-out community for over thirty years and who preached on both sides of the river. The issue for the "frum" cohort moving forward—no matter what side of the Ashley River they called home—was an endemic brain drain of their youngsters who attended the first-rate elementary day school. Lacking a critical mass of students to support a secondary school, most of their youngsters leave town as teenagers and do not return. I ended my virtual visit and the "Charleston book" with some questions about the future of the community as the long-time rabbi retired and a new man took his place.[13]

Turning back to Charleston in 2013, I found that many of the problematics that stunt the growth of Orthodoxy in that city remain, but two different religious establishments address them now. In 2012, the JCC-based minyan that actually began in private homes and was known for a while to locals as SHLEP (Shabbat Learning and Experience Program)—perhaps a fine play on words in acknowledging the issue of Sabbath traveling—broke away, with some "60-70 adult worshippers" in tow, from the long standing BSBI. During the week, those interested in praying in a minyan still repaired to the congregation of long-standing. As with so many splits within synagogues nationally, the fissure was reportedly rife with "acrimonious disagreements." Those who founded Congregation Dor Tikvah believed that the days of the established synagogue were numbered and that the future of Orthodox life had to be centered where they lived. "Suburban living is more appealing to families," one member explained to a local reporter. "Facts on the ground caused this to happen." Believing that their city could not support two separate Orthodox synagogues, the grand plan—that was backed by several of the erstwhile leaders of BSBI and the new young rabbi who had arrived in town in 2005—was for BSBI to leave the historic district and to resettle west of the Ashley River. The advocates for migration argued "in many other cities, downtown synagogues are defunct because the next generation moved to suburbs…That's what's happening in Charleston." However, stalwart supporters of BSBI in the historic district demurred and "resisted" the proposed change of venue. For them, arguably, BSBI downtown was their ancestors' congregation, and a strong sense of devotion to family traditions kept them close to the old venue even if to get to services these Tentative Orthodox Jews chose—as always—to drive to services on holy days. [14]

One supporter of the old time shul added that maintenance of the synagogue "along with the Ashley Hall School anchors the neighborhood . . . and it's walking distance from the College of Charleston's Jewish Studies Center which hosts many public events." Besides which, "Jews live throughout the tri-county area, and many of the Orthodox would have to drive on the Sabbath no matter where the synagogue is located. He did "not care" if these Tentative Orthodox "drive, just so we get them to come."[15]

Within this new configuration, in April 2013, Rabbi Michael Z. Davies was elected to serve Dor Tikvah. Concomitantly, a rabbi with a similar-sounding last name, Moshe Davis—who came into town just six months earlier—began addressing the challenges of spiritual leadership of BSBI. They also had in common the fact that they were both trained at Yeshiva University's rabbinical school. Davis was called to his post after a spirited competition against a YCT graduate—a portion of which I observed first hand when I attended services at BSBI during David Wolkenfeld's try-out weekend. Even more equivalently, Davies and Davis minister to, for the most part, comparable majorities of Tentative Orthodox Jews. As of October, 2013, Davies estimated that of the "50 family units" who have affiliated, only "10-15% were Shomer Shabbat, although not many [drive their cars to shul on Shabbat] since they live within walking distance of the shul." Davis' estimate of the levels of observance breakdown in his congregation is that "of approximately 230 family units, perhaps there are thirty shomer Shabbat families, some 10-15%"—a proportionality that is just like Dor Tikvah. And also like Davies, Davis is "welcoming of all and we don't ask how people get to shul [though] some presumably drive."

Understandably, both rabbis likewise harbor the common goal of increasing their memberships, either through attracting the tentative and the more observant Orthodox to their fold. For Davis, with his start-up congregation now having a spiritual leader in place and Dor Tikvah initiating attractive "social programming," he believes that the religious outpost across the Ashley has the potential to bring in "unaffiliated, indigenous Charleston Jews" through "the welcoming nature of the shul, bringing in people of all stripes." Adopting the rhetoric of inclusion of the times—a statement that Herzfeld might have made back up north—Davies asserted that ours "is an Orthodox congregation but a congregation that is open to all denominations across the spectrum." And while Dor Tikvah is "not looking to poach" from other local synagogues, the congregation and rabbi are determined "to put our best foot forward." These strides, Davies contends, augur well for his institution, Jews from outside of Charleston who are attracted as visitors to one of America's prime vacation spots and who determine once they encounter the warmth of Charleston that the Palmetto City is a place where they would want to reside permanently.

Back at BSBI, Davis has been more aggressive in pursuing one of his own "core groups": young retirees. In his first year at the helm, he noticed that "almost on a weekly basis" he received inquiries from Jews who wanted to visit South Carolina and who wondered about the availability of kosher food—the small kosher "Pita Place" in town folded before Davis arrived—and about the possibility of Sabbath lodging. To accommodate these tourists and to showcase his synagogue and community, in May 2013, Davis ran with wife Ariela's brainstorm and, with his wife, organized a Shavuot retreat in town with full accommodations. Advertised nationally, this event attracted some fifty visitors. He hoped that these folks would talk up Charleston to their friends and relatives as a place to settle and live vibrant senior years. Looking at his present shul demographics, Davis observed that every retiree who now belongs to the shul—some of whom are among the most active—began as a tourist. Significantly, this cohort of congregants include those who "walk and those who drive on a regular basis to services." One of BSBI's long-time members added: "we're not going after people with 10-12 year old children".

Nonetheless, Davis also hopes to attract to BSBI—regardless of their religious values—a second cadre of "young professionals and those right out of college" as he asserts that for this age group, this city is a "hip-trendy town." Yet for the more observant among these folks, the issue of intensive Jewish day schooling and the "brain drain" remains a major challenge. A high school, he believes, "would be ideal," but in the meantime, until "we are ready for that . . . [we] need to strengthen the elementary and middle school." He also hopes that such improvements might conceivably reverse the brain drain as BSBI would attract the sons and daughters of the more observant congregants back to their hometown who then build their own loyal homes in Charleston. But "we need amenities," he said, to convince them to stay over the long haul.

Dor Tikvah's Rabbi Davies is somewhat more sanguine about the possibility of "significant growth educationally" in town, even as he has fully "embraced the transient nature of the community." Indeed, he assumed his post clear-headed about the "aging out" conundrum. During his try-out weekend, he was told by some of those who interviewed him and who wanted him in town that they were "leaving in a couple of years." Yet, with tempered optimism, he noted that the Addlestone Academy was "moving into a new building" and that there have been "positive conversations about the future of the day school." One possibility towards reaching the high school "ideal" that captivates the rabbi is the potentiality of "blended education." Under this modality, significant portions of the curriculum could be made available online with the assistance of educational innovators from his and Davis's alma mater. For itself, Yeshiva University has expended resources and sent its student ambassadors to Dor Tikvah and BSBI on holidays to strengthen the religious spirit of the locales, both the tentative and the more observant.[16]

At our third and final revisited venue, the challenges facing Orthodoxy in Omaha, Nebraska are comparable, even if that community apparently has been spared Jewish intra-denominational competition within its limited constituency. When I took my readers there in 2008, I described how the Tentative Orthodox predominated and were ministered to by yet another young rabbi who had pledged to uphold Beth Israel's mission to "welcome all persons of the Jewish faith . . . and accepts the diversity of practice and thought among its members." There, a significant portion of his regular attendees at Sabbath services—"120 [worshippers] on a big *shabbes* and 70 regularly"—drive to synagogue, especially those who remained in the downtown section of town after the synagogue relocated some years earlier. In this community too, long-term allegiances to parental shuls affect the choice of synagogue. There were only "twenty to thirty" Sabbath-observant families out of a congregational body of two hundred; the "tentatives" were most visible at High Holiday services. But even as Rabbi Jonathan Gross was open to all in his Orthodoxy and asserted "for the record" that he "became a rabbi to be a rabbi in Omaha," he hoped to build his more observant constituency. And he too faced a brain drain, as the local community day school was small and his minority of more committed Orthodox Jews tended to either leave town—just like Charleston—as their children grew older. Or they sent their teenage youngsters to such cities as Chicago, Cleveland or Memphis. Only some return to build their own families in town.

The critical logistical issue for him in building community was the need to have an eruv. That was his prime concern and objective when he signed his five-year contract in 2007. But the time had to be ripe for such a critical construction. His sense then was "until recently we did not have a critical mass of young families that would warrant the expense. It does not pay to build an eruv so that a few people can carry their keys to shul." As a stopgap measure, Gross took a lenient halakhic position on "carrying." He ruled that it was "permissible to employ a [Gentile] baby sitter to push a stroller to and from shul." He also noted that this had long been "accepted halakhah in Omaha." Still, the lure of an eruv was "an imperative" for him, as he counted "all these little children" around him, and prayed that "please God we will have one very soon."[17]

By 2012, Rabbi Gross succeeded in having an eruv constructed in his community. But though they built it, large numbers of deeply committed members have yet to come. Rabbi Gross had predicted that with local "low unemployment and low cost of living" and the attractions of his "beautiful new shul [building], the day school . . . a kosher bagel store and the Rose Blumkin Jewish Home [that] operates a deli every Friday for lunch and a few times a month in the evenings"—and, of course, with the eruv—"all the stars have aligned for our Omaha Jewish community." However as late as October 2013, Gross admitted that he was still ministering to a small, fluctuating and often transient "shomer shabbes" constituency. He then estimated that of a congregation of some "200 family units, 25" were deeply committed—almost an identical proportionality as seven years earlier. (Sounding much like his colleagues in Charleston, Gross averred that all people are welcome and that he does not concern himself with how congregants find their way to services on holy days.) Still, such a limited base could ill afford a core constituent family moving to Israel or seeking employment out of his town. The facts on the ground moved him to realize that an eruv "was not enough of a draw"; and with a day school that only educated its some sixty students up to the sixth grade, "the big question," as Gross put it, "is how we are going to educate our kids."

However, as much as he hoped that more shomer shabbes families would eventually populate his pews, as a quintessential rabbi to the Tentative Orthodox, Gross redoubled his efforts towards that marginal cohort through a creative tweaking of his Sabbath morning services—a novel approach, albeit within halakhic boundaries.

Gross's own "pew survey [of Omaha Jewry]"—a play on words referencing a contemporary Jewish identity study—"judging whether or not Jews show up at their houses of worship on any given shabbes, unless there is a bar or bat mitzvah," has revealed that "only 2% of our community show up anywhere." While there are some 6,000 Jews in the city, only "120 families have synagogue attendance as part of their [weekly] routine, it is not part of our culture." For him, one of the cruel ironies in his community is that while Omaha Jews are "extraordinarily generous" in building their institutions, they do not regularly attend their shuls, nor—as critically—send the vast majority of their children to its day school. Perhaps the most attractive locale is the Jewish Community Center campus, with its welter of cultural and athletic activities within the same sprawling campus that houses the Blumkin Home and the day school.[18]

For Gross, one of the impediments to ongoing attendance at all synagogues is "that people are tired of Rabbis standing at pulpits and talking to them. So at Beth Israel, we traded in our pulpit for a desk and chairs, swapped the sermon for an opening monologue and booked a full season of amazing guests." The program, called "Good Shabbos Nebraska—America's first Shabbos morning synagogue talk show"—is situated in the traditional "sermon slot:" after the Torah reading and before the Musaf prayers. During this interruption, men and women sit together on one side of the *mehitzah* in "a forum that talks with you, not at you." The guest stars in the fall of 2013 included out-of-towners like a foreign policy expert and the Christian outreach director of AIPAC (American Israel Public Affairs Committee), "renowned scholar" Rabbi Dr. Jonathan Rosenbaum, Avital Chizik, a journalist from *Haaretz*, and the well-known and controversial public rabbi Shmuel Boteach. The Sabbath of October 26, 2013 was designated "Pink Shabbes," in recognition of Breast Cancer Awareness Month. In some cases, the ever-generous Omahans covered the travel expenses and honoraria for the speakers. And significantly, in some cases, the patrons also attended the events that they supported. Rabbi Gross has estimated that this program has doubled the attendance at his services, although some of those who are intrigued by the talk show do not remain for the conclusion of services. Nonetheless, Gross is hopeful that many of those who come to the initiative will eventually become more engaged in the prayers. In all events, everyone is invited to the Kiddush that follows at a synagogue that boasts that "every Shabbes is a Shabbaton [special Sabbath]." Gross believed that his plan could be duplicated within many communities nationally that face the problems that he—and for that matter his colleagues in Charleston and Portland—presently faces.[19]

But as it turned out, three months before Portland's Herzfeld decided to make aliyah, in March 2014, Gross of Omaha accepted a call to become an assistant rabbi at Baltimore's large Congregation Beth T'filoh, a synagogue of 1,300 members. Although in this position he was no longer the community's lead rabbi, he was moving back east for family reasons. In his published "Farewell," the rabbi acknowledged that "we are blessed with great synagogues, great rabbis, resources and, of course, warm and friendly people," and that there was a "wonderful day school where" his wife and he "would have been proud to send our children;" ultimately, though, Baltimore "offers something to our children that Omaha can never offer: grandparents." Gross stated that while "there is something special to raising children in smaller Jewish communities that gives them a sense of pride and joy in being Jewish that is harder to come by in larger Jewish communities, these emotions were trumped by understandable personal reasons." In the year after Gross left Omaha, the synagogue had still not found a permanent replacement.[20]

Thus, all told from our inspection update tour, it is clear that even in an era of Orthodox triumphalism and the appearance of statistics and anecdotal evidence about an increasingly punctilious Orthodox community in America, there are Jews out on the hustings who as of yet—and perhaps never will—harbor staunch traditional religious values. And there are rabbis willing to attempt to make personal sacrifices to reach them. But personal considerations may limit their ability to stay and continue the good fight for the faith. What is also striking to me is the commonality of the "openness" of the Orthodoxy of each of these young men in their approaches to congregational life, be they ordained by YCT or Yeshiva University. They all use that same welcoming, accepting, and non-judgmental bywords of our time in ministering to those whom they hope to attract. Arguably, their positions reflect a disposition that YCT explicitly embraces and which Yeshiva University perforce has come to understand as they too prepare their disciples to meet the communal and personal challenges of continuity in locales that are far removed from Orthodoxy's epicenters.

NOTES

1. Jeffrey S. Gurock, *Orthodox Jews in America* (Bloomington and Indianapolis: Indiana University Press, 2009), 312-324.
2. For the origins of the historiographical tradition of non-observance within American Orthodoxy, see Charles S. Liebman, " Orthodoxy in American Jewish Life," *American Jewish Year Book* 66 (1965): 27-90. For a more recent definition of "non-observance" which follows Liebman's conceptualization, see Jacob J. Schacter, "Preface," *in Jewish Tradition and the Non-traditional Jew* (ed. Schacter; Northvale, N.J.: Jason Aronson, 1962), xiv-xvii. See also the many essays in the

Schacter collection that reflect that point of view.

3. For my re-evaluation of my views of non-observance as a category of analysis, see Gurock, "Rethinking the History of Nonobservance as an American Orthodox Jewish Lifestyle," in *New Essays in American Jewish History: Commemorating the Sixtieth Anniversary of the Founding of the American Jewish Archives* (ed.s Pamela S. Nadell, Jonathan D. Sarna and Lance J. Sussman; Cincinnati: American Jewish Archives, 2010), 305-324.
4. On Shaarey Tphiloh's mission see, "our Philosophy," www.mainesynagogue.org
5. For a sense of the debate within Orthodox circles today about the nature of Kabbalat Shabbat as a prayer service, see, for example, http://morethodoxy.org/2013/01/25/partnership-minyanim-a-defense-and-encomium .
6. For Goldfinger's version of what transpired and what it meant, see "Because I'm the Mommy and I Say So . . . ." (December 1, 2011) and " I am Woman Hear Me Roar," (December 4, 2011) on her blog Brainstorm.
7. Interview with Rabbi Avika Herzfeld, September 23, 2013.
8. Abigail Jones, "The Rabbi Who Inspired You Most," *Forward* (March 21, 2013): on-line edition.
9. For a representative sample of blogger responses, see "How Did a Modern Orthodox Rabbi Find Himself On A List of America's Most Inspiring Rabbis," *Failedmessiah.com* (March 20, 2013.)
10. As a rabbinical student, in 2007 Herzfeld began working in Maine on a once a month basis. In 2008, upon ordination, he doubled as Portland's modern Orthodox rabbi and as the Orthodox rabbinical Advisor at Harvard's Hillel. By 2009, he was full-time in Portland. The calculations of membership are soft numbers. Herzfeld reports that when he arrived there were 12-13 paying members. The numbers have increased to approximately 65—the majority older worshippers, but including also some families with children. See interview with Herzfeld.
11. Herzfeld to Gurock, email (May 19, 2014); Ruthie Simon to Gurock, email (July 27, 2015).
12. Gurock, *Orthodoxy in Charleston: Brith Sholom Beth Israel and American Jewish History* (Charleston, S.C.: College of Charleston, 2004), 73-74, 81-83. See also *ibid.*, 315-16. I have also kept tabs on the synagogue through belonging to its listserv.
13. Ibid., 81-82, 84-87.
14. Leah F. Chase, "Dor Tikvah is Third Incarnation," *Charleston Jewish Voice* (November, 2012):16; Adam Parker, " New Synagogue Born in West Ashley," *Post and Courier* (September 2, 2012): G1-3
15. Parker, G3
16. Interview with Rabbi Michael Davies, October 17, 2013; interview with Rabbi Moshe Davis, October 24, 2013. For a report on the retreat weekend in Charleston, see Rukhl Schaechter, "Move Over Florida, Charleston is New Hot Place for Jewish Couples: Shavuot Retreat Highlights Strong Jewish Community," *Forward* (May 25, 2013): online edition. Davies has established a close working relationship with Rabbi Ari Sytner, who preceded Davis as BSBI rabbi and who now works for Yeshiva University's Center for the Jewish Future.
17. Gurock, *Orthodox Jews*, 316-17. Jonathan Gross, "There is an Eruv in Omaha!!!," www.amerabbica.com/2022/01
18. Interview with Rabbi Jonathan Gross, October 26, 2013.
19. "Good Shabbos Nebraska—America's Favorite Shabbos Morning Talk Show," www.goodshabbesnebraska.com; interview with Rabbi Gross.
20. "Farewell," www.amerrabbics.com/2014/03/farewell.html

EUGENE KORN

The Open Torah of Maimonides: Rambam on Halakhah, Ethics and Humanity

"The issue of negative blessings[1] *is no small matter. In many ways, these blessings represent three areas that distinguish Open Orthodoxy—our attitude toward the gentile, the most vulnerable and women. For many people, articulating them in the negative sends a wrong message—that we don't care about them."*[2]

AVRAHAM WEISS

I DO NOT KNOW IF RABBI AVI WEISS coined the term "Open Orthodoxy," but he surely is the one who conceptualized and actualized it. More importantly, Rav Avi made it a compelling reality for Modern Orthodox Jews. We are people who are touched by modernity and who strive to relate to all of God's creatures with sensitivity, ethical integrity and religious meaning. Rav Avi has provided a necessary and vital spiritual option for many of us, and for this alone we are enormously indebted to him.

Is the religious vision of Open Orthodoxy a novelty breaking away from the traditional Orthodox understanding of Torah, mitzvot and halakhah? Some claim this is so, yet Maimonides, the greatest religious thinker *and*

EUGENE KORN is Academic Director of The Center for Jewish-Christian Understanding and Cooperation in Israel and Senior Research Fellow at Beit Morasha of Jerusalem's Institute for Religion and Society. He was editor of the Edah Journal/Meorot for 13 years. He received semikhah from the Israeli rabbinate and earned a doctorate in philosophy from Columbia University. His recent publications include *Returning to Zion: Christian and Jewish Perspectives* (CJCUC, 2015), *Plowshares into Swords? Reflections on Religion and Violence* (CJCUC, 2014), *Jewish Theology and World Religions* (Littman Library, 2012) and *Covenant and Hope* (Eerdmans, 2012). His writings have been translated into Hebrew, Italian, Spanish and German.

master of halakhah in all our glorious history, espoused a conception of Torah and religious life that mirrors some of the same values of Open Orthodoxy. Like Rav Avi, Rambam believed that living the ideals of God's Torah demands that Jews relate to every human being with dignity, compassion and *hesed*. Both Rambam's and Rav Avi's spiritual universe include all people—Jews and gentiles, men and women, the free and those trapped in servitude.

Rambam's soaring spiritual message on this point is found not in his philosophic opus, *Moreh Nevukhim*, but in his halakhic code, *Mishneh Torah* (henceforth MT). It appears in *Hilkhot Avadim* (The Laws of Servants), Chapter 9, section 8. I consider it the most beautiful passage in all that magisterial work:

> It is permissible to work a gentile servant harshly. Even though this is the law, the attribute of piety and the way of wisdom dictate that a person be compassionate and pursue justice, not make his slaves carry a heavy yoke, nor cause them distress. He should allow them to partake of all the food and drink he serves. This was the practice of the Sages of the first generations who would give their slaves from every dish of which they themselves would partake. And they would provide food for their animals and slaves before partaking of their own meals. And so, it is written (Psalms 123:2): "As the eyes of slaves to their master's hand, and like the eyes of a maid-servant to her mistress' hand, so are our eyes to God."
>
> Thus we should not embarrass a servant by our deeds or with words, for the Torah gave them over for service, not for humiliation. Nor should one shout or vent anger upon them. Rather, one should speak to them gently and listen to their claims. This is explicitly stated with regard to the good paths of Job for which he was praised (Job 31:13-15): "Have I ever shunned justice for my slave and maid-servant when they quarreled with me. . . . Did not He who made me in the belly make him? Was it not the One who prepared us in the womb?
>
> Cruelty and arrogance are found only among idol-worshipping gentiles. By contrast, the descendants of Abraham our patriarch, the Jews, whom the Holy One, blessed be He, influenced via the goodness of the Torah and commanded to observe righteous statutes and judgments, (they) are compassionate to all.
>
> Similarly, with regard to the attributes of the Holy One, blessed be He, which He commanded us to emulate, it is written (Psalms 145:9): "His compassion is upon all of His works." And whoever shows compassion to others will in turn be showered with compassion, as it is written (Deut. 13:18): "He will show you compassion, and be compassionate to you and multiply you.

The placement of this passage in MT is not arbitrary. Scholars have noted that Rambam systematically places the most important message of each book of the MT in the book's final passage.[3] This message is the book's philosophic summation, its spiritual lodestar, and it is each last sweeping teaching that Rambam wants the reader to remember when he closes the halakhic code. This passage from *Hilkhot Avadim* is an instance of this technique, appearing as the very last halakhah of *Sefer Qinyan* (The Book of Acquisitions).

The passage is a guide for the Jew attempting to nurture a sensitive religious personality and lead a spiritual life. It makes three fundamental points essential to Torah values and religious philosophy, and I would like to analyze it for its power, nuance and message to Orthodox Jews. As is well known, the Torah significantly ameliorated the ancient institution of slavery and decreed that a Jewish master must free his slaves after six years of service (Ex 21:2). It also limited the duration and type of work that a Jewish master may order a slave to perform.[4] Both limitations serve to preserve the slave's intrinsic dignity. Through these legal and moral restrictions, the Torah transformed the institution of *avdut* to make it more similar to a system of indentured servitude rather than the slavery of antiquity in which the slave had no rights and the master owned the slave's body.

Yet the Torah is explicit that these ameliorating limitations apply with reference to a Jewish servant (*Eved Ivri)* and not a gentile slave (*Eved Cana'ani*) serving a Jewish master. The same passages that limit the permitted duration and workload of the Jewish servant explicitly remove these limitations from gentile servitude. This is codified halakhah over which there is no debate. A Jewish master does not free his gentile slave in the seventh year and he is legally free to work him as harshly (*b'farekh*) as he wishes.

Rather than restrict himself to the strict legal definition of gentile slavery as one would think in this halakhic work, in this passage Rambam rejects the halakhic standard and forcefully asserts, "Even though this is the law, the attribute of piety and the way of wisdom dictate that a person be merciful and pursue justice, not make his slaves carry a heavy yoke, nor cause them distress." Here Rambam declares that there are two levels of behavioral norms for the religious Jew: (1) the strict halakhah (*din*), and (2) the ethical demands of piety (*hasidut)* and wisdom (*hokhmah*)—stressing that the latter are no less imperative for Torah Jews. Crucially, Rambam insists that is the meta-halakhic ethical value that defines the religious ideal.

Rabbi Joseph B. Soloveitchik was fond of saying, "Halakhah is the floor, but ethics is the ceiling," yet according to this text of Rambam, the strict halakhah governing the practice of gentile slavery falls below the acceptable minimal standard for a pious Jew. How serious is the failing when a Jew follows the strict parameters of *din* exclusively and neglects super-legal kindness (מידת חסידות)[5], practical wisdom (דרכי חכמה) and basic fairness (צדק) toward other people? Rambam's language is extreme, shocking the reader who is used to Rambam's otherwise moderate and balanced style throughout MT: "Cruelty [i.e. the absence of *hesed*] and arrogance are found only among idol-worshippers." No matter how "halakhic," a Jew's actions bereft of *hesed* takes him out of the community of the pious and places him in the community of immoral idolators. Nor is this mere hyperbolic rhetoric: Elsewhere Rambam rules that a Jew who is cruel, hates others or who lacks compassion toward another person is suspect, and consequently his Jewish lineage should be investigated.[6]

Rambam's insistence on the insufficiency of strict halakhic obedience for Jewish behavior is the normative rabbinic view that is shared by others from the Talmud through the Middle Ages. For *Hazal*, it was the exclusive compliance with narrow halakhic standards that led to the destruction of the Second Temple;[7] according to the first century talmudic sage Shimon ben Shetah, myopic concern for the letter of the halakhah yields barbaric behavior;[8] and for Nahmanides (Ramban) in medieval times, narrow minded pan-legalism produces a Jew who is "a scoundrel within the domain of Torah."[9] While it is commonplace to hear some religious Jews today defining Torah as a pan-halakhic system and claiming that halakhah defines all Jewish values, clearly both Ramban and Rambam disagree—and vehemently so. For them, there are essential religions values outside of strict halakhah, and when a Jew ignores these values he fails miserably to live a correct Torah life.

The second major thesis of Rambam in this halakhah is that Jews are members of universal humanity. For Maimonides, there is no genetic or ontological difference between Jews and gentiles. He insists that all humans are identical in their essence. Indeed, Jews and gentiles *are* different, but it is the influence of the teachings and values of Torah that separates Jews from gentiles, not any innate or genetic property: "By contrast [to gentiles], the descendants of Abraham our patriarch, [and his descendants, who are] Israel, whom the Holy One, blessed be He, influenced via the goodness of the Torah and commanded to observe righteous statutes and judgments, are merciful to all."

Rambam participated vigorously in the philosophical debate that began in the Middle Ages and that continues in Orthodox circles today:[10] Is there a common humanity, or are Jews fundamentally different from gentiles? Rambam's answer to this question is unambiguous and consistent, as he writes repeatedly throughout his many works that Jews and gentiles share the same defining human characteristics and are part of the same humanity.[11] For Rambam, what differentiates Jews from gentiles is "software" acquired by learning Torah, not "hardware" inherited genetically or spiritually.[12] Rambam poignantly cites Job to drive home this point: "Did not He who made me in the belly make him? Was it not the One who prepared us in the womb?" Maimonides' citation of Job reflects Rambam's conceptual elegance and reinforces this point: in rabbinic tradition there is no consensus regarding whether Job is Jew or gentile, a historical personality or a mere literary persona. Job is everyman, the prototypical universal figure of humanity.[13] In both Job's and Rambam's eyes, we are all children of the same universal God of Heaven and Earth who creates Jews and gentiles identically in the same womb.

The insistence that there are no innate differences between Jews and gentiles reflects on the glory and importance of the Torah. Were Jews ontologically different from gentiles, we would not need Torah to preserve our uniqueness and ensure our spiritual survival.[14] According to Rambam, Jewish identity is neither an ethnic nor a racial category. Jews are a spiritual and moral community shaped by the values of Torah. Again, some traditionalists today may believe that Jews comprise a different species, that they have different DNA (be it physical or "spiritual") and that this essential difference justifies religious Jews closing themselves off to the rest of humanity—both to gentiles as well as to heterodox Jews. Yet for religious, philosophic and communal reasons, Rambam could never have pursued this policy.

At times, some Jews went to great lengths to "correct" Rambam's belief that Jews have a shared humanity and a common human destiny with gentiles. Scholars know that there are varying manuscripts of MT. One instance of a textual variation that carries significant implications is the very last halakhah of MT (Laws of Kings and their Wars, 12:5), the soaring crescendo of the entire work. Most of our printed texts read:

> ובאותו הזמן לא יהיה שם לא רעב ולא מלחמה ולא קנאה ותחרות, שהטובה תהיה מושפעת הרבה וכל המעדנים מצויין כעפר. ולא יהיה עסק כל העולם אלא לדעת את ה' בלבד. ולפיכך יהיו ישראל חכמים גדולים ויודעים דברים הסתומים, וישיגו דעת בוראם כפי כח האדם שנאמר "כי מלאה הארץ דעה את ה' כמים לים מסכים."

All logical and bibliographical evidence indicates that this is a corrupted version of Rambam's words. This version's ending limitation that only Israel will be great sages who reach the apex of human wisdom about God is manifestly inconsistent with the stunning universal vision ("ולא יהיה עסק כל העולם אלא לדעת את ה' בלבד.") that Rambam paints earlier in the passage. Hence it should be no surprise that all early reliable manuscripts indicate that Rambam never used the word "ישראל" here. Instead he wrote:

ולפיכך יהיו חכמים גדולים ויודעים דברים הסתומים, וישיגו דעת בוראם כפי כח האדם שנאמר "דעה את ה' כמים לים מכסים".

Evidently, a particularist Jew inserted the word "ישראל" convinced that that Rambam could not have believed in a common humanity or universal spiritual destiny.[15] Yet Rambam did believe precisely that, as our passage in *Hilkhot Avadim* indicates.

Third, Rambam closes by insisting that that the defining and most crucial personality trait of a Torah Jew is *rahamim*—empathetic compassion. If there is one essential characteristic of the faithful Jew, it is to be motivated by *rahamim* that expresses itself in acts of *hesed* toward all people. While having social and communal implications, the virtue of *rahamim* is nevertheless fundamentally religious and theological. The ultimate objective of the religious Torah life is to come close to God, and we achieve this by cultivating a personality of kindness and empathy that opens us up to sensitive relations with all human beings ("ורחמיו על כל מעשיו"). The God-intoxicated Jew is a *rahamim* personality who acts with unbounded *hesed* toward all God's creatures.

Because Rambam was a masterful pedagogue who knew his audience well, he was undoubtedly aware of how difficult it is for most people to act from virtue alone (*lishmah*). There are times when each one of us needs the promise of tangible reward to motivate us to act properly, thus Rambam adds, "וכל המרחם מרחמים עליו, שנאמר "נתן לך רחמים ורחמך"—"and all who show compassion toward others, are in turn showered with compassion", to give us practical incentive to show lovingkindness and compassion to all.

If the purpose of mitzvot and our halakhic duties is to draw us nearer to the Creator, then the test of successful halakhic obedience must be judged by the extent to which we are open to and compassionate toward all others—Jew and gentile, man and woman, superior and subordinate, free person or servant. For Rambam, lack of compassion in a Torah Jew is impossible—a contradiction in terms,[16] and the signal theological indication of a person's distance from his nurturing Creator.

In Rambam's eyes, closing oneself off to God's world and His creatures is simply not an option for the religious Jew. When we display empathy and openness, we approach the Divine, fulfill the ideal of *imitatio Dei* ("וכן במדותיו של הקב"ה שצונו להדמות בהם") and help bring God's immanent presence (*Shekkinah*) to earth. This is the character of the ideal religious life, and as such it is an end in itself.[17]

• • •

The twentieth century philosopher Leo Strauss maintained that "genuine fidelity to a tradition is not the same as literalist traditionalism, and is in fact, incompatible with it. It consists of preserving not simply the tradition but the continuity of tradition."[18]

Eight hundred years before Strauss, Rambam understood this concept of fidelity to tradition. Maimonides was both a great leader and an authority in rabbinic history, but Rambam was also a monumentally controversial figure. His universalism and openness to all human wisdom, his insistence that strict halakhah does not define Torah nor exhaust Jewish religious obligations, and his belief that philosophical inquiry was necessary to understand religious truth all generated conflict within the Jewish community. Because he rejected "literalist traditionalism," some of his books were banned and later burned. Rambam knew deeply that correctly understanding Torah and religious life demands rethinking common religious assumptions of the day, and sometimes entails changes in attitude and practice— while resolutely holding fast to the fundamental values of Torah and halakhah he articulated in *Hilkhot Avadim* 9:8.

This is also Rabbi Avi Weiss' understanding of Torah tradition. The courageous path of Open Orthodoxy that Rav Avi is blazing follows the model of Rambam. Rav Avi understands that to make Torah life-affirming and meaningful in our world today, we must bring acute moral sensibilities to the issues of our time. Unlike the eras of our ancestors, many God-intoxicated and Torah-oriented Jewish women today thirst for dignity and equality in Jewish communal life and practice. Heterodox Jews do not aim to assimilate out of our people, nor is their motive rebellion against God and His Torah. And modern Jews regularly interact with gentiles who are not enemies of our people and whose religions cannot be properly understood as idolatry. These new realities demand that faithful Orthodox Jews open up new horizons in Torah—horizons that include women's voices, *K'lal Yisrael* and all human beings. They entail rethinking some of our liturgy and practices, while we continue to hold fast to the deepest values of Torah life, thought and ethics.

After the storms that Rambam created calmed, he became the spiritual inspiration for generations of Jews who cherish Torah, who are faithful to halakhah and who work to bring God into the world. May Rav Avi's legacy follow that of Rambam, and may he continue to inspire *K'lal Yisrael* to lead lives dedicated to Torah, halakhah and what God requests of all Jews—Orthodox and heterodox, men and women, religious and secular alike.

NOTES

1. "Blessed are You, Lord our God, King of the Universe, who has not made me a heathen." "Blessed are You, Lord our God, King of the Universe, who has not made me a slave." "Blessed are You, Lord our God, King of the Universe, who has not made me a woman." These blessings are recited daily by Orthodox Jews in the morning liturgy.
2. "*Shlo Asani Isha*: An Orthodox Rabbi Reflects on Integrity, Continuity and Inclusivity," *Conversations*, Autumn 2013 (Institute for Jewish Ideas and Ideals, NY, 2013) p. 156.
3. See Isadore Twersky, *Introduction to the Code of Maimonides (Mishneh Torah)* (New Haven, CT: Yale, 1980), 371-373, and the forthcoming, *The Universalist Horizons of Maimonides' Mishneh Torah*, by Menachem Kellner and David Gillis (London: Littman Library of Jewish Civilization). For other examples of significant perorations in MT, see final passages of *Sefer Mada*, *Sefer Zemanim* and *Sefer Shoftim*.
4. Lev 25:44 forbids working an *Eved Ivri* harshly (*b'farekh*). Rabbinic tradition defined harsh labor in specific terms in Sifra, *Behar*, ch. 6, *halakhot* 2-3. Rambam repeated this delineation in *Hilkhot Avadim* 1:6-7.
5. *Hesed* is frequently associated conceptually and in actual cases with *lifnim m'shurat hadin*, i.e. acting beyond the strict requirement of halakhah. See my *Legal Floors and Moral Ceilings: A Jewish Understanding of Law and Ethics*, The Edah Journal 2:2, Tammuz 5762 at http://www.yctorah.org/images/stories/about_us/edah%20journal%202_2.pdf.
6. MT, Laws of Forbidden Relations 19:17.
7. *b. Bava Metsi'a* 30b.
8. *y. Bava Metsi'a* 2:5; 8c.
9. Commentary on Lev 19:2.
10. The most famous advocates of the idea that Jews are ontologically different from gentiles are Yehuda Halevi, who maintained that even after gentiles convert to Judaism, they remain spiritually inferior to Jews, and the authors of the Zohar and the Tanya, who maintained that gentiles possess only an animal soul ("*nefesh behamit*") while Jews also possess an additional divine soul ("*nefesh Elokit*"). Shockingly, it is common today to hear even *roshei yeshiva* in rationalist Lithuanian yeshivot espouse this mystical non-rational claim.
11. See MT, Laws of *Shmitah v'Yovel* 13:13, Laws of Kings 8:11, *Moreh Nevukhim* 1:1, "Letter to Ovadiah the Proselyte in Ya'akov Shilat," in *Iggerot ha-Rambam* vol. 1 (Jerusalem: Ma'aliyot, 1988), 231-241, "Eight Chapters," in *The Ethical Writings of Maimonides* (NY: Dover, 1983). For a fuller treatment of this thesis, see Menachem Kellner, *Maimonides on Judaism and the Jewish People* (Albany, NY: SUNY Press, 1991), particularly chs. 4-6,10.
12. Kellner (ibid., 5) attributes this accurate metaphor to Daniel Lasker.
13. The talmudic rabbis (*b. Bava Batra* 15a-b) disagree whether Job is Jewish or gentile, and whether the story is fact or fiction. According to Maimonides, Job may only be a literary personality (*Moreh Nevukhim*, III: 22) or a gentile ("Epistle to Yemen," in *Epistles of Maimonides: Crisis and Leadership* (trans. Abraham Halkin; Jerusalem: Jewish Publication Society, 1985), 110-112. I thank Menachem Kellner for pointing out these references to me.

14. Rambam's insistence that there is no fundamental difference between Jews and gentiles is also sadly confirmed by how easily modern Jews assimilate into gentile culture and lose their Jewish identity in open pluralistic societies. Were the difference ontological, it would be immutable and ineradicable, and hence complete assimilation of an individual Jew to non-Jewish identity would be impossible.
15. See Kellner, "*Farteitcht un Farbessert*—On Correcting Maimonides," *Meorot* 6:2 at http://www.yctorah.org/content/view/330/10.
16. Rambam was not naïve, and he surely encountered the phenomenon of Jews acting without compassion. In this passage he formulates this painful failure as impossible for pedagogical emphasis, in effect admonishing reader, "If you do not act with compassion toward all, you do not deserve to be called a Jew."
17. Rambam also expresses this religious principle as an ultimate theological truth of in the culmination of his philosophic work in III:54 of *Moreh Nevukhim*. There, he insists that the sign of intellectual perfection is the acquisition of *hesed*, defined III:53 as "*haflagah*" (overflow), i.e. autonomous free expression of the ideal human being. Interestingly, *hesed* here is in direct contrast to *gevurah* as limitation or constraint imposed upon a person by heteronomous authority, law, or communal convention.
18. Strauss, *Spinoza's Critique of Religion* (NY: Schocken, 1965), 24.

DOV LINZER

Beit Din's Presence in the Mikveh Room for Conversion: A Case Study in Values and Worldview in the Psak of Rav Ovadya Yosef

THE QUESTION ABOUT whether a *beit din* of three men must be in the mikveh room when a prospective convert is immersing for the sake of conversion is a matter of halakhic debate. A number of responsa have been written on this recently, but this is not the first time this issue has arisen. The last hundred years have seen responsa on this topic by a number of poskim, some ruling leniently and others, such as Rav Ovadya Yosef, ruling strictly.

For those who are strict, the possibility exists to rule that such an immersion would be invalid even after the fact.[1] However, many poskim concede that *bi'di'eved*—that is, *post facto*—the conversion would be valid, but rule that it would be strictly forbidden to do *lichat'hila*—that is, *ab initio*. This seems to be the position of Rav Ovadya Yosef. Once this point is granted, however, it opens the door to argue that *sha'at ha'dehak ki'bi'dieved dami*—exigent circumstances are treated as a *post facto* situation—and thus such an immersion should be allowed to be performed in a *sha'at ha'dehak*. In the contemporary context, many prospective converts have had deeply disturbing, if not at times traumatic, experiences when immersing before a court, and it is felt by many converts and non-converts alike that this requirement violates

RABBI DOV LINZER is the Rosh HaYeshiva of Yeshivat Chovevei Torah Rabbinical School, and the primary architect of its groundbreaking curriculum of Torah, Halakhah, pastoral counseling, and professional training. He teaches regular classes in advanced Talmud, advanced Halakhah, and the thought of Modern Orthodoxy, and has been a leading rabbinic voice in the Modern Orthodox community for over 20 years. He teaches a Daf Yomi shiur which is available on YouTube and iTunes, and was most recently the convener of the 2012 Modern Orthodox Siyyum HaShas.

standards of modesty. This reality would seem to constitute a *sha'at ha'dehak*. Thus, any posek who concedes that such an immersion is valid, at least after the fact, could in principle be used to argue that such an immersion could be done *li'chat'hila* in today's circumstances.

The crux of the issue is whether today's circumstances, or ones like them, constitute a *sha'at ha'dehak*.[2] Rav Ovadya Yosef rules categorically that they do not. In the responsum that we consider in this paper, he does not give any quantifiable or technical parameters for this determination. Rather, what he makes quite clear is that he does not find concerns of this type religiously valid. Similarly, he states that the possibility that potential converts will be discouraged from converting as a result is of no concern to him, because he generally is not in favor of conversion nowadays. The crucial question, then, of whether to consider this case a *sha'at ha'dehak*, is assessed by Rav Ovadya through the lens of the values and the worldview that he brings to this issue.

The role of worldview in the process of *psak* is something that might have come as a surprise in the case of Rav Ovadya Yosef. Rav Ovadya is known for being a posek who tabulates all the opinions on a matter and uses the weight of these previous rulings to arrive at his conclusions, and we thus tend to assume that his conclusions are simply a matter of "doing the arithmetic." Nevertheless, we will see that values and worldview do indeed play a role in how Rav Ovadya assesses policy and *sha'at ha'dehak* considerations. This is perhaps to be expected. Less expected, however, is how these factors may exert an influence even in how he cites and presents his sources. Our analysis will show that there are times when a cited source, as he presents it, differs significantly from its meaning in its original context.

Sha'at Ha'Dehak

Let us look at the responsum directly. In his discussion, Rav Ovadya records those who believe that the *beit din*'s presence in the mikveh room violates standards of propriety:

> והנה אף על פי שהיו כמה אנשים מודרנים (אשר הם חכמים בעיניהם), שהתנגדו לזה בכל תוקף. ובאו בטענה, שאין זה נאה והוגן לחברי בית הדין, להכנס בבית הטבילה של נשים בכלל, בשעה שיש אשה במקוה. . . .

> Behold, although there are some modern people (who are wise in their own eyes), who have vigorously opposed this practice, and have come with the charge that it is not fitting nor appropriate for the members of the beit din to enter into the women's immersion room at all during the time when a woman is in the mikveh . . . .

This complaint, he goes on to say in a parenthetical comment, is absurd, inasmuch as

> ורק לרופא פרוץ מותר לו לבדוק נשים אפילו ערומות, בגלל איזה מיחוש וכיוצא, משא"כ לת"ח צנועים זאת תורת המודרנים הללו, היפך תורתנו הקדושה... ואת הישרה יעקשו, ולא תהיה תורה שלמה שלנו כשיחה בטלה שלהם.

> It is only [acceptable in their eyes] for an immodest doctor to examine women even when they are naked, due to some discomfort or the like that they are experiencing, but it is not acceptable for modest Torah scholars [to act in a similar professional capacity]. This is the Torah of these moderns, the antithesis of our holy Torah... They pervert the straight path, and our perfect Torah should not be treated like their worthless chatter.
>
> (*Yabia Omer*, Yoreh Deah 1:19, section 12)

In Rav Ovadya's eyes, concerns for impropriety emerge from a modern sensibility that is perverse and antithetical to Torah values. By rejecting these concerns as religiously invalid, he concludes that they cannot be the basis for changing what he rules to be the required practice. It goes without saying that such concerns would not constitute a *sha'at ha'dehak*.

Rav Ovadya is not just taking umbrage at any possible aspersions that may be being cast on some particular *dayyanim* by conceding to these concerns. It runs deeper than that. For if this practice—which has been followed for centuries (although the number of converts was considerably smaller in the past)—is seen as immodest or unethical in any way, then it would raise questions as to the behavior of *dayyanim* of hundreds of years. Moreover, since this is a halakhic requirement, acknowledging these concerns would be tantamount to challenging the morality of the halakhah itself. It is thus imperative for him to categorically reject even the possibility that any problem of morality of modesty can exist.

Policy Considerations — Shelo Tin'ol Delet

However, whether the sense of impropriety is legitimate or not, the reality is that people do have these sensitivities, and potential converts might be scared away. This would seem to create a real problem that needs to be addressed. Beyond *sha'at ha'dehak* issues, such concerns could raise policy considerations. In a number of places the Gemara states that certain legal accommodations are made for certain groups so as "not to lock the door in their face"—that is, so as to not create undue obstacles for them. One group that this is said in reference to is converts. If so, perhaps this policy consideration should mandate, or at least allow, leniency in this case. This is indeed the position of Rabbi Ben Zion Uziel (*Mishpitei Uziel* YD 1:13). Rav Ovadya, however, disagrees:

> ולפע"ד אינה ראיה כלל, דהתם כשתנעול הדלת מטעם מומחים, אין גרים בכלל בזה"ז, מכיון שאין לנו מומחים, שפיר חששו לנעילת דלת כזאת. אבל הכא שאין נעילת דלת אלא במקום מסויים, מפני שנתקלים שם באיזה נסיבות, לא מצינו שום קולא בזה. ובייחוד להרכיב קולא מדעתינו במה שלא נזכר בגמ' ופוסקים, זו ודאי לא שמענו ולא ראינו . . . אבל הכא שאין מי שיאמר דהיכא דלא אפשר מותר להטביל שלא בפני שלשה, מי הוא זה אשר ימלאנו לבו לעשות מעשה מטעם זה.
>
> In my humble estimation this is not relevant here at all (lit., this is no proof), for in the case of the Gemara were we to "lock the door" and require "expert rabbis" (with semikhah going back to Moshe), there would be no converts nowadays, since we have no such "expert rabbis," and it makes sense for the Rabbis to have been concerned for such a "locking of the door." But in this case, where there will only be a "locking of the door" in specific circumstances (i.e., a convert who is scared away by the demand that beit din be in the immersion room), we have no precedent for being lenient [due to policy considerations]. How much more so when it comes to grafting on a leniency of our own, one not found in the Gemara and halakhic authorities, we have never seen nor heard of such a thing.... For in this case, where there is no authority who says that a convert may immerse without three judges present when it is possible to do so, who would have the audacity to say that we can act [contrary to this] on the basis of this [policy] consideration?
>
> (*Yabia Omer*, YD 1:19, section 18)

Rav Ovadya makes two straightforward points: (1) The policy of "not locking the door in the face of converts" is applied in the Gemara only when it will actually make it impossible for anyone to convert—whereas this is not the case here; and (2) the leniency of immersion not in the presence of a court has no precedent, and policy considerations cannot allow us to use such an unprecedented leniency.

However, the matter is not so simple. First, the argument that this leniency has no precedent is a curious one, since there is almost full consensus that such an immersion works *post facto*, and this is Rav Ovadya's position as well. Thus, while it is hard to find those who would allow this *ab initio* under normal circumstances, it would seem that due to its acknowledged efficacy, it is a practice that could be adopted based on policy considerations. This is how such a policy is meant to function: to allow practices that otherwise would not be allowed because of the overriding concerns. We are left wondering whether this point in Rav Ovadya's argument was influenced by his stated objection to the motive that lies behind suggesting such a change in the first place—a concern for the propriety of the practice.

Turning to his first point, that *shelo tin'ol delet* only applies when all converts will be excluded, Rav Ovadya in the next section clarifies that there are other reasons why he is not willing to consider this policy here:

> ועכ"פ בודאי דאנן לא אמרינן הכי מדעתינו, והיכא דאיתמר איתמר, היכא דלא איתמר לא איתמר. וכ"ש האידנא דאחסור דרי ורוב הגיורות אין כוונתן לשם שמים רק לשם אישות וכיו"ב, ודי לנו להקל בעצם הגרות, שאנו מוכרחים לקבלן כשבאים אלינו להתגייר . . . .
>
> אבל להוסיף עוד קולות כגון לטבול שלא בפני ב"ד, כדי שלא תנעול דלת בפני גרים, חלילה לומר כן, אדרבה מי יתן וננעלה דלת בפניהם, ומכ"ש שאחר הגרות ע"פ הרוב זה דרכם כסל למו, ואיש לדרכו פנה, ומחללין שבת, וכו', וקשין לישראל יותר מספחת. ואינם ראויים הללו לחוס עליהם ולהקל נגד דברי חכמים.
>
> Nevertheless, we certainly cannot apply this policy on our own authority, for where it was said, it was said, and where it was not said, it was not said. All the more so nowadays when the generations are on a lower religious level and when the majority of the women who convert are not sincerely religiously motivated, but are only doing it for the sake of marriage and the like. It is sufficient for us to be lenient in allowing the conversion itself, that we are compelled to accept them when they come to us to convert . . . .
>
> But to add other leniencies, for example to immerse not in the presence of the beit din so as not to slam the door in the face of converts, God forbid that we should say this! The opposite is the case—if only we could slam the door in their faces! How much more so [should we not find ways to open the door] considering that in the majority of cases this path of theirs (the converts) is a foolhardy one, and each person goes his own way (in terms of observance), and they desecrate the Sabbath, etc., and converts are more troublesome to the Jewish people than a scab (cf. b. *Yevamot* 109b). It is not fitting to have compassion on them and to be lenient against the rulings of the Sages.
>
> (Ibid., section 19).

Here we see that just as Rav Ovadya rejected the legitimacy of concerns around impropriety, he likewise rejects a general welcoming and encouraging attitude towards converts. He is in fact happy to turn away converts nowadays. Given this, one cannot also help wondering whether his argument of the inapplicability of the policy to "not lock the door in their face" in the current case is one that has been arrived at dispassionately, or whether it has been influenced by his negative attitude towards present-day converts.

In fact, Rav Ovadya's distinction between a "locking of the door" that is universal, and thus justified, as opposed to one that is of more limited scope, and thus not justified, is not borne out by the sources. In the Gemara, the principle of *shelo tin'ol delet* does not appear regarding converts. It is applied most frequently to explain rulings and procedures enacted for the sake of borrowers, to ensure that lenders would continue to lend money (*b. Yevamot* 152b,*b. Gittin* 50a, *b. Baba Batra* 176a). In the absence of these rulings, some creditors would choose to no longer lend money, but it is clear that certainly others would continue to do so. The application to converts occurs in Tosafot (*b. Yevamot* 46b, *s.v. Mishpat*), where an analogy is made to the case of creditors. Thus, if we are concerned even by creating obstacles for some creditors, we should likewise be concerned about creating obstacles that would exclude some, even if not all, potential converts.

Interestingly, this principle does appear in the Talmudic literature regarding converts in a midrashic context. In *Sifre Bamidbar* (on 10:31), the midrash has Moshe saying to Yitro: "If you abandon us, you will lock the door in the face of future converts, who will say, 'If the father-in-law of the king did not convert, certainly we should not do so'." While this passage is aggadic, it speaks directly to the concern that certain practices would discourage some, but by no means all, potential converts.

Finally, in a different responsum (*Even Ha'Ezer* 2:2), Rav Ovadya advises a man who had an affair with a married woman to not tell her husband about the affair, although according to halakhah she is forbidden to live with her husband. He bases himself on the principle of "not locking the door" in the face of those coming to repent from their sins. Here he uses this principle in a specific and not universal case (by no means will all potential repentants be discouraged), and he also applies it to new circumstances and with leniencies not found in the Gemara.

Given the evidence of the sources and Rav Ovadya's own rulings, it is clear that what is really at play here in his rejection of the principle of *shelo tin'ol delet* is not his analytic distinction between a universal and specific case, or between precedented and unprecedented leniencies, but rather his general worldview regarding converts and conversion.

In contrast, Rabbi Ben-Zion Uziel (*Mishpetei Uziel* 1:13) had a welcoming approach to converts, as is evident in his other responsa.[3] In line with this, Rav Uziel believed that the principle of *shelo tin'ol delet* was quite relevant, and felt compelled to find a way to allow immersion not in the presence of the *beit din*. It probably would not be debated that his worldview and attitude towards converts led him to conclude that there is a mandate of *shelo tin'ol delet* in this case. What now seems clear is that Rav Ovadya was likewise influenced by *his* worldview, only in the opposite direction.

Citation of Sources

a) Rav Uziel

So far, we have seen how Rav Ovadya's values and perspective shaped, or at least contributed to, how he determined whether the situation was one of a *sha'at hadehak* and whether other policy considerations such as *shelo tin'ol delet* should weigh in. On reflection, we might have anticipated that the definition of *sha'at ha'dehak* would incorporate value judgments, and that the decision of whether to apply *shelo tin'ol delet* would likewise be evaluated through the lens of one's assessment of the society, its values, and its priorities. Nevertheless, it is instructive to see it stated explicitly. Beyond the case at hand, this should sensitize us to the role that values and attitudes could be playing beneath the surface whenever *sha'at ha'dehak* and similar principles are invoked.

But policy and value considerations seem to play a role in Rav Ovadya's teshuvot in other ways as well. A close reading of some of the responsa quoted by Rav Ovadya Yosef shows how Rav Ovadya sometimes reads a source in a way that diverges from its original meaning. Often, Rav Ovadya's reading differs from the original meaning in a way that parallels the difference between his worldview and that of the author of the source.

Consider how Rav Uziel explains the circumstances that compel him to find a leniency to allow the judges to be outside the mikveh room:

> בהיותי משרת בקדש בעוב"י סאלניקו יע"א נשאלתי אם אפשר להכשיר טבילת הגיורת שלא במעמד בית דין כי היות ומקוה טהרה נמצא במרחצאות של לא יהודים ובו מתרחצות תמיד גם נשים לא יהודיות וזילותא גדולה היא לבית דין להכנס במרחץ זה והוא דבר זר לעיני הרואים ....
> (משפטי עוזיאל, יו"ד, ס' י"ג)

> When I was serving as a rabbi in Salonika, I was asked if it is possible to permit the immersion of a female convert to take place not in the presence of the *beit din*, inasmuch as the mikveh is located in the bathhouse of non-Jews, and non-Jewish women regularly bathe there, and it is a matter of great embarrassment for the *beit din* to enter the bathhouse and it is a bizarre practice in the eyes of others. . . .

Rav Uziel mentions that given the circumstances of the mikveh's location in a non-Jewish bathhouse, it would be an embarrassment for the *beit din* to enter in there. Presumably, the embarrassment is not for the *beit din* to enter a mikveh room, which itself would be acceptable, but for them to enter a bathhouse where partially and fully undressed women are present. However, the statement that it is a bizarre matter in the eyes of others points to a different issue. The point here seems to be that because there are non-Jews present, they will see that a *beit din* observes a woman when she is immersing, and this, in itself, from an outside perspective seems quite inappropriate.

Now let's see how Rav Ovadya quotes this passage:

ותבט עיני בשו"ת משפטי עוזיאל ח"א (חיו"ד סי" יג), שנשאל בהיותו הרב דסאלוניקי, במה שהמקוה נמצא בבית המרחץ של גוים, ונשי עכו"ם מתרחצות שם, וזילותא גדולה להב"ד להכנס בו, אם אפשר להקל ולהכשיר טבילת הגיורת שלא במעמד ב"ד.
(יביע אומר, יו"ד י"ט, אות ט"ז)

> I have seen in *Mishpitei Uziel* (YD 13), who was asked when he was the rabbi of Salonika, regarding a mikveh that was found in a bathhouse of non-Jews, and the non-Jewish women bathed there, and it was a great embarrassment for the *beit din* to enter there, if it is possible to be lenient to allow a convert to immerse not in the present of the *beit din*.

Notice that Rav Ovadya dropped the second point (that the matter seems bizarre in the eyes of others). Given that Rav Ovadya rejects any concern for the morality or perceived morality of this practice, it would be difficult for him to cite this concern in the responsum he is quoting. He thus quotes only the concern of embarrassment, specifically connected to the mikveh's location, and does not quote the concern that this entire practice is seen as bizarre.

We find a similar truncation in Rav Ovadya's citation of a later passage. In a further description of the case, Rav Uziel writes:

הואיל ובבית המרחץ שבו המקוה נמצאות תמיד נשים שמתרחצות בו ועמידת בית דין על ידי הטובלת גורמת לזות שפתים מצד הנשים המתרחצות ומצד הקהל והואיל ומצד הדין והמוסר לא הותר לכל אדם, ומכל שכן לרבני ישראל, להכנס לתוך מרחץ של נשים בשעה שהן מתרחצות. . . .
וכאשר נכנסים אל המרחץ שיש בו נשים אחרות שמתרחצות או אפילו מתלבשות לא ימלט דבר זה שלא במתכוין, וכיון שכן נעשתה טבילת גיורת במעמד בית דין לדבר שאי אפשר, ובמקום שאי אפשר כזה קרוב הדבר לומר שלכל הדעות מהניא טבילתה שלא בפני בית דין אפילו להשיאה לישראל.

Since in the bathhouse where the mikveh is located, there are constantly women present who are bathing there, and having the beit din stand by the woman who is immersing causes perverse talk from the perspective of the women who bathe there and from the perspective of the community; and since from the perspective of law and ethics it is not permissible for any man (lit., person), and certainly not Jewish rabbis, to enter into the bathhouse of women when they are bathing. . . .

And when the judges enter into the bathhouse where there are other women who are bathing there, or even getting dressed there, it is not possible to avoid this thing (seeing women not fully clothed), even without intention to do so. Thus, the immersion of a convert in the presence of the beit din has become a matter that is impossible ("*ee efshar*"), and in situations such as this where it is impossible otherwise, it can be argued that all opinions would agree that to immerse not in the presence of beit din would be valid.

The first concern that Rav Uziel notes is the perverse talk that will arise from the *beit din*'s presence in the women's bathhouse; people would gossip about the bizarre and inappropriate nature of this practice. The phrase "from the perspective of the women . . . and from the perspective of the community" make it clear that this action will be seen as inappropriate based on communal standards. This is reinforced by his statement that for a man to enter into the bathhouse would go against both legal and ethical standards. In short, such behavior is inherently problematic. It is only after all of this that he states the halakhic concern of seeing women in a not-fully clothed state, and that thus the case should be considered one of *ee efshar*—that is, impossible from a halakhic perspective, to demand that a *beit din* be present.

Here's how Rav Ovadya quotes the passage:

מפני שבבית המרחץ של גוים הנ"ל שבתוכו נמצאת המקוה, ישנן נשים ערומות, וא"א בשום אופן שאנשים ובפרט רבנים יכנסו לתוכו.

[Rav Uziel concludes to be lenient] since in the bathhouse of non-Jews, where the mikveh is located, there are naked women, and it is impossible under any circumstances from men, and in particular rabbis, to enter there. (Section 17)

Notice again what Rav Ovadya quotes and what he does not quote. He cites the concern of the judges seeing naked women, but he does not cite the concern about violating community standards or improper activity from a moral perspective. Perhaps it is possible that Rav Uziel intended nothing more by these additional phrases than to underscore the problem of the judges seeing other women in various states of undress, but it is significant that Rav Ovadya in two places drops these suggestive phrases. In his quoting of Rav Uziel he presents only those factors that he himself believes would be relevant in assessing whether this case should warrant special consideration.

b) Shut Beit Avraham

Rav Ovadya's selective citation of sources can be seen again in a teshuvah that he deals with at the end of this responsum. Rabbi Avraham Ever Hirshovitz (Melbourne, Australia, 1840-1924), in *Shut Beit Avraham* (p. 47), discusses a case where there were no other options (*ee efshar*) but to immerse without the *beit din* present. Here's how Rabbi Hirshovitz describe the circumstances of his case:

> דבר זה קשה מאד פה במדינה באשר מקוה לבנות ישראל אין פה תחת יד ישראל ... רק הצניעות ילכו לטבול בים אשר שם אוהל מוקף מחיצות אשר לא יבא שם איש ולא יראה לעין איש ואם יזיד ח"ו איש לשחד את השומרת לתתו לבא שמה בשעה שנשים רוחצות שם בנפשם היא כי ענוש יענשו קשה על פי חוקי המדינה.

> This matter (for a *beit din* to be present) is very difficult in this country, since there is no mikveh for Jewish women that is under Jewish auspices. . . . However, the scrupulous (lit., modest) women will go to immerse in an ocean where there is a tent surrounded by curtains, and where no man is allowed to go there, and where they cannot be seen by any man. And if a man were to willfully, God forbid, bribe the woman who guards the place to allow him to enter at a time when the woman are bathing there, they [sic] are taking a serious risk upon themselves, because they will be heavily punished according to the laws of the country.

As Rabbi Hirshovitz describes it, it is "very difficult" for the *beit din* to be present, but not literally impossible. The obstacle indicated so far is that this would risk serious punishment from the authorities. But then he goes on:

> ומה גם דייני ישראל יגרמו בזה ח"ה גדול ר"ל לחשוב את דייני ישראל למפירי חוק המוסרי הנקדש בעיני העמים פה, ילמדנו מו"ר איך להתנהג פה במדינה ששורר חופש האמונה, האם נאמר גם בזה כדאמרינן (נדה ס"ז) גבי חפיפה היכא דאפשר אפשר והיכא דלא אפשר לא אפשר ונסמך על הרבה מהראשונים דס"ל דטבילה בדיעבד סגי בלא ב"ד....

> The Jewish *dayyanim* [were they to witness the immersion] will cause a great desecration of the Divine Name, God forbid, for people will think

> that the Jewish *dayyanim* violate the ethical standards that have been sanctified by the non-Jews here. Let our master teach us how to act here in this country where freedom of belief prevails, can we say like we say elsewhere (*b. Niddah* 67), "Where it is possible, we do what is possible, and where it is not possible, it is not possible," and rely on the many Rishonim who hold that *bi'di'eved* it suffices even without a *beit din* [for immersion]?

The factor that makes this not only "very difficult" but actually "impossible," *ee efshar*, is that to do so would create a *hilul haShem*. That is to say, that if not physically impossible, it is religiously impossible because of what this would communicate to people about the ethics of halakhah.

Without asserting that this act would be a genuine ethical problem, Rabbi Hirshovitz is sensitive to the perception that it is such, and that leads him to assess the situation as one of no alternative. It was exactly considerations such as these that Rav Ovadya dismissed as illegitimate, and it will be interesting to see how Rav Ovdaya will treat the case. But let us first look at how other poskim did so.

Rabbi Hirshovitz turned to other rabbonim with this question. Rabbi Yaakov Reinowitz, the senior member of the Beit Din of London (1818-1893), responded that if there are truly no other options—במקום שאי אפשר בשום אופן—then the case would be considered a *bi'di'eved*, and the position that such an immersion is kosher can be relied upon (p. 48). It seems that Rabbi Reinowitz was not prepared to rule on whether the circumstances actually were *ee efshar*; he most likely believed that this could only be determined by the rabbi who was involved in the actual case.

Rabbi Smuel Salant, the then-Ashkenazi Chief Rabbi of Jerusalem, also responded to this question. He described the case as one where שאין רשות לאנשים להכנס בבית הרחצה, men do not have permission to enter into the immersion room (p. 49). He concludes that in such a case, the *beit din* can indeed be outside the space where the immersion is being done. The salient point for our discussion is that he completely brackets the concerns of *hilul HaShem* and the impression that this would create regarding the ethics of halakhah; presumably, it is not a material consideration for him. It is only the legal restrictions which make this case one of *ee efshar*.

Let us now look at Rav Ovadya's citation of this responsum. He starts by paraphrasing and partially quoting Rabbi Hirshovitz's description:

> שבעירו אין שום אפשרות לחברי בית הדין לגשת אל מקום הטבילה הנמצא ברשות העכו"ם, ואיש הבא שם בנפשו הוא, וענוש יענש ע"פ חקי המדינה, וכ"ש שאם ילכו שם דייני ישראל יגרמו חלול ה' בזה.

> For in his city there was not the possibility for the members of the *beit din* to enter into the place of immersion which was under non-Jewish control, and any man who would go there would be taking a serious risk upon himself, because he will be heavily punished according to the laws of the country. And certainly [this is a problem], for if the Jewish *dayanim* go there, it will lead to a *hilul HaShem* in this matter.

Rav Ovadya accurately references the *hilul HaShem* concern, but similar to what we have seen in the case of Rav Uziel, he does so only in a truncated form. He quotes the first part of the sentence, that to have the *beit din* witness the immersion would lead to a *hilul Hashem*, but he fails to quote the second part of the sentence, where Rav Hirshovitz explains that the *hilul Hashem* would result from the perception that this practice violates ethical standards. By not explicating what the *hilul haShem* would be, Rav Ovadya avoids having to give any legitimacy to the concern that this practice is or appears to be unethical. As we know, Rav Ovadya thinks that to raise ethical concerns in this case is "an antithesis of our holy Torah" which "perverts the straight path." One is left assuming that the *hilul haShem* emerges from the presence of other women, as in the case of Rav Uziel, or from the violation of the secular law restricting such entry, and not from the perception that the practice is inherently problematic.

Beyond this, while Rav Hirshovitz considered the *hilul haShem* factor to be primary in defining the case as *ee efshar*, Rav Ovadya, like Rabbi Salant before him, brackets its halakhic relevance and focuses only on the legal and practical impossibility of the court to be present. However, here too we find a divergence from the original source. Rabbi Salant, remember, described the case only as one where the court was not allowed to enter the location of immersion. Neither he nor Rav Hirschovitz said it would be impossible to do so. This is inconvenient for Rav Ovadya, whose halakhic position is that an immersion not in the presence of a *beit din* can never be allowed if it is at all possible for the *beit din* to be present.

Rather than dismiss the ruling of Rabbi Salant, Rav Ovadya reframes it:

> ומ"מ פשוט שלא התיר הגאון ז"ל אלא בנידונו שיש סכנה לגשת שם, שהוא חשוב כדיעבד גמור, משא"כ כשישנה איזו אפשרות שהיא להכנס שם, אין להתיר כלל.

> Nevertheless, it is obvious that the gaon did not allow such a practice except in a case such as his, where there is a danger [for men] to go there. Such a case is to be considered a complete *bi'di'eved*. This, however, would not be the case when there exists a possibility to enter. In such a case, one cannot allow this practice at all. (Section 21)

Rav Ovadya states that in this case it would have been a danger for the *dayyanim* to enter there. Here, he diverges from the original source. The original responsum had only said that the men would be subject to heavy punishment—most likely monetary—as the phrase ענוש יענשו appears in the biblical context in regards to monetary payment (Shemot 21:22). Even if such a man would have risked jail time, there is no basis for Rav Ovadya to assume that such a person would be under true danger. (The word *sakanah* without a modifier usually implies life-threatening danger.)

Consistent with the original teshuvah, Rav Salant, in his paraphrase of the case, described the situation only as one of אין רשות—that there was "no permission" for the judges to enter. In Rav Ovadya's framing, this became a case of סכנה, danger. The reason to frame the circumstances as he did is obvious: it significantly narrows the application of Rav Salant's ruling, a ruling that does not conform to Rav Ovadya's stance on the matter.

What emerges from this analysis is that even for Rav Ovadya Yosef, whose responsa present a wealth of sources and emphasize a tabulation of the existing halakhic opinions on a matter, his values and worldview can play a role in his halakhic process. This is certainly true when it comes to assessing situations as *sha'at hadehak*, or whether to be concerned with certain policy issues, such as scaring off potential converts. More significantly, his worldview can also be seen to exert influence in his citation of sources. In his selective quoting, interpreting, framing and paraphrasing of a source, Rav Ovadya may at times present a source in a way that differs from its original meaning in its salient features. This can lead to putting a particular source on one side of an issue when it more properly belongs on the other side. None of this proves whether this influence is a conscious or subconcious one. But what is clear, is that we cannot discount the role that values and interpretation play even in a halakhic process that emphasizes citation and tabulation.

NOTES

1. Rav Moshe Feinstein in two *teshuvot* (Yoreh Deah 1:160, 2:127) considers this possibility.
2. Related questions are: (a) what degree of *sha'at ha'dehak* is necessary to be considered equivalent to a *bi'di'eved* situation, and (b) whether the principle *sha'at ha'dehak ki'bi'di'eved dami* is always applicable. We will not explore these questions in this article.
3. See *Mishpetei Uziel* vol. 1, YD 14; vol. 2 YD 53, 65, 66; and *Piskei Uziel, Sheilot HaZman*, 65. However, see also *Piskei Uziel, Sheilot HaZman*, 63.

BEZALEL NAOR

The Scribal Art of Rabbi Meir: A Study in Metanomianism

(Rav Kook's Pre-Purim Talk 5677/1917)
Translation and Commentary by Bezalel Naor

Introduction

IN A PERSONAL LETTER to his son Zevi Yehudah, dated "11 Adar, 5677," Rav Abraham Isaac Hakohen Kook shared a talk he delivered the previous Sabbath (*Parashat Zakhor*) before a London audience, concerning the commandment to erase or obliterate Amalek.[1] The hero of this discourse is the second-century sage Rabbi Meir. By cobbling together various references to Rabbi Meir in Talmud Bavli, Yerushalmi and Midrash Rabbah, Rav Kook is able to deftly paint a vivid portrait of the *tanna* (sage of the Mishnah) Rabbi Meir. It is possible that some of what Rav Kook arrived at concerning writing and erasing will jibe with postmodern deconstructionist literary theory.[2]

Before we launch into study of the actual discourse, we should point out that which, though unstated, may be obvious to some readers, namely that Rav Kook identifies with the protagonist. This is of extreme interest because just four years later, the Hasidic Rebbe of Gur (Gora Kalwaria, Poland), Abraham Mordechai Alter, in a letter to his family, published in the Jewish press of the day, would compare Rav Kook to—Rabbi Meir. It is highly unlikely that the Rebbe read our epistle of Rav Kook to his son. How did the Rebbe so uncannily size up the situation? Was it something that Rav Kook let

BEZALEL NAOR is the President of Orot, an organization dedicated to the dissemination of Rav Kook's teachings. He is the author of many works of Jewish Thought; his latest book, *Mahol la-Tsaddikim* (2015), analyzes the controversy between Rabbi Moses Hayyim Luzzatto and Rabbi Eizik of Homel concerning the true kabbalistic understanding of the purpose of Creation (*takhlit ha-beri'ah*) drop in conversation? Did the *tsaddik* (just man) read the "root" of Rav Kook's soul? (In Kabbalah, the term would be "*shoresh haNeshamah.*") Whatever the answer, the Rebbe took it with him to his eternal reward.

I quote the Rebbe of Gur's impression of Rav Kook, whom he had just met for the first time in Jerusalem in Nissan of 1921:

The Rav, the Gaon, R. Avraham Kook, may he live, is a man of many-sided talents in Torah, and noble traits. However, his love of Zion surpasses all limit and he "declares the impure pure and adduces proof to it,"[3] reminiscent of the one [=Rabbi Meir] who the rabbis said in the first chapter of *'Eruvin* (13b) "had no equal in his generation," and therefore, "the final halakhah did not follow his opinion."[4]

Text

> I spoke this holy Sabbath before an attentive audience concerning the erasing of Amalek, as a means of purifying all the values of existence; all the systems laden with the burden of the impurities, the pollution of wickedness, that extends from the "first of nations" [i.e., Amalek][5] even into the contents of the holy—which are corrupted by the evil influence of the wicked of the world.
>
> This is the reason[6] for the prohibition of putting *kankantum*[7] into the ink.[8] The law requires "'And he shall write . . . and he shall erase'—a writing that is able to be erased."[9] [This is] on account of the particles of wickedness that infect the values of holiness. If the hand of wickedness would pollute the entire foundation [of holiness] with its actions, then we would burn it [i.e., the Torah scroll] and the names of God contained therein, so as not to preserve the memory[10] of the sectarians and their deeds.[11] [But] the totality of the holy is merely *touched* by wickedness, as Jacob was touched by the man who wrestled him,[12] and for the purpose of this erasure there suffices a *potential* erasing (*mehiyah kohanit*), "a writing that is able to be erased."[13]
>
> In the Torah scroll written by Rabbi Meir, "whose contemporaries were not able to fathom his thinking,"[14] instead of "*kotenot 'or*" (with an *'ayin*), "tunics of skin," it was written "*kotenot 'or*" (with an *aleph*), "tunics of light."[15] And in the Jerusalem Talmud, he referred to himself by saying: "Here is your Messiah."[16] In other words, the illumination of his soul was from the [future] state that the world will ascend to after the light of Messiah will shine "and the wickedness will be consumed as smoke."[17]

In the case of Rabbi Meir, there was no need to prevent the placing of *kankantum* [in the ink]. (We could even go so far as to say that without *kankantum*, something would have been missing.) The very possibility and capability of erasing stands in opposition to the pure light, the supernal light,[18] "that illumines and lights up the eyes of the sages in Halakhah."[19] So, true to his character, Rabbi Meir used to put *kankantum* into the ink.

But Rabbi Akiva[20] said to him that the [present] state of the world still requires—even in the values of holiness—the potential of erasure, so that there might ramify from it the absolute erasure: the erasure of the memory of Amalek in all its branchings, and the existence of the darkness of Amalek. [This darkness consists of] the spread of all the evil characteristics (*hamiddot hara'ot*) in the national soul of every people,[21] which brings about all the tragedies, individual and collective.[22] In the words of the *Pesikta*: "As long as there is Amalek in the world, a wing (*kanaf*) covers the face [of God]. Only with its erasing, will it be said, "No longer shall your Teacher be hidden (*yikanef*)."[23]

• • •

At that time, the light of the Oral Torah shall unite with [the light of] the Written Torah; the lights shall interpenetrate.

"Write this a remembrance in the book"—Written Torah. "And place in the ears of Joshua"—Oral Torah.[24]

We are not allowed to write any of the Written Torah [from memory] without having an exemplar of the Scripture before us[25]—so as not to confuse [the realms of] scripture and orality. This concept [of not confusing the written with the oral] is explained in the *Yerushalmi*, [Tractate] *Megillah*.[26]

But none of this applies to the great of stature, "who see their eternity in their lifetime."[27] "Whoever possesses knowledge, it is as if the Holy Temple were rebuilt in his days."[28] And the light of Messiah shines upon him. And [thus] Rabbi Meir, concerning whom it is said, "And your eyelids [look] straight before you,"[29] wrote [by heart] without consulting Scripture[30]—just as he placed *kankantum* into the ink.

And in the days of Purim, when the erasing of Amalek intensified, the foundation of the Oral Torah was united with the Written Torah. The Torah that had been accepted under duress on Mount Sinai, was once again accepted *willingly* in the days of

Ahashverosh.[31] In the well-known words of the [Midrash] *Tanhuma*, the coercion on Mount Sinai was directed at the Oral Torah.[32]

(Igrot Rayah, vol. III [Jerusalem, 1965], Letter 808 [86-87])

Commentary

Rabbi Meir was a *lavlar* or scribe by profession.[33] Rav Kook, by marrying two *sugyot* of the Talmud (*'Eruvin* 13a and *Megillah* 18b) drew a composite sketch of Rabbi Meir, whereby he deviated from the norms prescribed by the sages in two respects: He added *kankantum* to his ink rendering it indelible; and wrote scripture from memory. The simple explanation for these deviations was his exceptional, flawless recall of the text of the Scripture. But Rav Kook chalks up Rabbi Meir's unusual behavior to the fact that his soul was from a future, Messianic time. (Thus, on one occasion Rabbi Meir referred to himself as the Messiah.) For that reason, in the verse in Genesis which narrates how after the Primordial Sin, the Lord fashioned for Adam and Eve tunics of animal skins, Rabbi Meir substituted in his Torah scroll "light" (*'or*) for "skin" (*'or*).[34] In Rabbi Meir's reality, the outer "*levushim*," or garments, have shed their opacity; they have become translucent.[35]

Our world is tainted by the wickedness of Amalek. So insidious is this influence of Amalek that it penetrates even into the inner precincts of holiness. Even our Torah has been infected by the corrupting influence of Amalek. *Horribile dictum*.

(Some years ago, there appeared a popular film, *The Matrix* (1999), which envisioned a dystopia whose reality had been thoroughly subverted by aliens.)

In this vein, Rav Kook interprets the prohibition of adding *kankantum* to the ink. In our present reality, the Torah is subject to corruption; therefore, the Torah must carry within itself the capability of being erased.

But Rabbi Meir's Torah is a scroll from the future, the Messianic future which basks in the light of the Face of God, no longer obscured by the wing of Amalek. That scroll is not subject to corruption and is in no need of erasure. Rabbi Meir adds *kankantum* to the ink, rendering it permanent.

Collateral damage resulting from the "wing of Amalek" is the wedge that it drives between Written and Oral Torah. Here it would be almost impossible to glean Rav Kook's meaning, were it not for a passage in the writings of his beloved disciple Rabbi Jacob Moses Harlap, which serves as a "Rosetta Stone" to decipher the master's allusion.

Employing Kabbalistic terminology, Rabbi Harlap informs us that the Written Torah is code for the "*kelim*" ("vessels"), while the Oral Torah is code for the "'*orot*" ("lights").[36] In other words, the Written Torah represents the outer manifestation, the material side of existence; the Oral Torah is evocative of the inner content, the spiritual aspect of existence.

Amalek drives a wedge between those two. And in an era in which the Face of God is eclipsed by the Wing of Amalek, we are told to maintain the separation of the two realms of Written Law and Oral Law. In the words of the Babylonian Talmud: "Words that are in writing, you are not permitted to recite orally; words that are oral, you are not permitted to commit to writing.[37] Once again, Rabbi Meir, who lives already in the Messianic Era, recognizes no such opacity. In his reality, the Written Torah and the Oral Torah collapse into one. In Rabbi Meir's world there is total transparency. The "tunics of skin" have been transcribed into "tunics of light."

On Mount Sinai, there yet existed separation of Torah into two distinct realms: the Written and the Oral. On Purim, with the erasing of Amalek, this gap between the Written Law and the Oral Law is bridged; the two dimensions dissolve into one.

Conclusion

Contained in this pre-Purim talk of Rav Kook is radical theology, the assertion that the Torah of our age—as opposed to the Torah of the eschatological future[38]—has been tainted by the evil of Amalek, and therefore requires by halakhic mandate (no less!) the potential of erasure. Rav Kook makes very clear that he is not referring to a Torah scroll written by a sectarian with improper intention (which the halakhah would have us consign to flames), but rather a "kosher" Torah scroll written with the most holy of intentions. The thought that the quintessence of holiness, the Torah, is subject to corruption, is a prospect so frightening as to cause us to shudder. But that very outlook may also be a source of hope, reminding us that "hardwired" into the script of the Torah is the capability of catharsis.

NOTES

1. See Exodus 17:14; Deuteronomy 25:19; Maimonides, *Sefer haMitsvot*, positive commandment 188; idem, *MT Hil. Melakhim* 5:5; and the anonymous *Sefer haHinnukh*, commandment 604.
2. Cf. Marc-Alain Ouaknin, *The Burnt Book: Reading the Talmud* (trans. Llewelyn Brown; Princeton, 1995).
3. For Rabbi Zadok Hakohen's thoughts regarding this passage in '*Eruvin* 13, see

Dover Tsedek (Piotrkow, 1911), 4a-c. In brief, Rabbi Meir had the power to reveal the underlying unity of all existence, and from that perspective of the divine unity, the duality of pure versus impure is transcended.

4. The letter was published in serial form in three successive issues of *Der Jud*, the Warsaw newspaper of the Agudat Yisrael movement (27 May, 3 June and 10 June, 1921 [English translation from my introduction to Rav Kook's *Orot*]). To this day, in at least some Agudist circles, the Rebbe of Gur's assessment of, and pronouncement upon Rav Kook is considered well-nigh authoritative.
5. Numbers 24:20. Cf. Rabbi Michael Forshlager, *Torat Michael* (Jerusalem, 1967), "*Derush be-'inyan mehiyat zikhro shel Amalek*," 250a: "'The first of nations is Amalek,' for he is the first of and includes all the evil." See infra, n 20.
6. The Hebrew word is "*ta'am*." Rav Kook contributed much in the area of "*Ta'amei haMitsvot*" (rationales of the commandments), beginning with his essay "*Afikim ba-Negev*," published in the Berlin journal *Ha-Peless* in 1903-1904 (reprinted in Rabbi Moshe Zuriel, *Otserot ha-Rayah*, vol. II [Tel-Aviv, 1988], 733-779), and continuing with his essay "*Talelei Orot*," published in the Bern journal *Tahkemoni* in 1910 (reprinted in *Ma'amrei ha-Rayah*, vol. I [Jerusalem, 1980], 18-28). See also the collection entitled *Orot ha-Mitsvot* in Rabbi Moshe Zuriel, *Otserot ha-Rayah*, vol. IV (Ashdod, 1992), 31-47. For a survey of the earlier literature, see Isaak Heinemann, *Ta'amei ha-Mitsvot be-Sifrut Yisrael* (Jerusalem, 1966). In this particular instance, I do not believe that Rav Kook intended to supplant the practical reason for the law forbidding adding *kankantum* to the ink, which is simply to allow erasure in the case of scribal error. Rather, it appears that Rav Kook wrote in a homiletic vein.
7. Medieval opinions were divided as to the identity of *kankantum*. Rabbi Nathan of Rome, *'Arukh*, s.v. *kalkantum*, and Rashbam opined that the substance is vitriol. See the various opinions in *Tosafot, b. 'Eruvin* 13a; idem, *b. Megillah* 18b; Rashi, *b. Shabbat* 104b; idem, *Sotah* 17b; Maimonides, *Commentary to the Mishnah, Shabbat* 12:4 (Kafah ed., 41); *Megillah* 2:1 (Kafah ed., 231); *Gittin* 2:3 (Kafah ed., 141); *Teshuvot haRambam* (ed. Freimann; Jerusalem, 1934), no. 126. For our purposes, we need not concern ourselves with the *realia*. However one identifies *kankantum*, the upshot is that it renders the ink indelible.
8. *b. 'Eruvin* 13a; *b. Sotah* 20a.
9. Numbers 5:23; *Mishnah, Sotah* 2:4; *b. 'Eruvin* 13a; *b. Sotah* 17b, 20a; Maimonides, *MT, Hil. Sotah* 3:8; 4:9.

   Originally stated in regard to the *Megillat Sotah* (the Scroll of the Suspected Adulteress), Rabbi Yishmael extended this requirement to the entire Torah scroll. *Tosafot* speculate by what Biblical exegesis Rabbi Yishmael accomplished this extrapolation. The alternative is that Rabbi Yishmael merely stated a matter of rabbinic law. See *Tosafot, b. 'Eruvin* 13a, s.v. *huts miparashat sotah*.

   Maimonides ruled that as a *mitsvah min hamuvhar*, *kankantum* (or in his reading, *kalkantum*) should not be added to the ink of the Torah scroll; however, those who would invalidate a Torah scroll written with indelible ink, err in their judgment. In both his *Commentary to the Mishnah* and in a responsum to Rabbenu Ephraim of Tyre, Maimonides fleshed out his decision by explaining that the halakhah follows the *lishna batra* (later statement) of the Talmud:

   > Rabbi Judah says, "Rabbi Meir used to say: 'For all [Scripture] we may place *kankantum* into the ink, except for the portion of the suspected adulteress (*parashat sotah*).'"

   See Maimonides, *Commentary to the Mishnah, Sotah* 2:4 (Kafah ed., 171-172);

MT, *Hil. Tefillin* 1:4; *Teshuvot haRambam* (ed. Freimann; Jerusalem, 1934), no. 126. *Par contre*, the admixture of *kankantum* to the ink of the *Megillat Sotah* (Scroll of the Suspected Adulteress) does invalidate the scroll. See Maimonides, *Hil. Sotah* 4:9.

10. Rav Kook wrote literally: "so as not to leave room" ("*kedei shelo lehoni'ah makom*"). However, the wording of Maimonides, *Hil. Yesodei haTorah* 6:8 (which is the source for Rav Kook's statement) is: "so as not to leave a name" ("*kedei shelo lehoni'ah shem*").
11. *b. Shabbat* 116a; *b. Gittin* 45b; Maimonides, *MT, Hil. Yesodei haTorah* 6:8; *Hil. Tefillin* 1:13. Rabbi Ahron Soloveichik wrote that in our contemporary society, burning a Torah scroll written by a heretic would be counterproductive. In so many words, Maimonides wrote that the reason for doing so would be to prevent Jews from being drawn to heresy. But today we have the opposite scenario. Burning the Torah scroll would make heresy that much more attractive!

> All this applies only in a situation where by burning the Torah scroll written by the heretic, Jews will be prevented from being drawn to heresy. But if there should arise a situation (such as ours today) that by burning the Torah written by the heretic, Jews with limited commitment to the commandments will be drawn to heresy, as a result of the influence of the Reform and Conservative rabbis, who will say that the "*gedolim*" (great men) are intolerant and wish to coerce everyone into performing the commandments against their will—not only is it not a *mitsvah* (commandment) to burn the Torah scroll written by the heretic, but this would be a great desecration of the Name (*hillul hashem*).
> (Rabbi Ahron Soloveichik, *Perah Mateh Aharon*, novellae to Maimonides, *Sefer Madda*' [Jerusalem, 1997], *Hil. Yesodei haTorah* 6:8, 49-50)

Rabbi Soloveichik cites as his source the by-now famous ruling of the sage of B'nei Berak, Rabbi Abraham Isaiah Karelitz (*Hazon Ish*) regarding the inapplicability of the law of "*moridin velo ma'alin*" in modern society:

> . . . But in the time of the concealment, when belief has been cut off from the feeble of the people, the act of *horadah* [elimination of heretics] does not constitute a fence against the breach, but rather an addition to the breach, for in their eyes it will appear as a wanton act of violence, God forbid. Since our whole striving is to remedy, the law does not apply at a time when this is no remedy. [Rather,] we must return them with cords of love and stand them in the light (*leha'amidem bekeren 'orah*), to the extent of our ability.
> (*Hazon Ish, Yoreh De'ah* 2:16; cited in *Perah Mateh Aharon*, 5)

See further Benjamin Brown, *The Hazon Ish: Halakhist, Believer and Leader of the Haredi Revolution* (Hebrew) (Jerusalem, 2011), 708-719. (The phrase "*leha'amidem bekeren 'orah*" derives from *b. Berakhot* 17a.)

In the Table of Contents, this chapter of *Perah Mateh Aharon* is summarized:

> If the burning of Torah scrolls of heretics will alienate Jews because of the impression of extremism, it is forbidden to burn them.

12. Genesis 32:25.
13. Although Rav Kook discusses the Torah scroll rather than the "*Megillat Sotah*" (Scroll of the Suspected Adulteress), it may interest the reader to learn that even in the latter regard (which is the source of our law), the verse "And he shall write

. . . and he shall erase" (Numbers 5:23) is interpreted strictly *in potentia* ("that the ink is *capable* of being erased"), but the actual total erasure is derived from another verse: "'And after he shall give drink' [Numbers 5:26]—provided that no imprint [of the writing] be discernible" (*b. Sotah* 19b). See the clarification in *Tosafot Sens* (ibid.)—which differs with our *Tosafot, Sotah* 19a, s.v. *ve'ahar yashkeh*; Rabbi Hayyim Joseph David Azulai, *Hayyim Sha'al*, vol. II (Livorno, 1795), No. 5(3) (to Maimonides, *MT Hil. Sotah* 4:14); Rabbi Pinhas Epstein, *Minhah Hareivah* (Jerusalem, 1923), *Sotah* 19a (93a). Concerning the two *Tosafot* to Tractate *Sotah* ("our" *Tosafot* versus *Tosafot Sens*), see *Hayyim Sha'al*, II, no. 41. (Azulai's father possessed a manuscript of *Tosafot Sens* and remarked to his son that *Piskei Tosafot, Sotah* are based on *Tosafot Sens*.)

14. *b. 'Eruvin* 13b.
15. Genesis 3:21; *Genesis Rabbah* 20:12. Cf. *Genesis Rabbah* 9:5: "In the Torah of Rabbi Meir they found written [for] *'Ve'hineh tov me'od'* ('And behold it was very good')—*'Ve'hineh tov mot'* (*'And behold it is good to die'*). Saul Lieberman discussed at length "the book of Rabbi Meir"; see his study, "The Texts of Scripture in the Early Rabbinic Period," in Saul Lieberman, *Hellenism in Jewish Palestine* (New York, 1994), 24-26.
16. *y. Kil'ayim* 9:3. The context was that Rabbi Meir, who had traveled to Asya, was about to die. He sent a message to his disciples in *Erets Yisrael* to bury him in the Land. The sense of his statement was: "Here is your rabbi." (See *P'nei Moshe* ad locum.) Rav Kook seizes upon Rabbi Meir's peculiar use of the word "Messiah."
17. From the prayer of Rosh Hashanah and Yom Kippur.
18. Aramaic, *nehora 'ila'ah*."
19. *b. Shabbat* 147b; *b. 'Eruvin* 13b.
20. It seems that Rav Kook's memory deceived him. It was not Rabbi Akiva but Rabbi Yishmael who had the exchange with Rabbi Meir. See *b. 'Eruvin* 13a and *b. Sotah* 20a. In the very different Yerushalmi account, "Said Rabbi Meir, 'All the days that I studied under Rabbi Yishmael, I did not place *kankantum* into the ink.'" See *y. Sotah* 2:4; quoted in *Tosafot, Sotah* 17b, s.v. *shene'emar*. Maimonides explained in a responsum to Rabbenu Ephraim of Tyre that the Yerushalmi refers to the practice of the student Rabbi Meir; later, the mature Rabbi Meir did add *kankantum* to the ink. See *Teshuvot haRambam* (Freimann ed.; Jerusalem, 1934), no. 126.
21. Cf. Rabbi Abraham Bornstein of Sokhatchov: "This is Amalek, 'the first of nations,' head of the seven evil characteristics" (*Ne'ot haDeshe*, vol. I [Tel-Aviv, 1983], *Parashat Zakhor*, 179, par. 6). The editor, Rabbi Aharon Israel Bornstein clarifies that the seven Canaanite nations symbolize the seven evil characteristics and Amalek is the first of these nations. Ibid., n. 45.
22. Rav Kook penned these lines at the height of World War One. He witnessed how the phenomenon of nationalism decimated Europe. Cf. *Orot*, *"HaMilhamah"* (*"The War"*).
23. Isaiah 30:20; *Pesikta Rabbati* (Warsaw, 1913), 12:9. Rav Kook paraphrased. The exact wording of the *Pesikta* reads: "As long as the seed of Amalek exists, the Face is covered, as it were; once his seed is removed from the world, the Face that was covered, is revealed. 'No longer shall your Teacher be hidden (*yikanef*), but your eyes shall see your Teacher' [Isaiah 30:20]."
24. Exodus 17:14. Cf. Rabbi Isaac Ze'ev Halevi Soloveitchik, *Hiddushei Maran RIZ Halevi 'al haTorah, Beshalah*, s.v. *Ketov zot zikaron basefer vesim be'oznei Yehoshua* (I).

The author juxtaposes the comment of the *Sifre, Pinhas*: "'*VeTsav et Yehoshua*' ('And charge Joshua') [Deuteronomy 3:28]—*Tsavehu 'al divrei Talmud* ['charge him concerning the Oral Law']." See '*Emek haNetsiv*, ad loc. Rabbi Soloveitchik (the "Brisker Rav") supposed that the *Sifre* is the source of Maimonides' statement in the Introduction to *Mishneh Torah*: "To Joshua, his disciple, Moses, our teacher, delivered the Oral Law and charged him concerning it." The verse in Exodus 17:14 follows upon Joshua's armed conflict with Amalek. Rav Kook suggests that the separation and bifurcation into two distinct entities of Written Law versus Oral Law came about under the spell of Amalek's influence.

25. *b. Megillah* 18b; *b. Menahot* 32b; Maimonides, *MT, Hil. Tefillin* 1:12.
26. *y. Megillah* 4:1:

> Rabbi Haggai said: "Rabbi Samuel bar Rav Yitshak entered the synagogue. He saw a scribe reading the *Targum* [the Aramaic translation of Scripture] from a book. He said to him: 'It is forbidden for you [to read the *Targum*—an oral transmission—from a book]. Words that were said orally, [must be transmitted] orally; words that were said in writing, [must be transmitted] from writing.'"

Cf. *b. Gittin* 60; *b. Temurah* 14b. Rav Kook might as well have made his point from the Talmud Bavli. Perhaps the *Yerushalmi Megillah* was uppermost in his mind, because his talk preceded Purim (and the incident concerning Rabbi Meir writing a Scroll of Esther by heart in Asya, occurs later in that passage of Yerushalmi). But there is another possibility. Alfasi transcribed the Yerushalmi in his *Halakhot, Megillah*, chap. 4 (14a). (See Rabbi Solomon ben Simon Duran, *She'elot uTeshuvot haRashbash* [Livorno, 1742], no. 277.) Perhaps Rav Kook, like his mentor Rabbi Naphtali Zevi Yehudah Berlin (Netsiv) of Volozhin, was especially conversant with Alfasi. (According to anecdote, one Friday night in the Volozhin Yeshiva, the lights went out, yet Netsiv was able to continue studying, having committed Alfasi to memory.) Confirmation of this theory comes from Rabbi Shim'on Glitzenstein, who acted as Rav Kook's secretary during the latter's stay in London. Glitzenstein attests that an Alfasi in small format never left the Rav's hands during his medically prescribed walks. The custom of daily study of Alfasi goes back to the Vilna Gaon. See Rabbi Moshe Zevi Neriyah, *Sihot haRAYH* (Jerusalem, 5755/2015), 184-185.

And then the question arises why Rabbi Isaac Alfasi (Rif) quoted the Yerushalmi and not the Bavli. This question was asked of Alfasi by Rabbi Chaim Zimmerman, *Binyan Halakhah* (New York, 1942), *Hakdamat haRambam* (2).

Here too (as above, n. 6), it is unwarranted to assume that Rav Kook rode roughshod over the simple reason for the sages' prohibition of writing Scripture from memory, namely to prevent scribal error. (See Rabbenu Menahem haMe'iri, *Beit haBehirah*, *Megillah* 18b.) Rather, Rav Kook wrote in a homiletic vein.

27. *b. Berakhot* 17a.
28. *b. Berakhot* 33a.
29. Proverbs 4:25; *b. Megillah* 18b.
30. *b. Megillah* 18b. Rav Kook stopped short of the *sugya*'s conclusion, which is that "an exigency is different" ("*she'at hadehak shanei*"). Provisionally, the Talmud assumed that Rabbi Meir, because of his phenomenal recall of Torah, was *sui generis* (as correctly quoted by Rav Kook). However, when challenged by the example of Rav Hananel, whose total command of Torah was certainly comparable to that of Rabbi Meir, the Talmud was forced to retract, attributing Rabbi Meir's writing

of Scripture (in the case in question, the Scroll of Esther) from memory to the extraordinary circumstances in which he found himself. In 'Asya, there simply was no preexisting *Megillah* to refer to.

In the final analysis, we may say that that there were two factors that contributed to Rabbi Meir's writing Scripture by heart: 1) "*she'at hadehak*" (exigency); and 2) the fact that Rabbi Meir was "*shalem she'bishelemim*" ("perfect among perfect"), in the words of Me'iri. See *Rabbenu Menahem haMe'iri, Beit haBehirah, Megillah* (ed. Hershler; Jerusalem, 1968), *b. Megillah* 18b (51).

Rabbi Ya'ir Hayyim Bachrach equated the waiving of the prohibition of writing scripture by heart in the case of *she'at hadehak* (*b. Megillah 18b*) to the waiving of the prohibition of writing down the *Agadeta* in an "'*et la'asot lAdonai—heferu toratekha,*" "A time to do for the [sake of] the Lord—they annulled your Torah" (Psalms 119:126; *b. Temurah* 14b.) The same permission that makes allowances for turning the oral into the written, allows turning the written into the oral in extenuating circumstances. They are but two sides of the same coin. See *Havot Ya'ir*, no. 175.

The parallel *sugya* in *Yerushalmi, Megillah* 4:1 offers an alternative solution to the problem of how Rabbi Meir in Asya could write the Scroll of Esther by heart. Besides "*Ein lemedin mi'she'at hadehak*" ("We do not learn from an exigency"), as in *Bavli*, there is proffered the following ingenious solution: "And some say that [Rabbi Meir] wrote two [*megillot*]; the first, he wrote by heart, and the second from the first, and archived (*ganaz*) the first."

Rabbenu Nissim (in pagination of Alfasi, *Megillah*, 5b, s.v. *heikhi damei mitnumnem*) ruled that other than a *she'at ha-dehak*, it is forbidden to read from Scripture that had been written by heart. Rabbenu Manoah, on the other hand, wrote that the law of not writing by heart is strictly at the outset (*lekhatchilah*), but the Scripture is not invalidated thereby. The two opinions are brought in Rabbi Joseph Karo, *Beit Yosef* on *Tur, Yoreh De'ah* 274.

31. *b. Shabbat* 88a.
32. *Midrash Tanhuma*, Noah, 3. According to the Talmud (*b. Shabbat* 88a), at Mount Sinai, God held the mountain over the heads of the people "as a vat" and threatened that if they did not accept the Torah, that would be their burial place. *Tosafot* (ibid.) raise the question that the Children of Israel had already willingly accepted the Torah by saying, "We shall do and we shall hearken (Exodus 24:7)." The *Midrash Tanhuma* resolves this difficulty by differentiating between Written and Oral Law. The Israelites' voluntary acceptance extended only to the Written Law; the heavy-handed tactic was required to force their submission to the Oral Law as well. On Purim, this situation was remedied, when the Jews lovingly committed to the Oral Law.
33. *b. 'Eruvin* 13a; *b. Sotah* 20a. See also *Ecclesiastes Rabbah* 2:17: "Rabbi Meir was an excellent scribe" ("*Rabbi Meir havah katvan tav muvhar*"). Quoted in Lieberman, op. cit., 25.
34. Genesis 3:21; *Genesis Rabbah* 20:12. Perhaps this Midrash was the inspiration for the phrase "rags of light" in Leonard Cohen's song "If It Be Your Will."
35. See Rabbi Zadok Hakohen Rabinowitz of Lublin, *Dover Tsedek* (Piotrkow, 1911), 4b.
36. Rabbi Jacob Moses Harlap, *Mei Marom*, vol. 10 (Leviticus) (Jerusalem, 1997), *ma'amar* 41, "*Ihud Torah shebikhetav 'im Torah shebe'al peh*" (131, par. 2). Earlier in that discourse, Rabbi Harlap writes: "The Written Torah is the essence of the worlds, the essence of all existence; and the Oral Torah, the light of existence...In

the hands of Israel is the power to unify the essence of existence with the light within, and combine them into one unit, with the result that existence itself will be synonymous with the light, the Oral Torah..." (128).

37. *b. Gittin* 60; *b. Temurah* 14b; Maimonides, *MT Hil. Tefillah* 12:8; idem, *Guide of the Perplexed*, vol. I (trans. Schwarz; Jerusalem, 2002), I, 71 (185-186). Rav Kook demonstrated an abiding interest in the problematic of committing the Oral Law to writing, revisiting this theme on more than one occasion in his halakhic *oeuvre*. On the issue of whether the prohibition of writing down the Oral Law is biblical or rabbinic in origin, he wavered. See Rav Kook's earliest halakhic work, *'Ittur Soferim*, vol. I (Vilna, 1888; photo offset Jerusalem, 1974), 7a (*"Lishkat haSha'ar"*) and 20a (*"Lishkat haSofer")*. See the earlier literature: Rabbi Eliezer of Metz, *Yere'im*, chap. 128; Rabbi Ya'ir Hayyim Bachrach, *Havot Ya'ir* (Frankfurt am Main, 1699), no. 175; Rabbi Hayyim Joseph David Azulai, *Birkei Yosef*, vol. I (Livorno, 1774), *Orah Hayyim*, chap. 49, par. 2; idem, *Mahazik Berakha* (Livorno, 1785), *Orah Hayyim*, chap. 49, par. 1.

    And then there is Rav Kook's scintillating explanation of the passage in Maimonides' Introduction to *Mishneh Torah*:

    > From the time of Moses to that of *Rabbenu haKadosh* [i.e., Rabbi Judah the Prince], no work had been composed from which the Oral Law was publicly taught. But in each generation, the head of the court or the prophet of that generation wrote down for his private use a memorandum of the traditions which he had heard from his teachers, while teaching orally in public.

    Rav Kook's commentary thereto was transcribed by Rabbi Ya'akov Filber in his work *Le'Oro* (Jerusalem, 1995), 164-167; reprinted (in a truncated version) in Rabbi Moshe Zuriel, *Otserot haRayah*, vol. II (Tel-Aviv, 1988), 849-850, and (in a lengthier version) in idem, *Otserot haRayah* (new, expanded edition), vol. III (Rishon leZion, 2002), 11-13. In both *'Ittur Soferim* (loc. cit.) and the commentary to Maimonides, Rav Kook probed whether the prohibition consists in the initial act of writing the Oral Law or in the subsequent act of teaching it in public from a written text, or both.

    For a scholarly treatment of the subject, see Saul Lieberman, "The Publication of the Mishnah," in idem, *Hellenism in Jewish Palestine* (New York, 1994), 83-89.

    Inter alia, in Jerusalem, in the 1930s, Rav Kook and the young, budding scholar Saul Lieberman studied together *behavruta* on a regular basis *Tur* with the commentary of *Beit Yosef*. The precondition for this arrangement was that neither would prepare the text beforehand. (Heard from Dov Zlotnick, disciple of Lieberman and executor of his will—BN.)

38. Cf. Rabbi Moses Hayyim Luzzatto, *Kalah Pithei Hokhmah* (ed. Spinner; Jerusalem, 1987), *petah* 30 (93-94), referencing Isaiah 51:4 and *Leviticus Rabbah* 13:3.

WALTER REICH

Speaking Truth to Power: What Avi Weiss Said to Jimmy Carter and Its Implications for the World Today

On May 1, 1978, some 600 Jewish leaders gathered on the South Lawn of the White House. They were there to mark the 30th anniversary of Israel's birth. Most of them were rabbis, and almost all of them were men.

The day was clear and cool. The guests sang the Israeli national anthem, *Hatikvah*, and *The Star-Spangled Banner*. Menachem Begin, Israel's prime minister at the time, had come to the United States for a speaking tour to commemorate the founding of his country, and the White House decided to invite him for a talk with President Jimmy Carter. In all, 1,200 Jewish leaders had been invited. That only 600 came was a poor showing for this grand occasion. Which Jewish leader wouldn't want to be there, and which wouldn't want to have a photo of himself shaking the president's hand?

But two reasons could have explained the low turnout. First of all, the Carter-Begin meeting itself had been arranged just a few days earlier, as had been the South Lawn ceremony, giving the invitees little time to make travel arrangements. Perhaps more importantly, the feelings of America's Jewish community toward Carter had turned sour. Carter had just decided to sell 60

Walter Reich is the Yitzhak Rabin Memorial Professor of International Affairs, Ethics and Human Behavior, and Professor of Psychiatry and Behavioral Sciences, at George Washington University. He is also a Senior Scholar at the Woodrow Wilson Center and a former Director of the United States Holocaust Memorial Museum. This is an expanded and updated version of an article that appeared in *Global Antisemitism: A Crisis of Modernity: Volume 5: Reflections*," edited by Charles A. Small. New York, ISGAP, 2013.

advanced F-15 warplanes to one of Israel's enemies, Saudi Arabia, and 30 other warplanes to Egypt,[1] leaving some Jewish leaders, presumably, reluctant to pay Carter obeisance by appearing instantly at his bidding.

Yet the crowd that did come seemed jubilant, expectant and, by some reports, pleased with themselves for having been chosen for the invitation. A number of them had declined to attend a demonstration at the White House to protest the arms sales to the Arabs.[2] At 1:30, Begin drove up to the entrance of the White House's West Wing in a limousine and was greeted by a grinning Zbigniew Brzezinski, Carter's National Security Adviser, who had been blamed by some Jews for what they saw as the Carter Administration's tilt toward the Arab states.[3] During the 30 minutes of the Begin-Carter meeting, the waiting guests on the lawn drank coffee and punch. One of the guests, Rabbi Avi Weiss, described in the *Washington Post's* report of the event as "an intense, young rabbi from Riverdale"—a neighborhood in The Bronx, in New York City—handed out "copies of a letter he had written to Carter. It opposed, in polite language, the proposed sales of warplanes to Saudi Arabia and Egypt."[4]

Finally, Carter and Begin showed up on the South Lawn. Carter announced that he was appointing a commission to recommend to him ways of memorializing the Holocaust—a commission that, eventually, recommended the creation of, among other things, the United States Holocaust Memorial Museum. It's very unlikely that Carter had such a large and permanent institution in mind when he announced the creation of the commission. He might have thought they'd recommend a statue or a ceremony, but in any case, coming soon after the airing of the 1978 NBC miniseries "Holocaust," seen by about 120 million[5] Americans and ultimately by about 220 million viewers in the U.S. and Europe,[6] and welcomed by the country's Jews, this seemed like an effective way to mollify an important Democratic Party constituency. After all, 70% of voting American Jews had cast their ballots for him; because of that lopsided percentage he'd won New York State, Ohio, and the national election.

In announcing the commission on the Holocaust, Carter described the Holocaust as "the ultimate in man's inhumanity to man." After Begin spoke about the Jews' struggle for survival and freedom, the crowd sang *Am Yisrael Chai*, "The People of Israel Live."

The receiving-line that formed to shake hands with Carter included the rabbi from The Bronx who would be described by the *Washington Post* as intense and young, Avi Weiss. "As I waited my turn," Weiss later recalled, "I wondered whether I could speak truth to power. Memorizing the words

I wanted to say to the president, in fear that I would freeze when meeting him, I finally clasped his hand and said, 'I was one of your strongest supporters, but I'm outraged by your disastrous tilt toward the Arabs. And Mr. President, don't give us the Holocaust at the expense of Israel.' The president looked incensed, but I felt good that access had not prompted me to compromise my principles."[7]

In that dramatic moment, that young and intense rabbi understood something that few other Jews—rabbis or not, communal leaders or not—have understood. He understood that the Holocaust could serve, for national and international statesmen, as a political sop. He understood that a bow to Holocaust memory would be greeted automatically with gratitude by Jews who wanted non-Jews to understand, or at least recognize, the reality of the immense atrocity that had befallen the Jewish people only a few decades before. And he understood that even a government or international organization that had done something to threaten the existence of the Jewish state could, by recognizing the Holocaust, and talking about its memory in lofty terms, immunize itself from the accusation that it was endangering—and, in extreme circumstances, ignoring, condoning or even endorsing lethally-intentioned hostility—toward the Jewish state.

Those who know anything about that young and intense rabbi—and I do, not least because I happen to be his brother-in-law—know that no one has been more committed than he to the honest preservation of Holocaust memory.

It was this rabbi who, in 1989, demonstrated against the use, as a convent, of a building at the Auschwitz death camp that had been used to store canisters containing crystals of Zyklon B, the very crystals that the Germans had tossed into the gas chambers of the crematoria in which well over 90% of the victims had been Jews; he saw the creation of that convent as part of the attempt to transform the memory of Auschwitz into a place of Polish Catholic martyrdom. Many Poles were indeed murdered at Auschwitz, but the primary purpose to which the Germans put it was the extermination of those European Jews who had not already been gassed in the other death camps or starved in ghettos or shot in extermination pits. Weiss saw the convent as part of an attempt to re-shape historical memory, and he went there to protest that attempt.

For the same reason, Weiss also protested, in the late 1990s, the use of the building that had housed the commandant of Birkenau, the largest part of the Auschwitz complex and the one that contained its gas chambers, as a parish church, with its crosses towering over the barracks and the remains of the barracks and the gassing centers,[8] just as he protested, also for the same reasons, the erection, amid the ashes of hundreds of thousands of Jews, numerous crosses.[9] In 2015, for the occasion of International Holocaust Remembrance Day, he once again protested, this time in the *Washington Post*, the continued presence of the church, with its crosses, in Birkenau.[10]

And Weiss protested the building, in 2003, of a memorial in another German death camp in southeast Poland, Belzec, where some 600,000 Jews were murdered upon arrival, with only two survivors—a memorial the building of which involved the desecration and destruction of the remains of those murdered Jews.[11][12] Alas, the Belzec memorial, doing exactly that, was built.[13]

Clearly, Weiss has committed much of his life to preserving Holocaust memory so that it would be true to Holocaust history and to protecting the physical remains of its victims. Yet, back in 1978, he wasn't willing to accept the sop that Carter had used as a political strategy to enable him to do what, Weiss believed, would endanger Israel. For him, the memory of dead Jews was sacred, but the survival of living Jews—the Jews of Israel, including many of the Holocaust's survivors—was immensely more important.

And, for Weiss and others, those living Jews are still more important than the lofty words, often uttered as rote platitudes, by world leaders in memory of the Holocaust dead—especially if those words ignore, or serve to mask, the efforts of other leaders to eliminate the Jewish state.

Which is why they're wary of the crop of commemorations, resolutions and exhibitions that have emerged in recent years from the United Nations. For example, in 2005, the U.N. commemorated the 60th anniversary of the liberation of Auschwitz;[14] during that same year, the General Assembly rejected the denial of the Holocaust as a historical event;[15] in 2007, its Secretary General established an "International Day of Commemoration in Memory of the Victims of the Holocaust";[16] and in February of that year its Department of Public Information's Holocaust and the United Nations outreach program collaborated with the International Raoul Wallenberg Foundation on a "Partners of Hope" concert at Carnegie Hall.[17]

Since then, the United Nations has sponsored an observance of an International Day of Commemoration in Memory of the Victims of the Holocaust. The proclamation of the observance in 2015 was introduced in terms that implied that the high principle that human rights must be protected for all people, which is supposed to be at the core of the United Nations itself, was "shaped by the experience of the Holocaust":

> Inspired by the theme "Liberty, Life and the Legacy of the Holocaust Survivors," the 2015 observance of the International Day of

> Commemoration in Memory of the Victims of the Holocaust coincides with the two milestone events: the 70th anniversary of the Second World War's end and the founding of the United Nations. The Organization's establishment seven decades ago in 1945 reflects how deeply it was shaped by the experience of the Holocaust. Both the Charter of the United Nations[18] and the Universal Declaration of Human Rights[19] enshrine the principles of human rights for all peoples around the world. This year's events include the annual ceremony, exhibits, a film screening, discussions and a special exhibit that recognizes the work of the Holocaust and the United Nations Outreach Programme since its creation 10 years ago by the United Nations General Assembly.[20]

In themselves, of course, those commemorations are laudable, and many of the speeches made at them have been quite moving. So it's not surprising that some Jewish organizations, as well as many Jews, including Holocaust survivors, have been touched by the U.N.-sponsored Holocaust-remembrance events and grateful to the world body for having carried them out.

But the fact that these attacks have been carried out by an institution many of whose members have for decades unrelentingly hijacked the U.N.'s bureaucratic machinery to demonize the Jewish state, and in recent years have increased the virulence of the U.N.'s focused attacks on Israel, makes those commemorations, resolutions and exhibitions, almost insignificant—and, at worst, has served to mask the U.N.'s constant attacks on the Jewish state. That the leader of one of those members, President Mahmoud Ahmadinejad of Iran, even threatened to "wipe Israel off the map,"[21] headed a country that was building a nuclear infrastructure that could do just that, and was warmly applauded by a large segment of the U.N. when that leader addresses it even as he excoriated the Jewish state and rejected its right to exist—highlights the hypocrisy, even the bitter mockery, that Holocaust commemorations have sometimes become. That this march toward nuclearization appears, as of this writing, to be achieving a status that enshrines that goal underscores the clash between the U.N.'s high principles, at least on paper, and the reality of its embrace of genocidal regimes and leaders. This clash is rendered even more striking by the fact that the leader who uttered those words about wiping Israel off the map was only one of the leaders of that country that promised a genocide of the Jews. These have included Supreme Leader Ayatollah Ali Khamenei, former President Mohammad Khatami, former President and Current Head of the Expediency Council Ayatollah Akbar Hashemi Rafsanjani, Revolutionary Guard General Yahya Rahim Safavi, and Revolutionary Guard General Mohammad-Ali Jafari.[22]

This is no small matter. Those unfair and one-sided attacks—organized by the U.N.'s bloc of 56 Islamic states and supported by an automatic bloc of additional, "non-aligned" states whose votes are captive to the power of the Islamic states—are constantly cited by Arab and other Muslim countries, as well as by terrorist groups, as proof that Israel is a demonic country—that it's the only violator of human rights in the world and that it doesn't have the right to exist. In some cases, they're cited as proof that not only Israel, and not only Israeli Jews, but *all* Jews don't have the right to exist.

A non-governmental organization, UN Watch, has carefully monitored what is, essentially, a war being carried out against Israel through statements and resolutions of its official bodies. One study it has published summarizes those statements and resolutions adopted by the UN Human Rights Council since its creation in June 2006. As UN Watch notes, this council "was designed as an improvement over the discredited Commission on Human Rights, but has tragically repeated and even intensified the same biases."[23] It notes:

> The council has criticized Israel on 27 separate occasions, in resolutions that grant effective impunity to Hamas, Hezbollah and their state sponsors. Obsessed with condemning Israel, the Council in its first year failed to condemn human rights violations occurring in any of the world's 191 other countries. In its second year, the Council finally criticized one other country when it "deplored" the situation in Burma, but only after it censored out initial language containing the word "condemn." It even praised Sudan for its "cooperation". . . . The Council's fixation with Israel is not limited to resolutions. Israel is the only country listed on the Council's permanent agenda. . . . Moreover, Israel is the only country subjected to an investigatory mandate that examines the actions of only one side, presumes those actions to be violations, and which is not subject to regular review.

Here are further examples—many of them compiled by UN Watch—of the ways in which the U.N. has, with extreme unfairness, attacked Israel in recent years, an unfairness that has been made to seem less unfair by the recent spate of Holocaust commemorations, as if they demonstrate that the U.N. isn't anti-Semitic or hasn't had its organizational structure hijacked to achieve the demonization and even the elimination of the Jewish state:[24]

- In 2007, the organization UN watch reported, only a few countries were criticized by the General Assembly, and in no case by more than a single resolution. Israel, on the other hand, was the target of 22 one-sided resolutions.

— In 2006-2007, *all* of the 11 condemnatory resolutions passed by the U.N. Human Rights Council—which was supposed to have been an improvement over the obsessively anti-Israel U.N. Human Rights Commission, which had embarrassed even U.N. staff members—were against Israel; *none* of them were against any of the remaining 191 member states of the U.N.—including Sudan, which is responsible for the genocide in Darfur (and which co-sponsored condemnations of Israel); Burma, with its severe political repression; China, with its repression of Tibetans; Saudi Arabia, with its severe religious intolerance, beheadings and discrimination against women; Iran, with its executions of homosexuals and calls for the elimination of a member state of the U.N., Israel; and a host of other countries that have murdered or suppressed their own populations.

— Also in 2006-2007, the Human Rights Council created one agenda item that is permanent—the "human rights situation in Palestine and other occupied Arab territories"[25]—again, despite the fact that the human rights situations in numerous countries are far more serious.

— In 2005, two U.N. bodies, the World Health Organization and the International Labour Organization, passed only one resolution against a specific country—Israel.

— A number of permanent organizations have been set up within the U.N., several with large staffs, that constantly spew out anti-Israel messages: the Special Committee to Investigate Israeli Practices Affecting the Human Rights of the Palestinian People and Other Arabs of the Occupied Territories (which was established in 1968); the General Assembly's Committee on the Exercise of the Inalienable Rights of the Palestinian People; and the U.N. Secretariat's Division for Palestinian Rights, which has a staff of 16.

— Louise Arbour never criticized anti-Semitism while she was the U.N.'s High Commissioner for Human Rights, nor did she take exception to the call by Mahmoud Ahmadinejad, the president of Iran, to "wipe Israel off the map." Indeed, she never responded to a plea by over 40 human rights organizations that she use the U.N.'s second annual Holocaust commemoration to condemn the Iranian government's Holocaust denial.[26] And the General Assembly has repeatedly condemned Islamophobia while ignoring the hatred of Jews or of Christians.

— The U.N.'s "International Day of Solidarity with the Palestinian People" in 2005 was marked by a map in which Palestine replaced Israel.[27]

— The most striking recent moment of anti-Israel frenzy by a U.N. organ was at the U.N. Human Right Council's Durban Review Conference in April 2009 in Geneva, which was addressed by Iranian President Mahmoud Ahmadinejad, who had urged that Israel should be "wiped off the map."

— In May 2010 Libya, a chronic violator of human rights, was elected to the U.N Human Rights Council—by a vote of 155 of the U.N.'s 192 members.[28]

The attacks against Israel are increasing at the U.N. The few apostrophes to Holocaust memory are welcome. But it's to them that the U.N., and some of its most rabidly anti-Israel members, point when confronted with the relentless anti-Israel bias in the world body—a bias that, as demonstrated above, results in anti-Israel condemnations that are cited to justify the argument that Israel is the world's worst violator of human rights and doesn't even deserve to exist.

Unfortunately I've grown accustomed to the practice, in the U.N., of holding ceremonies to remember the Holocaust, but often as a cover to engage in activities that attempt to delegitimize the Jewish state, and remain silent, or even support, the threats to annihilate it.

But I'm disturbed when even friends of Israel—who are deeply troubled by the attempts to delegitimize it, and fear the possibility of a future Holocaust perpetrated against Israel's more than six million Jews carried out by Iran—fail to seize opportunities, especially at Holocaust commemorations. I'm troubled that such an opportunity was missed in Washington, during the Days of Remembrance Ceremony in the Capitol Rotunda on April 23, 2009. The ceremony was dedicated to the theme of individual responsibility, to the idea that all human beings must be individually responsible to make sure that an event like the Holocaust never happens again. President Barack Obama, the main speaker, said all the right words, but never mentioned the threats of annihilation against Israel by a nuclearizing Iran. Sadly, none of Jews who spoke there mentioned the Iranian threat either. No one noted that Hitler's 1939 "prophecy" that the Jews would be exterminated was being repeated, seventy years later, by a national leader whose country was, by all accounts, building nuclear weapons, denied that the Holocaust ever happened and threatened the elimination of Israel—and who, in his speech a few days earlier, at the UN's "anti-racism" Durban Review Conference in Geneva, called the Holocaust an "ambiguous and dubious question" and a "pretext of Jewish sufferings." These Jews, who are at the forefront of Holocaust commemoration in America, had, as their captive audience, the President of the United States, and still they said nothing directly about the danger of a second Holocaust.

When, in 1978, Jimmy Carter played the Holocaust card in order to mollify his Jewish critics and mask his acts that endangered the Jewish state, at least he set in motion the creation of what was ultimately a useful product—the United States Holocaust Memorial Museum. At the U.N., though, the Holocaust card—the occasional commemorations and exhibits evoking the memory of the Holocaust dead—is unlikely to have any redeeming outcomes.

One wishes that a young, intense rabbi would, at some Holocaust remembrance ceremony, tell the U.N.'s Secretary-General, "Don't give us the Holocaust at the expense of Israel." But even if he did, and even if the Secretary-General were to respond sympathetically, it's unlikely that the U.N. member states that are busy undermining Israel's existence would, even during some obligatory moment of silence, stop their efforts to delegitimize or eliminate the Jewish state.

And one wishes that *any* Jewish figure—whether old or young, intense or laid-back, a member of the establishment of Jewish organizations or outside of it, famous or not—would tell a U.S. president who has come to commemorate the Holocaust to say the right thing about the Holocaust that was, but also to *do* the right thing about the even *more* important task of preventing a Holocaust-to-come. Rabbi Avi Weiss would still do that. He would speak truth to power. Would future rabbis—younger, and facing even fiercer odds, also do it? By creating a new rabbinical seminary, Yeshivat Chovevei Torah, Rabbi Weiss created an institution that encourages such courage. That is YCT's hope—and its challenge.

NOTES

1. "Will America's Jews thank Carter in the end?" *The Economist*, April 29, 1978, 47.
2. Avraham Weiss, *Principles of Spiritual Activism* (Hoboken, N.J.: KTAV, 2002), 166.
3. Edward Walsh, "A Day of Emotion for Carter, Begin; Unity Gesture on Israeli Anniversary," *Washington Post*, May 2, 1978, 2.
4. Edward Walsh, "A Day of Emotion for Carter, Begin; Unity Gesture on Israeli Anniversary," *Washington Post*, May 2, 1978, 2.
5. Alan L. Mintz, *Popular Culture and the Shaping of Holocaust Memory in America* (Seattle: Univ. of Washington Press, 2001), 23.
6. http://www.museum.tv/archives/etv/H/htmlH/holocaust/holocaust.htm
7. Avraham Weiss, *Principles of Spiritual Activism*, 167.
8. Avi Weiss, "What price memory," *Jerusalem Post*, January 6, 1999, 8.

9. See "President promises Jews Auschwitz site will be protected by law," BBC Summary of World Broadcasts, January 12, 1999, from Polish Radio 1, Warsaw, in Polish 1800 gmt 10 Jan 99.
10. Avi Weiss, "Auschwitz is a sacred place of Jewish memory. It's no place for a Catholic church." *Washington Post*, January 28, 2015, http://www.washingtonpost.com/posteverything/wp/2015/01/28/auschwitz-is-a-sacred-place-of-jewish-memory-its-no-place-for-a-catholic-church/
11. Tom Martin, "Pensioner to Sue for Nazi Site Memorial," *Sunday Express*, August 10, 2003, 44.
12. Avi Weiss, "A Monumental Failure at Belzec," The Forward, April 11, 2003. See also http://www.hir.org/amcha/belzec.html.
13. Walter Reich, "A Trench Runs Through It," *New York Times*, June 12, 2004, http://www.nytimes.com/2004/06/12/opinion/a-trench-runs-through-it.html.
14. Warren Hoge, "UN Listens to Pledges of "Never Again," International Herald Tribune, January 26, 2005, http://www.iht.com/articles/2005/01/25/news/un.php.
15. http://www.un.org/holocaustremembrance/docs/res607.shtml
16. http://www.un.org/holocaustremembrance/2007/index.shtml
17. http://www.un.org/holocaustremembrance/2007/concert.shtml
18. http://www.un.org/en/documents/charter/
19. http://www.un.org/en/documents/udhr/
20. United Nations, 2015 Calendar of Holocaust Remembrance Events "Liberty, Life and the Legacy of the Holocaust Survivors," http://www.un.org/en/holocaustremembrance/2015/calendar2015.html.
21. Ewen MacAskill and Chris McGreal, "Israel should be wiped off map, says Iran's president," *The Guardian*, October 26, 2005, http://www.theguardian.com/world/2005/oct/27/israel.iran
22. Joshua Teitelbaum and Michael Segall, "The Iranian Leadership's Continuing Declarations of Intent to Destroy Israel, 2009-2012, Jerusalem Center for Public Affairs, 2013, http://jcpa.org/wp-content/uploads/2012/05/IransIntent2012b.pdf
23. UN Watch, "Anti-Israel Resolutions at the HRC, at http://www.unwatch.org/site/c.bdKKISNqEmG/b.3820041/
24. http://www.unwatch.org/atf/cf/%7B6DEB65DA-BE5B-4CAE-8056-8BF0BEDF4D17%7D/UNW_THE_UN_AND_ANTI_SEMITISM_04_07_REPORT_CARD.PDF
25. Jackson Diehl, "A Shadow on the Human Rights Movement," *Washington Post*, June 25, 2007, A19.
26. http://www.unwatch.org/site/apps/nl/content2.asp?c=bdKKISNqEmG&b=1330819&ct=4566483.
27. http://www.eyeontheun.org/view.asp?l=21&p=142
28. Neil MacFarquehar, "New Members Elected for Human Rights Council," *New York Times*, May 13, 2010.

JONATHAN D. SARNA

"The Last Years Were the Most Difficult" A First-Person Account of a Mission to the Soviet Union in March 1986

IN HIS MEMOIR, *Open Up the Iron Door*, Rabbi Avi Weiss recounts that many in the Soviet Jewry movement considered the release of Natan Sharansky, on February 11, 1986, "an indication that the struggle for Soviet Jewry was nearly won." He, however, thought differently. "From the activist perspective," he recalls, "the opposite was the case. Indeed, the last years were the most difficult."[1]

The document that follows captures the bleak period for Soviet Jews that followed the Sharansky release. It consists of a letter[2] that I wrote to my parents, Professors Nahum and Helen Sarna, on the airplane departing Moscow for Cincinnati, where I then lived, after spending one week (March 20-27, 1986) visiting with refuseniks. The late historian Professor Martin Gilbert had laid the groundwork for this visit, when he wrote to me in 1985 and asked me to correspond with a young Leningrad Jewish historian named Igor Kotler, with whom he was working on a bibliography of the Holocaust in German-occupied Russia.[3] Kotler and I struck up a careful correspondence,

JONATHAN D. SARNA is the University Professor and Joseph H. & Belle R. Braun Professor of American Jewish History at Brandeis University, and chairs its Hornstein Jewish Professional Leadership Program. He also is a past president of the Association for Jewish Studies and Chief Historian of the National Museum of American Jewish History in Philadelphia. Author or editor of more than thirty books on American Jewish history and life, his *American Judaism: A History* won six awards including the 2004 "Everett Jewish Book of the Year Award" from the Jewish Book Council. Sarna is a fellow of the American Academy of Arts and Sciences and of the American Academy of Jewish Research. His most recent books are *When General Grant Expelled the Jews* and *Lincoln & the Jews: A History* (with Benjamin Shapell).

and I passed his letters on to Sandy Spinner, then the director of the Cincinnati Council for Soviet Jews. The Council soon decided that I should travel to Leningrad to meet Kotler in person. My good friend, Professor Benny Kraut (1947-2008), then director of Jewish Studies at the University of Cincinnati,[4] accompanied me.

Our mission to the Soviet Union, like so many missions sponsored by the Union of Councils, had multiple goals. Besides the immediate aim of meeting with Kotler, we carried a coded list of other people to visit in Moscow and Leningrad—refuseniks, family members of imprisoned refuseniks, teachers, scholars and more. Our goal was to offer moral support and collect intelligence; we also carried gifts that could help some in tangible ways. In addition, we were instructed to attend synagogue services on Purim in Leningrad to offer support to those who were there and to report on how they were treated. Finally, we were advised to "go with the flow." It was not easy to predict what we would find, whom we would see, and what dangers we might face. The goal was to make maximum use of our one week in the Soviet Union to benefit the refusenik community and to return with as much information as possible for the Union of Councils.

We arrived in Moscow amid a crack-down on refuseniks. On March 14, 1986, Alexei Magarik, a Moscow Hebrew teacher, was arrested on trumped-up charges of narcotics possessions.[5] In Leningrad, Vladimir Lifshitz, a Hebrew teacher, was on trial for anti-Soviet activity.[6] As it turned out, we would play a role in bringing news of his trial to the west. Other refuseniks had been interrogated by the KGB, the Soviet secret police. Overall, only a dismally small forty-seven Jews emigrated from the Soviet Union in March 1986.[7] To those (like Avi Weiss) who looked upon emigration statistics as a barometer of Soviet intensions, the low figure served as proof that Soviet president Vladimir Gorbachev was no more interested than his predecessors had been in extending human rights to Soviet Jews. While history surprised us—as it turned out, twenty times more Jews emigrated in 1988 than in 1986, and some two hundred times as many Jews emigrated in 1990—that certainly could not have been predicted when Benny and I flew out of the Soviet Union on March 27th. Our confidential report to the Union of Councils made for grim reading.[8]

Before working on that official report, I used the long plane ride out of Moscow to compose a long letter to my parents providing details of our trip. My parents were naturally worried about my mission, particularly since I was engaged to be married to my then fiancée, Ruth Langer, on June 8th. I was glad to be able to reassure them that everything had ended well. While confidentiality issues prevented me from revealing all that we had accomplished, the letter does offer a vivid account not only of our activities but of the refusenik community and its mood in the difficult weeks following Natan Sharansky's release. It is a privilege to dedicate the publication of this letter, with annotations, to Rabbi Avi Weiss, whose untiring activism did so much to shape and strengthen the movement to free Soviet Jews.

• • •

Somewhere between Moscow & Paris
Dad's birthday [March 27, 1986]

Dear Mom & Dad,

As promised, I have (almost) returned safe and sound (as well as wiser, moved and saddened) from behind the iron curtain. I will prepare a full description of Benny's and my adventures which I will send you. I also have with me some choice Soviet volumes on the horrors of Zionism and its practitioners given me by my friend Igor Kotler.[9] Finally, we have important films (this is strictly confidential) which, we hope, will come out.[10] In short the trip was an outstanding success.

Before proceeding, you will no doubt be interested to know that a Jew in Leningrad[11]—a remarkable, charismatic, self-taught *ba'al teshuvah* with *tsitsit* and a gartel, who teaches Jewish texts and photographs copies of *Talmud* for his students—asked me if I was related to the author of *Understanding Genesis*. I failed to learn what he thought of the volume (I suspect he read it 'on the way' to his current more Hassidic phase), but I informed him of the sequel.[12]

Two people in Moscow knew the work of my future father-in-law.[13] One, a physicist, proudly took out Jim Langer's article and asked me to pass along his contributions to the same field; the other had spent time with Langer when he was in Moscow.[14]

We began in Moscow, where we met two types of Jews: activists and intellectuals. The news is not good: arrests, investigations, fear, but one is in awe of the courage displayed. For the anniversary of *Rambam*,[15] a special joint meeting of two refusenik seminars was held (one seminar in physics & math, the other in biology & medicine)—the first joint seminar and the first venture into humanities since the arrest of Victor Brailavsky.[16] The Moscow Jews, as we later learned, are much divided internally, yet wives of prisoners of conscience—a distinct group of astonishingly courageous yet war-weary women—are respected and helped by everyone. They live thanks to ongoing connections with the West: visitors, phone calls, packages, mail.

We spent *Shabbat* walking around Moscow. It was our only day 'off' and I think the rest and mental relaxation did us both good. Russian architecture is remarkable (post-1917 building, by contrast, is mostly dull and coarse), and I am pleased to have seen Red Square & the Kremlin. We also witnessed two religious rites: the pilgrimage to St. Lenin's tomb (long lines which we passed up), and the bridal pilgrimage to WWII shrines—in mid-wedding—to place flowers (I presume a functional equivalent to old customs of grave-visiting). We saw dozens of these wedding parties line up (everybody lines up in Moscow, and nobody talks in line), and little emotion. Benny noticed that almost everyone had 1-2 children—not more. In fact, when he mentioned to someone that he had three kids, they were astonished—how rash, they thought, especially in the modern age! Actually, Russian apartments are so small, and refuseniks so poor, that the restraint is understandable. But that does not account for other Russians.

We left Moscow on Sunday night. Neither of us were sorry to bid the Intourist Hotel farewell: if that is first class one wonders what second class must be! Two beds and our cases filled the room (most of our luggage included food and 'supplies'.[17] We ate nothing out, both because Benny doesn't eat out and because we could not afford, on our schedule, to get the usual maladies.) Flying Aeroflot is an experience—especially internally. The planes are like our busses: grubby, stark, noisy. People sit anywhere, put packages on overhead racks, and sit on hard chairs. This is lowest-common-denominator Socialism—but since some workers are better than others, there is a much nicer First Class section that gets on last and off first. I do not know who sits there. On our flight was one other American-looking couple. We did not exchange comments, but they turned up in the Leningrad Synagogue on Purim. I presume they had a similar errand as we had.

The situation in Leningrad is worse than Moscow. Vladimir Lifshitz has just been sentenced to three years; houses of numerous activists, Hebrew teachers, political intellectuals and religious figures have been searched; and leadership of the movement has fallen to the very young—a critical person (probably soon to be arrested) is only twenty![18]

The city itself is beautiful. St. Petersburg on the Neva River was impressive two centuries ago and the palaces and monuments remain—now supplemented by numerous new ones dedicated to St. Lenin. We took a compulsory ½ day trip with a private guide and were both deeply impressed. The subway system is magnificent, clear, fast (Moscow's is even better) and most people use public transit to get around. I have never seen a city with so few cars. The Hotel Leningrad was also much better in quality, although we were rarely in to enjoy it.

Our first ½ day (Sunday) in Leningrad was the most frustrating of all: nobody was home. We spent six hours travelling back and forth to different apartments with heavy packs on our sore backs, and finally gave up and went home to a midnight dinner. On Monday, we took our compulsory tour and then went to visit Evgeny Lein, a leading activist, who has been imprisoned and is clearly on the vanguard of refusenik activities.[19] We had missed him twice; now Benny saw him in the street leaving his apartment, recognized him from his photo in M[artin] Gilbert's book,[20] and we caught him. He proved a fount of information and a valuable entrée into all circles: activist (including the most secret activities reminding me of old spy movies), religious, intellectual, wives of refuseniks, Hebrew teachers. As we walked with Lein, the militia appeared. We ducked into a hallway. While speaking in his small, dark, poorly furnished flat, a knock on the door was heard. I thought the people outside would hear my pounding heart, but in fact it was only the inspector making sure that Lein was "working" (parasitism is a crime; most refuseniks are watchmen, and jokingly call themselves *shomer yisrael* [Watchmen of Israel]. We sat still in the back room; one of two times that we had to do this (I hear that several visiting professors including [Michael] Yudkin of Oxford[21] have been picked up by the KGB and later released to consuls. Recently Lubavitch emissaries have been expelled). Lein gave us full details of the Lifshitz trial and told us how to go the schule for Purim (which he, not being religious, had forgotten about.)

Monday night at 6:30 we arrived at the Leningrad synagogue. It is an imposing structure, off a main street, and consists of an old little *Beit Midrash*—one that looks like something out of old Yiddish movies and must date back at least 150 years—which is found in a back red building where only the ultra-froum (mostly old) go, and the great synagogue, which is very well kept up, no doubt for tourists' benefit.[22] Young and old milled around outside and in the ante room; the middle-aged 'lost' generation was conspicuously absent. We entered the synagogue and saw TV cameras and lights set up—the show was being taped for propaganda (I heard different versions of *who* was to be given the propaganda. I doubt anybody really knew). This infuriated the young and many left. Services began with an old *Hazan* and choir (the young rabbi on the left, an anti-Zionist quisling, said nothing), and TV lights went on. When cameras faced front, Jews moved to [the] back, when they turned around, Jews left. A few went upstairs. Men and women sat together (apparently *only* on Purim) and left together. Most of the crowd had no idea how to follow the service; few had *siddurim* much less copies of the *megillah*. The early chapters of *Esther* were well read, but people were forever 'thinking' they heard *Haman* and so they made noise. Incidentally, Leningrad follows *Nusach Ari*—an old tradition in the city (I presume from mid or early 19th century) that solves a puzzle re practices of some Russian Jewish emigrants [to the United States] early in [the] 20th Century.

About 2 chapters into the *megillah* a young activist[23] came up to us and asked if we could read the *megillah*. They had decided that a "*megillah* TV show" was treife and wanted to symbolically secede. I have never read the *megillah* in public, but I know some of it, and Benny had a text. After much pressuring I agreed ("recklessly") to read. It is hard to describe the feeling of reading the *megillah* in a back room of the Leningrad Synagogue on Purim. Did my *arur Haman* ["cursed be Haman"] have special conviction? Were the sentences in *Eichah trop* [verses sung to the traditional cantillation of the Book of Lamentations] particularly sad? Did I detect special joy and delight in the last *perek* [chapter]?[24] No matter the mistakes (Benny corrected every *dagesh)*, no matter the made up trop—it was an unforgettable experience and the crowd went wild. We were taken to a Purim party and gained entry into all circles.

Next day we missed *megillah* to have a secret meeting with Anna Lifshitz (wife of the imprisoned Vladimir) and several others in a Leningrad hideaway.[25] We then went to the home of Chaim Burshtein, who, at 20, is a leader of the religious refuseniks. He is a *baal teshuvah,* wise beyond his years, but wild and revolutionary—a true son of the City of Lenin. One day, since his grandmother was born in England, he decided that he was English and staged a 'work-strike'. He was arrested and went on hunger strike. But he has numerous foreign contacts, a sharp mind, and unbelievable courage. So he has been repeatedly warned, his parents' apartment searched, and often harassed. Most people assume that he will be the next to be tried; for now, he spends his time telephoning (from secret locations; his own phones—and those of many refuseniks—have been disconnected) all over Russia and to many in the US spreading information. His English and Hebrew is good, and we learned much about the religious activists, the circle of teachers of texts (distinct from Hebrew teachers, about 30 in all, not all of whom are official refuseniks, though all would leave if they could), and the general situation. Chaim's father, who lost his car and job when he sought to emigrate, and who shares little of his son's religion and none of his linguistic abilities, looked with obvious awe on his son. He boasted to me in broken English of how much *Chaim* had learned in 6 years on his own, how much he had achieved & done—so it must been in Russia c. 1881. Burshtein's father also pointed out to me that the older generation all have Russian names (and some them, Russian identity cards); the youngsters have all taken on Jewish names.

Chaim took us to Purim *seudah* at the home of Grigorii Wasserman, the 38 year old *Mara D'Atra* of Leningrad.[26] Wasserman looks and dresses like a rebbe, has an infectious smile, and a fair Jewish library. He is the one who had read your book. Sixteen Jews were present, none of them dressed like Wasserman, and none of them as learned. He led the proceedings, with humor, Torah, *mussar,* and, of course, food. I ate only starches myself and excused myself from the vodka. Benny gave a *D'var Torah* that nobody seemed to understand in translation. But we did speak to many at the table and came away with heartrending tales: of an 18 year old girl whose father wants to stay, [while] mother and she want to go — "I wish I had not been born, so my Mother could have left for Israel." She seeks a pseudo father in Israel. Another 18 year old girl, a Hebrew teacher who speaks magnificent Hebrew and English, and is studying other languages, fears to apply to emigrate, lest she be expelled (but she may be expelled anyway for teaching Hebrew . . .), but obviously wants a western husband.[27] Others recounted similar tales of harassment and hope, courage and fear. We enjoyed a traditional *se'udah*, but had to keep our voices low: a neighbor's complaint is the usual excuse for breaking up such gatherings.

Wednesday we had another secret meeting and then a long afternoon with another young religious teacher ([Elimelech] Rochlin)[28] who has a *mezuzah* on his door, a wife with a *sheitl,* a full beard, and speaks a good Hebrew—we could have been in *Kiryat Moshe*. This teacher seeks a whole library of religious books and wants news of Israel, [and] news of the Jewish world. Only the disconnected phone and the job—another *shomer yisrael*—reminds us where we are.

How to sum all this up? First I learn that there is not a *single* refusenik movement. There are different circles:

(1) Activists who collect documents, petition the government, and are eager to get legal and political assistance from abroad. They keep in touch with foreign bodies and know what is going on. They are full of theories, and often argue among themselves—in good traditional Russian fashion. In the Zionist days, Jabotinsky must have been such a type.

(2) Intellectuals—they have advanced training in science or history and are most interested in their own seminars and work. They want to leave, are eager for news, but make their contribution by helping one another. My friend Igor Kotler in Leningrad, whom we visited, researches Jewish names

and the history of Jews in remote Soviet republics. Others have other fields. They fear too much publicity lest they lose more than they can gain.

(3) Hebrew teachers—they want to keep Jewish learning alive and Zionist sparks burning by educating Jews in the language of their people. Literature and language—not necessarily religion—is their bent, and some are not official refuseniks. Echoes of *Ahad Ha-am*.

(4) Religious leaders—they practice and preach Judaism, teach traditional texts, maintain contact with Lubavitch and *Agudah* and generally see the future in religious (even fanatical) terms. They are much influenced by US *baalei teshuvah*, mouth anti-Reform slogans, and feverishly devote themselves to collecting and teaching traditional sources.

(5) Relatives of prisoners of conscience—they are a specific class devoted to helping their husbands, sons, etc. They travel to distant camps to see them, get food, medicine and clothing for them, collect documents, send petitions, and generally attempt to ensure that *their* relative is kept alive and kept in the minds of the authorities.

Beyond this, there are obvious internal disputes between:

(1) Those who seek maximum activity, publicity and noise, and those who prefer to avoid publicity and work internally to strengthen the Jewish community. Some believe that publicity helps, others insist that it hurts. Some wanted us to photograph them, others did not.

(2) Those who want to go to Israel, those who want to go to US.

(3) Different views of/on Israel, and on religion.

I could go on and on, but this plane is about to land. You'll have the full report[29] when I write it!

Love,
Jonathan

NOTES

1. Avi Weiss, *Open Up the Iron Door: Memoirs of a Soviet Jewry Activist* (New Milford, CT: Toby Press, 2015), 195.
2. My parents preserved the handwritten letter and it came to me after they passed away. The original is now at the Jacob Rader Marcus Center of the American Jewish Archives in Cincinnati, which kindly made available a scan to me. In transcribing the letter, I have silently corrected minor spelling errors. Italicized words were in Hebrew in the original.
3. Igor Kotler was a member of the circle of Jewish historians in Leningrad. Subsequent to our visit, Hebrew Union College-Jewish Institute of Religion awarded him a fellowship, funded by Proctor & Gamble, which allowed Kotler and his family to emigrate to Cincinnati, where he arrived on November 3, 1987. He subsequently pursued graduate study in Jewish history in California, brought many of his relatives to the United States, and worked at the Museum of Jewish Heritage in New York. He is currently President and Executive Director of the Museum of Human Rights, Freedom and Tolerance in New York.
4. Stephen J. Whitfield, "In Memoriam, Benny Kraut, 1947-2008," *American Jewish History* 94 (December 2008), 331-334; Jonathan D. Sarna, "Foreword," in *The Greening of American Orthodox Judaism: Yavneh in the 1960s*, by Benny Kraut (Cincinnati: Hebrew Union College Press, 2011), xi-xviii.
5. Philip Spiegel, *Triumph Over Tyranny: The Heroic Campaigns that Saved 2,000,000 Soviet Jews* (New York: Devora Publishing, 2008), 159.
6. Ibid., 259.
7. Gal Beckerman, *When They Come for Us We'll Be Gone: The Epic Struggle to Save Soviet Jewry* (New York: Houghton Mifflin, 2010), 489.
8. The report is available at http://www.brandeis.edu/hornstein/sarna/contemporary-jewishlife/Mission-to-the-Soviet-Union_1986_B.Kraut-and-J.D.Sarna.pdf
9. On Kotler, see above, n.3. The volumes were Igor Yaroslavtsev, *Zionism Stands Accused* (Moscow: Progress Publishers, 1985) and *Zionism: Enemy of Peace and Social Progress* (Moscow: Progress Publishers, 1983).
10. This refers to various documents and tapes connected to the trial of Hebrew teacher Vladimir Lifshitz in Leningrad, which we smuggled out of the Soviet Union and turned over to the Union of Councils. The trial was monitored by Daniel Grossman, US consul in Leningrad (March 1985-October 1986); see Spiegel, *Triumph Over Tyranny*, 259.
11. Grigorii (Grisha) Wasserman studied with Ilya Esses and became a religious leader in 1979. He moved to Israel in January 1988; *Spiegel, Triumph Over Tyranny*, 414-5, 419-20.
12. The sequel refers to Nahum M. Sarna, *Exploring Exodus: The Heritage of Biblical Israel* (New York: Schocken, 1986).
13. James S. Langer, then Director of the [Kavli] Institute for Theoretical Physics, University of California, Santa Barbara. Langer had earlier visited Moscow to participate in scientific seminars organized by Andrei Sakharov and refusenik Mark Azbel.
14. The physicists were Michael Reizer and Alexander Ioffe.
15. The 850th anniversary of Moses Maimonides' birth was commemorated around the world in 1985.

16. Victor Brailovsky, a prominent mathematician and computer scientist, hosted scientific seminars for refuseniks in his home until his arrest in 1980. He served time in prison and was finally allowed to emigrate to Israel in 1987.
17. A reference to items that we brought with us as gifts for the refuseniks. Many of these gifts were sold for cash on the black market, allowing refuseniks, who could only hold menial jobs, to pay their bills.
18. Albert (Chaim) Burshtein; see below, n.24.
19. Evgeny Lein, an applied mathematician, became a refusenik in 1978. He served two years of forced labor in Siberia, was released in 1982, and emigrated to Israel in 1989; see his autobiography, Lest We Forget (Jerusalem: Jerusalem Publishing Center, 1997), portions of which are online at http://www.soviet-jews-exodus.com/English/Memory_s/MemoryLein_1Text.shtml; Spiegel, *Triumph Over Tyranny*, 151-54; Beckerman, *When They Come for Us We'll Be Gone*, 422-423.
20. Martin Gilbert, *The Jews of Hope* (New York: Viking, 1985), 78.
21. Michael Yudkin was professor of biochemistry at Oxford. He briefly described some of his activities on behalf of Soviet Jews in an essay available at http://www.oxford-chabad.org/templates/blog/post_cdo/AID/708481/PostID/44107.
22. Actually, the smaller prayer house in the courtyard was consecrated in 1886 and the main [Choral] synagogue in 1893; see Mikhail Beizer, *The Jews of St. Petersburg: Excursions Through A Noble Past* (Philadelphia: Jewish Publication Society, 1989), 30.
23. Chaim Albert Burshtein, on whom see more below.
24. Burshtein (1985-) later emigrated to Israel and became a rabbi. He currently lives in Beitar Illit and serves as Chief Rabbi of the Jewish community of Lithuania. See https://www.facebook.com/chaim.burshtein.7?fref=ts.
25. The hideaway was the home of Boris Yelkin, an engineer who lost his job when he applied to move to Israel, where his father lived. The Yelkin apartment had special locks and sound proofing and was the nerve-center of the refusenik community. One room in the apartment had special lighting and equipment for filming documents. Many of the documents connected with the Lifshitz trial were filmed there. We carried those films back with us to the United States.
26. On Wasserman, see above, n. 11.
27. Several young women whom we met hoped to find Western husbands (or "temporary husbands") among the tourists who visited. This, they thought, would make it possible for them to emigrate.
28. Elimelech Rochlin, a chemist, was part of the circle connected to Gregorii Wasserman and attended the trial of Vladimir Lifshitz. He subsequently emigrated to Israel and resumed his scientific work, publishing numerous articles and receiving several patents. See Gilbert, *Jews of Hope*, 169, 175-76.
29. See above, n.8.

DANIEL SPERBER

Some Comments Relating to Halakhic Feminism

Introduction

RABBI AVI WEISS, the exemplary and iconic orthodox Jewish activist,[1] has many a notable achievement to his credit. The one that I should like to highlight is his pioneering contribution to orthodox feminism. From his early publication of *Women at Prayer* in 1990[2] to his establishment of *Yeshivat Maharat* and the ordination of several female halakhic community clergy,[3] he has consistently contributed to broadening the scope of women's participation in orthodox ritual and communal leadership. The seeds he sowed over two decades ago have grown and flourished, nurturing new models of orthodox synagogual worship in the form of the so-called "*partnership minyanim*".

All these activities, and the burgeoning Jewish orthodox feminist movement have, as was to be expected, provoked considerable opposition. Criticisms of various kinds have been voiced; some serious halakhic discussions have evolved,[4] while others, far less serious, and even disparaging and lambasting, have made their way into the "blogger literature". Some of these criticisms have encouraged renewed examination of the issues involved and subsequent responses,[5] while others hardly bear our consideration. However, the polemic dialogue is an ongoing affair and clearly requires constant attention.

Having also played a part in these various, innovative developments and having written copiously both on the ritual aspects of orthodox feminism[6] as well as upon the leadership issue,[7] and having had my own share of both

RABBI PROFESSOR DANIEL SPERBER is Professor Emeritus of Talmud at Bar-Ilan University, and presently President of the Institute of Advanced Torah Studies at Bar-Ilan University. He received the Israel Prize for his Talmudic researches in 1992, and is the author of over 30 books in Hebrew and English on a wide variety of rabbinic topics as well as on classical philology and art history. He has also published copiously on the subject of feminist rights according to the halakhah.

constructive and destructive criticism, I should like here to make a number of short responses to some of the objections raised.

1. The Kabbalat Shabbat Memorandum

The recent and rather acrid debate led by a certain rabbi on women leading the Kabbalat Shabbat service appeared at first to be primarily a halakhic one. But it soon overflowed into additional areas, revealing it as a clearly political polemic. Indeed, I found the whole discussion—which appeared on a whole series of blogs and a major published article—most astonishing.[8] We are not talking about women reading the Torah and/or having aliyot. I can well appreciate the criticisms raised against this practice, though I disagree with them and have sought to refute them. But here we are talking about a practice first established in the latter years of the sixteenth century among a small group of people, disciples of the Ari haKadosh in Safed, which took place outside the confines of the synagogue looking over the hills and comprised watching the sunset and reciting some psalms and piyyutim. It gradually spread to other venues, first being practiced outside the synagogue in the courtyard, and later, when in the synagogue, came to be recited at the *bimah* rather than at the chazan's lecturn—clearly in order to emphasize its different status from the *Maariv* service.[9] In many communities there is no *sheliah tzibbur* leading the service; rather, the congregants sing the Psalms together. Indeed, in small communities, the service often begins even before there is a *minyan* of ten men, and the congregation waits for the requisite number in order to say *Barkhu*.

But the debate about *Kabbalat Shabbat* was intended to have far broader implications, for, by the same argument, it would also disallow women to lead *Pesukei deZimra*, for example. Indeed, this clearly tendentious aim is overtly revealed by yet another argument put forward, namely that a *Shaliah tzibbur* must have a *full beard*—something that clearly excludes women (*Shulhan Arukh*, Orah Hayyim 53:6). The reason given is because of the *dignity of the congregation, kevod hatzibbur*, which is clearly irrelevant in present day society. Moreover, both the Maharam MiRothenberg and the Rashba agree that the congregation can waive this requirement. Furthermore, the original ruling only applied to permanent *shlihei tzibbur*, not to occasional readers, and, on occasion, even a thirteen-year-old, who has reached maturity, may lead the service (*Shulhan Arukh*, ibid., 8). Additionally, the *Biur Halachah* (ad loc.) writes that this requirement may be waived when there is no one else to fulfill this function. And finally, this restriction referred to very specific prayers, such as *Keriat Shema*, prayers on fast-days in Eretz Yisrael because of drought, and High Holidays prayers. (See *Lehem Mishnah* to the Rambam, *Hilkhot Tefillah* 8:11; *Peri Megadim* to *Shulhan Arukh*, ad loc.) In any case, nowadays, hardly any synagogue requires its reader to be bearded; even American Rabbis are often clean-shaven, because the plain meaning of that ruling is that a service should be led by one who is mature, i.e., post-bar mitzvah. And a thirty-year-old without a beard is fully eligible to serve as a *shaliah tzibbur*. Indeed some of the greatest hazzanim were beardless, such as the Koussevitzky brothers, Mosheh, David, Jacob and Simhah, Leibele Waldman, Leib Glanz, Zavel Kwartin, Shmuel Malavsky, to list only a few of the best-known names.

This is surely because many *Rishonim* are of the view that if the congregation does not mind having a *sheliah tzibbur* who has no beard, then the beard is not a requirement.[10]

Three additional arguments were put forward. First, that for *Kabbalat Shabbat* the *shaliah tzibbur* wears a *tallit*. This, of course, is the case where there is a *shaliah tzibbur*. Now, according to the *Magen Avraham* (*Orah Hayyim* 18:1), citing the *Bayit Hadash* (*Bah*), one really should remove the *tallit* one is wearing when one says *Barkhu* since it is night and one does not wear *tzitzit* at night. And so too, many *Aharonim* specifically rebuked those who wore a *tallit* at night. However, those who did so did so because of kabbalistic reasons related to *kevod Shabbat*, and not *kevod hatzibbur*. Indeed, there were even those who wore a *tallit* for *kiddush* at home, and *kiddush* at home is hardly a *tefillat tzibbur* or *rabbim*.[11]

The second point raised was, curiously enough, from the writings of my grandfather, R. David Sperber.[12] He says that if one cannot find a *minyan*, one should at least try to pray with two other people, since this would constitute a *tefillat rabbim*, which is more readily accepted by God. He derives this from a passage in *Hayyei Adam* (*Klal* 68:11) who says that every mitzvah which can be done *behaburah*, in a group, should be so done, and not as an individual, because "the greater the number of people, the greater is the honour to the king" (Proverbs 14:28). So, this rabbi argues, *Kabbalat Shabbat*, which is normally recited in a *tzibur*, becomes *tefillat rabim*, which a woman cannot lead. But if three people give *tzedakah*, does that make it a *rabbim*? If three people declaim Psalms together, does that make it a *tefillat rabbim*? Surely the term my grandfather zt"l used was not intended to give a special status to the group of three, but merely to say that such a mitzvah or prayer is more acceptable before the Holy One Blessed be He than that of a single individual.[13]

Perhaps this point should be further amplified. The principle "the greater the number of people the greater the honour to the king" applies even to a mitzvah which is incumbent upon an individual (*mitzvat Yahid*)—even in such a case it is preferable to involve others. Thus, for example, Cohanim would participate in the lifting (*tenufah*) of the "breast and thigh" (*hazeh vashok*), or the innards of the *Shelamim* offering: the one who brought them from the place of slaughter handed them to the Cohen, who lifted them; the one who lifted them, and one who received them from the "lifter," placed them on the altar, in order that it be in a greater number to honor the king.[14] All these actions could have been done by a single Cohen; nonetheless, there was an additional "value," as it were, in involving others. Similarly, we learn from the Mishnah in *Pesahim* 5:5, that the Cohanim stood in rows, starting with place of the slaughter of the paschal lamb up to the altar, and one handed over the sprinkling bowl full of blood to another, though this could be done by a single Cohen, again for the same reason (*b. Pesahim* 64b). Although these are not exact parallels to our case, they clearly reveal the fact that involving more people in a mitzvah which can be legitimately carried out by an individual is seen as having additional value. This is certainly the case with prayer (see, e.g., *b. Berakhot* 8a), and, as we have just seen, even if the addition is minimal, such as up to three, this is considered an upgrading of the mitzvah, and this is to what my grandfather was alluding. (We might add, incidentally, that during the Ten Days of Repentance, the prayer of an individual is as effective as that of a *tzibbur*; see *b. Rosh haShanah* 18a; Rambam, *Hilkhot Teshuvah* 2:6.)

(On a personal note, I might add that in order fully to understand my sainted grandfather's ruling, one has to appreciate his particular brand of hassidic piety, which was a unique blend of halakhah, kabbalah and a special brand of hassidut. His belief in the efficacy of prayers was also evident to anyone who saw him in prayer. I personally served him in his latter years and received my *semikhah* from him.)[15]

A third argument was put forward: namely, that the recitation of *Kaddish Yatom* after *Mizmor Shir leYom ha-Shabbat*, etc., turns the preceding prayers into a *tefillat rabim*. It should, however, be noted that this particular *Kaddish* is not found in early sources. So, for example, it is not found in the *Tur* (*Orah Hayyim*, 237), and seems to have been introduced by the Ari haKadosh.[16] It certainly does not effect the status of the preceding section. And, of course, women themselves can say *Kaddish Yatom*.[17]

Now, my learned colleague knew all these facts which are plainly evident to anyone who is conversant with the relevant sources. Nonetheless, he chose to disregard them, or to reinterpret them in the most forced fashion.

Looking more closely at the discussion, it becomes patently evident that, rather than this being a genuinely halakhic debate, it is more a tendentious, socio-political polemic, but delivered on shaky grounds and dressed in a somewhat misleading garb of halakhic disquisition.

Now, I can well understand someone of the opinion that a certain kind of change from traditional practice, while not necessarily halakhically prohibited, is nonetheless somewhat unacceptable. Indeed, the Steipler, R. Yaakov Yisrael Kanievsky (1899-1985), in his *Karyana delgarta*,[18] already stated (as Marc Shapiro pointed out in his *Seforim Blog* post of May 26, 2013), that:

> There are some things which a Hakham has no ability to prohibit, even though they are in no way correct (i.e., acceptable).

But this is usually a matter of *hashkafah*—opinion, outlook, and policy—rather than *halakhah*. And in this regard, it is prudent to take notice of R. Hayyim Ozer's position (in his *Igrot* 2:51) where he made a "clear distinction between *halakhah* and policy", demanding absolute accuracy and precision when it comes to *halakhah*.

> If a behavior is halakhically permissible, but regarded by distinguished rabbis as destructive either personally or communally, it must be presented as such, but not as halakhically prohibited. To do so would be akin to heresy in terms of the Maharshal's view [*Yam Shel Shlomoh* to *Baba Kama*].[19]

Or as Marc Shapiro more generally pointed out: a week argument is worse than no argument.

2. Another Note on Women's Aliyot

One of the central points of controversy between those who permit women's *aliyot* and those who do not, is the understanding of the critical text in the Talmud (*b. Megillah* 23a) which states that "all are counted among the seven *aliyot*, even women and children. But the Rabbis said: 'A woman should not read the Torah because of the dignity of the community'". It is this final section that is the main source of the controversy. Some have claimed that "but the Rabbis said: A woman should not read . . ." is an absolute decree that cannot be changed. Others—myself included—have argued that this is advice, rather than a decree, and is limited by the principle of "the dignity of the community." That is to say, if there is no such slight on the community, the suggestion becomes irrelevant. I argued that most of the places where the phrase "But the Rabbis said" may be understood as "advice" and not "decree." Recently, Ephraim Bezalel Halivni sought to show that in many instances "but the Rabbis said" should clearly be understood as a "decree" formulation.[20] However, he himself[21] agrees that there are examples where this phrase can be understood as "advice." Hence, even according to his position, he will have to agree that *it is possible* that in our Megillah text "but the Rabbis said" may be advice. In other words, there is an element of uncertainty (*safek*) as to the precise interpretation of that text.

And even if we were to interpret it, as have some, as a decree, it is a decree with a reason. Now, there exists a well-known controversy between Rambam and Raavad as to whether, when the reason for a decree is no longer relevant, the decree is still in force; Rambam says yes, and Raavad disagrees.[22] It is true that in such controversies we follow the Rambam; however, it is equally true that it is not *certain* that he is correct. Perhaps the Raavad's position is more correct. In other words, there still exists an element of uncertainty (a *safek*) as to who is right. It is just that in accordance with certain pragmatic rules of halakhic adjudications (*pesak*) we follow the ruling of Rambam.[23]

There is yet another point of uncertainty. I pointed out elsewhere that several authorities hold the opinion that a *tzibbur* [community] can forgo their dignity (*mehilat kevodam*), while others differ on this point.[24] While it seems clear that the former is the dominant opinion, making the *Kevod hatzibbur* argument largely irrelevant, even if we were to side with the latter opinion, here again this would only be a pragmatic decision, which does not do away with the element of uncertainty as to which is *actually* the correct view. We have, thus, one more element of *safek* to take into account.

Moreover, R. Yosef Messas added yet a further consideration, arguing that even according to the view of Rambam, this principle only applies where there is a fear that the original reason could be relevant in the future. But in a case where there is little or no reason to think that the reason will resurface, the original prohibitions may be disregarded.[25] Here too, we may be fairly certain that in our modern society the dignity of the community will not be impugned by a woman's *aliyah* even in the future, in addition to which we have already pointed out that a community can, according to both the Maharam MiRothenberg and the Rashba, forgo their dignity should they so wish.

Now, even if I could not be sure that R. Messas' interpretation is necessarily correct, and I would not be absolutely certain of his ruling, that would imply that there exists yet another *safek*—in fact, at least a triple *sfek sfeka* and perhaps even many more: what is the correct interpretation of the Gemara in Megillah's phrase; whether to rule like Rambam or the Raavad; and even if one follows Rambam, whether we should accept R. Messas' interpretation thereof.

Furthermore, the Rambam himself did away with the *takana* that the *shaliah tzibbur* repeat the *Amidah* prayer (at *Shaharit*, *Musaf* and *Minhah*) for the benefit of those who had not said it, or could not do so.[26] So too, R. Ovadiah Yosef ruled[27] to annul the Rambam's *takanah* and to reestablish the *hazarat hashatz*, again explaining that the times and circumstances had changed! And see further Rav Kook's responsum in his *Orah Mishpat* to *Orah Hayyim* no. 58, on the ability to change or annul a *takanah* under certain circumstances. He formulates his argument as follows:

> . . . Nonetheless, in order to annul a *takanah*, it is sufficient if there is another reason, according to which it would not have been worthwhile establishing the *takanah* [in the first place].[28]

We should further add that the Radbaz on the Rambam[29] is even more lenient than the Raavad, for he states that "if the *takanah* was clearly stated to have been enacted for a given reason, and that reason no longer obtains, then the *takanah* is annulled. And the Rosh[30] goes even so far as to rule that even if the reason for the *takanah* was not expressly stated to be its determining factor, if nonetheless the reason was known and is no longer relevant, the *takanah* is annulled.

Given the above, surely the present state of feminine discomfort with the absence of greater participation in synagogue ritual is sufficient to annul what may have been *takanah* of old, even according to the view of the Rambam.

Without going into all the details of the very complex *kuntres sfek-sfeka*, surely here we should rule *sfek sfeka le-kula*—most leniently—admitting the permissibility of women's aliyot, especially when added to all our other arguments.[31]

But in point of fact, although R. Messas' ruling may appear to be very innovative, i.e., a great *hiddush*, it is actually well-attested in a number of different halakhic contexts. Here we shall bring one such example.

The Mishnah in Terumot 8:4 rules that:

> . . . Those liquids become forbidden through being uncovered: water, wine, and milk. . . . How long must they have remained [uncovered] to become forbidden? Such time as it could take a serpent to come forth from a place near by and drink.

The Rambam in *Hilkhot Rotzeah* 11:11 expands this ruling, stating that:

> All liquids that were uncovered, whether by day or night, are forbidden, even if a person slept next to them, because the creeping creatures fear not a sleeping person.

This ruling is followed by the *Tur Yoreh Deah* 116, who explains that the Rabbis forbade things which they regarded as dangerous, such as uncovered liquids, for they feared that a snake put its poison in them. But, adds the *Tur*, "nowadays it is the custom to be lenient in this matter, even if it is certain that the liquids remained uncovered, because such poisonous creatures are not to be found now". He continues to explain why the Rabbis' ruling can, in effect be annulled, arguing that the original enactment was instituted because of the fear of snake-poison, and since now there are no longer such snakes around, the enactment no longer applies. And this indeed is how the *Shulhan Arukh* rules.[32]

However, the *Pri Hadash*[33] comments that in the Magreb there are many places where snakes and scorpions are to be found, and in these places people are careful not to drink uncovered water. And in Jerusalem, and its surroundings, even though snakes are not common, since there are some, people should take heed of this prohibition. And so too, R. Yosef Hayyim of Bagdhad (1833-1909), in his famous *Ben Ish Hai*,[34] despite the lenient ruling of the *Shulhan Arukh*, nonetheless cautions his community to take heed of this ruling; and so too does the Hungarian, Shlomo Ganzfried (1804-1886), in his highly popular *Kitzur Shulhan Arukh* 33:5.[35]

We see, then, that despite the fact that the Rabbis instituted a prohibitional regulation (*gezerah*) when (and where) the reason for its enactment was no longer applicable, the prohibition was ignored or rejected with the consent of the Rabbis. Indeed, there are many other such examples of halakhic regulations enacted because of the fear of some sort of danger—*mishum sakanah* (or *mishum hashasha*)—that subsequently became regarded as irrelevant and fell into desuetude, again with the approbation of the Rabbis.

Or, in the words of Schepansky:

> That which [the Rabbis] forbade *mi-shum hashasha*, out of fear or apprehension (of some kind), even if they enacted it *be-minyan*, i.e., through the agency of a court of law (*beit din*), if that fear is now allayed, one does not require a court of law to permit it.[36]

He then gives the example we have cited above, adding that nowadays we do not observe strictly the practice of *mayyim aharonim*, (rinsing the hands at the end of the meal), required by the Talmud (*b. Hulin* 106a), because we no longer use *melah sedomit*, a kind of salt which if left on one's hands and touched to one's eyes might blind them (Tosafot, *b. Berakhot* 53b).[37]

So too, in our own case, the "fear" (*hashasha*) of impugning the congregation is no longer present, and the *gezerah*, (or *takanah*, if so it be), may now be annulled without recourse to a beit din (minyan).

Furthermore, one of my key arguments was that *kevod haberiot*, the dignity of the individual has greater halakhic weight than *kevod hatzibbur*, the dignity of the community, for the Talmud tells us that "so great is the dignity of the individual that it annuls (*doheh*) even biblical prohibitions". I cited sources and gave some examples to prove this point. Here, I should like briefly, and almost telegraphically, to amplify this argument.[38] The principle of dignity of the individual comes into force when someone may be shamed, and even when the shame devolves upon one and not upon others because, for example, of their difference in status—and a *mitzvah* can be rejected (*nidheit*) for this reason.[39] Hence, if some women feel offended by not receiving *aliyot*, even if others do not, this is sufficient for those that do. And, of course, the fact that men are not so offended, because they do get *aliyot*, while women are because they do not, merely strengthens this argument.[40]

The shame and affront does not necessarily have to be acute. Even a slight shame (*genai katan*) is enough to bring this principle into force.[41] And should one argue that there are alternative and conflicting views on all these issues (though I have highlighted the dominant opinions), I would reply, continuing the aforementioned line of argumentation, that all these components of the halakhic question may introduce the element of uncertainty [*safek*]; hence, here we have yet another integer to add to our complex equation with its ever-increasing list of uncertainties.

The cumulative effect of all these various considerations legitimately leads us to take the path of leniency, and permit the practice of women's *aliyot* in the synagogue.[42]

3. On the Maharat Debate

As briefly alluded to in our introductory note, on Sunday June 16, 2013, three woman graduates of Yeshivat Maharat were ordained as members of the clergy and "decisors" in a very emotionally charged historic ceremony. This was followed, and actually had been preceded, by a number of sharply-worded criticisms by members of the "orthodox" rabbinic establishment, and specifically the R.C.A.[43]

Already in 2010, in the wake of the sharp polemic censure that flared up in the wake of Ms. Sara Hurvitz's ordination, I wrote an extensive article in *Meorot* 8 (1-12) justifying and legitimating the appointment of women to Rabbinic leadership positions. Now, after the most recent ordination ceremony I was asked to present an abbreviated version of my study in a more simplified style, for a more widely disseminated public. (Hence, I have not burdened the reader with references and footnotes, as they may be found in my *Meorot* article.)

What then are the halakhic problems involved in women serving as "rabbis" or judges—"*dayyanot*"? The Mishnah (Niddah 6:4) and the Talmud Yerushalmi (*Yoma* 6:1) indicate that since a woman cannot serve as a witness, she cannot serve as a judge, i.e., cannot give halakhic rulings. The Tosafot (to *b. Niddah* 50a) asked: How can this be? Surely Devorah the Prophetess served as a judge (Judges 4:4-5)! One of the answers given is that she herself did not give judgments, but taught the judges the laws. So clearly a woman can teach the law and its rulings if so required.

Now, rabbis can give two different types of rulings. They can say such and such is the case, and the client-requester is obligated to follow that reply and may not go shopping around for more convenient replies. Or they can say: "This is my opinion," or "This is my advice to you," which leaves the client with the option to decide for himself or herself or to go and get a different opinion. In the latter case, the rabbi is really teaching rather than ruling, which as we have seen is permissible for a woman to do. And should she wish to give a ruling, rather than an opinion, which is usually the less common response, she may be limited in the spectrum of the cases she can deal with because of her ineligibility to serve as a witness. However, there are many categories of testimony that she may give—I listed some eight of them—and in all of these she should be eligible to give rulings.

But even if she were not qualified to give testimony, she could still answer questions with which she was capable of dealing.[44]

Furthermore, strictly speaking, one is not required to have an official *semikhah* for ruling halakhic questions in the area of *Orah Hayyim* and *Yoreh Deah*.[45] The Rambam (ibid.) and the *Tur* (*Yoreh Deah* 242) and the *Shulhan Aruch* (ibid., 242:3) rule that a disciple requires his mentor's permission to rule, i.e., this is the modern form of *semikhah*. However, in matter of *issur veheter* there is apparently no *semikhah* requirement; so states the *Rema* explicitly.[46] Indeed, he writes that since the institution of *semikhah* no longer exists: "today's *semikhah* is nothing but *netilat reshut* (receiving permission to give a halachic ruling), and whatever one is capable of ruling is sufficient [ground for giving a *psak halakhah*]."[47]

Furthermore, a number of authorities claimed that this limitation is only applicable to a woman who is appointed by the Sanhedrin, or by a non-democratically appointed board. But if the congregation appoints her, accepts and trusts her, their acceptance gives her position legitimacy—*kabbalah mehania.* Indeed, trust and acceptance are obviously a key element in leadership.[48]

In actual fact, many questions put before a rabbi are of a technical nature, and the questioner could easily find the answer in a halakhic book, if he were competent to deal with such literature. And so in all so many cases, the rabbi's answer is almost the equivalent of opening a book, but for some people the Rabbi's reply is easier and more readily available. Today, halakhic books are more or less the equivalent of rabbis.[49] Clearly, the element of trust again clearly comes into play, and the answer is much in the nature of a testimony. And since the answer can always be checked out, such a class of testimony is acceptable from a woman too.

This position would seem to be borne out by an early responsum of *Ri Migash* (R. Yosef Ibn Megas, 1077-1141).[50] He was asked:

> What would you say, Our Master, about a man who has never in his life studied halakhah under a Rabbi, and does not know the way of halakhah and its ways of interpretation, on how to read [such literature], but he saw many responsa of the Geonim and books of regulations (*dinim*)?

The answer he gives is as follows:

> Know that this person is more suited to be given permission to give rulings than many other people who have given themselves authority to give rulings in our time; for most of them have neither of two requirements, that is to say: an understanding of halakhah, and a knowledge of the opinions of the Geonim. And those who think they can rule out of their own study of halakhah and because of the strength of the study of Talmud, it is they who should be prevented from [giving rulings], as in our times there is no one who is worthy of this, and [even] one who has reached the wisdom of the Talmud may not rule out the results of his personal study unless he be acquainted with the views of the Geonim. But, on the other hand, he who rules out of a knowledge of the Geonim and relies upon them, even if he does not understand Talmud, he is more suitable and praiseworthy, than he who thinks he knows Talmud and relies upon himself.

This remarkable statement clearly expresses the preference for one acquainted with the writings of the authoritative sources, to one who relies on his own judgment but does not base himself on the authorities. In our days, the authoritative sources are readily available in books and other media, so that, provided the answers given are based on and consonant with these sources, they may be given even by a less learned individual.

See further *Shut Maharshdam* (R. Shmuel de-Medina, Salonika 1506-1589), *Hoshen Mishpat* 1:

> . . . In our days the scholar only rules in accordance with the book. And if we see that he is expert and experienced in studying [the sources] and has a healthy sense of reason (*u-baal sevara yodea daat u-meivin*), it is obvious that he can give rulings . . . even when there is someone greater [in learning] than him in his locale.[51]

However, it should also be borne in mind that he has to choose the books he uses with great care, and be sure of the author's status and the accuracy of the traditions cited, etc.[52]

It has been argued that the rabbi exerts an element of leadership control, or "authority," and the Rambam rules that women may not serve in a position of authority.[53] However, latter-day authorities, who found no source for the Rambam's ruling, rejected it, or again stated that this is not relevant when a woman is democratically appointed. Again, the community has, as it were, formed a contractual agreement to accept that authority. And indeed, this seems to be the clear meaning of the Sifrei to Deut. 17:15,[54] which states that "one does not appoint a woman as a *parnasa* over the community." However, the *community* can appoint her as such. In parenthesis, we may add that usually the Rabbi is not a *parnas over* the community (parnas *al hatzibbur*), but *serves* the community (*parnas latzibbur*).

As to the issue of serving as a judge, it is known that if the litigants agree to accept the rulings of an appointee, his rulings are binding even if he is a relative, or would appear to have a tendentious objective, or any other reason that might disqualify him. Such practice is called *borerut*, arbitration.

There has been a considerable body of literature that has recently appeared on this subject which may be consulted for further and more detailed analysis. But in the final analysis, it makes little sense that while a woman can be a supreme court judge, and even president of that court, she cannot give halakhic opinions; that while she can serve as a member of Knesset, or even as a prime minister, she cannot serve on the synagogue board of governors.[55] We are not arguing that because she can do the one, she is automatically eligible for the other, but rather that since she does the one, if it is basically permissible to do the other, then it is legitimate to do so, even if this appears to be an innovation. Because as social changes take place in our society, we need to uncover those areas in which we can accommodate the legitimate responses to the challenges posed by these societal developments.[56]

Final Note

And finally, a somewhat pedagogical comment. The Beit Yosef, of R. Yosef Caro, in *Yoreh Deah* 242, states:

> It is forbidden for a *hakham* to give a ruling permitting something which looks strange, for the masses will see this as permitting the forbidden.

He bases himself on *Hagahot Maimoniyot* to Rambam, *Hilkhot Talmud Torah* chapter 5 sect. 6. Now almost all innovations look strange, and can easily be understood as permitting the forbidden. And indeed, this is the ruling in *Shulhan Arukh Yoreh Deah* 242:10. (And see *Beur haGra*, ibid., sect. 21 for Talmudic sources.) But the *Shakh* (*Siftei Cohen*) ad loc. sect. 17 modifies this statement as follows:

> It would appear that this [refers to a case] where he permitted [something] without any explanation [for his ruling]—*setam*—and indeed so it appears from the proofs he brings from *Hagahot Maimoniyot* and b. *Sanhedrin* 5ab . . . and b. *Nidah* 20a . . . and the beginning of b. *Berachot* (3b). . . . But if he tells the questioner the reason for his ruling, and explains to him his arguments (ומראה לו פנים), or if he brings evidence from the book, it is permitted.

And the *Beer Heiteiv* cites this in abbreviated form.[57] Indeed, this was already stated in a responsum of R. Shlomoh b. R. Shimon ben Tzemah Duran (*Rashbash*, 1401-1470), *Shut Rashbash* (Jerusalem: 1998), no.513, 423 (and cf. *Sedei Hemed*, by R. Hayyim Hezkiahu Medini, vol.2, 337-338).

This indicates to us very clearly that all changes such as those we are advocating must not only be firmly based in our canonic sources, but must also be clearly presented and openly justified and documented to the general public.

Therefore, we need to be sensitive to those societal charges which bring serious challenges in their wake, proactively search out viable solutions, and present them to the public in a convincing manner, as indeed Rabbi Weiss has been doing for the past several decades.

NOTES

1. See Avraham Weiss, *Principles of Spiritual Activism*, (Hoboken, NJ: KTAV, 2001). In 1992, Rabbi Avi Weiss created AMCHA, a Coalition for Jewish concern engaged in Jewish activism, in addition to establishing Yeshivat Chovevei Torah in 1999 and Yeshivat Maharat in 2001.
2. Avraham Weiss, *Women at Prayer: A Halakhic Analysis of Women's Prayer Groups* (Hoboken, NJ: KTAV, 1990), and see my review in *Gesher* 34:127-128 (1989), 147-148. Already in 1977 he coined the term "open orthodoxy" which R. Steven Pruzansky claimed was similar to 20 cent. Conservatism.
3. On June 16, 2013.
4. See the classic study of A.A. Frimer and D. Frimer, "Women's Prayer Services—Theory and Practice," *Tradition* 32:2 (1998), 5-118. (This was only Part 1, and regretfully, we have not yet been treated to Part 2.) Gideon Rothstein wrote an interesting critique in *Tradition* 39:2 (2005), 30-52, entitled "Women's Aliyot in Contemporary Synagogues," and Michael J. Broyde published a fine summary of the issues, entitled "Women Receiving Aliyot? A Short Halakhic Analysis, in Leib Moscovitz and Yosef Rivlin, eds., "*Wisdom and Understanding*": *Studies in Honour of Bernard Jackson, Jewish Law Association* 2 (2012), with a useful bibliography of previous discussions in note 1. Of late, the literature on this subject has become very copious and has appeared in a variety of literary media, and thus cannot be fully referenced within this context. However, a very fine summarizing study was published by Professor Roberta Kwall, entitled "The Cultural Analysis Paradigm: Women and Synagogue Ritual as a Case Story," *Cardozo Law Review* 34:2 (2012), 609-667.
5. Such as those of Shlomo Riskin and Eliav Shochetman, in *Congregational Prayer: Halakhic Perspectives*, ed. Chaim Trachtman (Hoboken, NJ: KTAV, 2010), 291-358, (Shochetman), and 359-388 (Riskin) with Mendel Shapiro's response to Riskin, ibid., 354-406, and Riskin to Shapiro, 407-411. Shochetman's essay is an abbreviated version of what he wrote in Hebrew in "Aliyyat Nashim leTorah," *Sinai* (2005), 271-349. See also Y.H. Henkin, "Qeriat Ha-Torah by Women: Where We Stand Today", *Edah Journal* 1 (2001).
6. See, inter alia, my extensive study entitled "Congregational Dignity and Human Dignity," which appeared in *Women and Men in Communal Prayer*, 27-205.
7. See my essay entitled "On Women in Rabbinic Leadership Position", *Meorot* 8 (2010), 1-12. It is interesting in this context to compare my conclusions with the nuanced ones in M.J. Broyde and Shlomo M. Brody, "Orthodox Women Rabbis? Tentative Thoughts that Distinguish Between the Timely and the Timeless," *Hakirah* 25 (2011), 52-53.
8. I am referring primarily to the extensive articles by Rabbi Dr. Barry Freundel, e.g., "Recited by the Community; But is it communal?" *Tradition* 44:2 (2011), 35-51; "Putting the Silent Partner Back into Partnership Minyanim," 1-35; "Kabbalat Shabbat"; and *Hirhurim-Musings*, Jan. 22, 2013; Jan. 27, 2013; Feb.12, 2013; Feb. 15, 2013; Feb. 27, 2012; March 5,2013 (6 parts), available at http:torahmusings com/2013/01/partnership-minyanim/. There have been a number of responses and reactions to his articles, notably those of Zev Farber, and some very significant comments by Professor Marc B. Shapiro in seforim.blogspot.co.2013/05.
9. See I.J. Cohen, "*Seder Kabbalat Shabbat u-Pizmon Lecha Dodi*", *Mekorot ve-Korot*

(Jerusalem: 1982), pp.74-106, and my *Minhagei Yisrael*, vol. 4 (Jerusalem: 1955), 1-7. Cohen's exhaustive study first appeared in *Sefer ha-Zikaron le-Adam Noah Braun* (Jerusalem: 1970). The sub-title is: *Mehkar Histori al Hitpashtut ha-Minhag, Keitzad Nitkabel bi-Tefutzot Yisrael ve-Eimatai Hunhag be-Aratzot Shonot*. See further Mosheh Hallamish, *Hanhagot Kabbaliot be-Shabbat* (Jerusalem: Orchot, 2006), 189-246; Reuven Kimelman, *Lecha Dodi ve-Kabbalat Shabbat: ha-Mashmaut ha-Mistit* (The Mystical Meaning of *Lekha Dodi* and *Kabbalat Shabbat*)(Jerusalem: Magnes, 2003), passim.

10. See *Magen Avraham* 53:9; *Entziklopediah Talmudit* vol. 26 (Jerusalem: 2004), 562-564, n. 140; and see E.B. Halivni, *Bein ha-Ish la-Ishah* (Jerusalem: 2007), English section, at 15. See Rambam, Responsa ed. Freiman, Jerusalem 1934, no.15, p.15, on the forty-year old who had no beard, but the Rambam allowed to act as a *hazzan*.
11. See Joseph Lewy, *Minhag Yisrael Torah*, Volume 1 (5 vols.)(Brooklyn: Pink Graphic, 1994), 87-88.
12. *Teshuvot: Afrakasta de-Anya*, 3rd ed. (Israel: 2002), vol. 4, at 215.
13. Freundel's other reference to vol. 2, 211 is quite irrelevant to this issue.
14. *b. Menahot* 62a; see *Entziklopedia Talmudit*, vol. 4 (Jerusalem: 1952), 196.
15. See the introduction of my father, Rabbi Shmuel Sperber, to my grandfather's *Michtam le-David* on the Torah, vol. 1 (Jerusalem: 1967).
16. See *Shaar haKavanot* 68b; *Siddur Tzelota deAvraham*, by A. Werdiger (Jerusalem: 1991), *Shabbat Kodesh*, 112-115. See also Hallamish, ibid., 251. We may add that *Kaddish Yatom* after the *Shaharit Mizmor Shir Hannukat haBayit* only occurs in some versions, and certainly does not make that section of *Shaharit* as *Tefillat rabbim*. Indeed, the introduction of this psalm is also the work of the Ari haKadosh; see M.Y. Weinstock, *Siddur ha-Geonim vehaMekubbalim*, vol. 2 (Jerusalem: 1970), 226. See the section on Kaddish in my *Minhagei Yisrael*, vol. 7, 139-140.
17. See my discussion in *Women and Men in Communal Prayer*, 178-179. This has most recently been reaffirmed by the Rabbinic Organization Beit Hillel, in a declaration of June 2013.
18. 2011 ed., vol. 2, no. 581.
19. See Berel Wein and Warren Goldstein, *The Legacy: Teachings for Life from the Great Lithuanian Rabbis* (New York: Maggid, 2012), 112-113.
20. See also E. Shochetman, *Women and Men in Communal Prayer*, 316-318, arguing that, as such, the ruling is in effect completely unalterable; and cf. ibid., 311-313, where he rejects my ensuing argument.
21. *Studies in Liturgy and Reading The Torah* (Jerusalem: 2012), 160
22. Rambam, *Hilkhot* Mumrim 2:2, and Raavad, ibid. Rambam, Responsa *Peer haDor* no.148, ed. David Yosef (Jerusalem: 1984), 291, and editor's notes, ibid. See in detail Israel Schepansky, *Ha-Takkanot be-Yisrael* (Jerusalem: New York, 1991), vol. 1, 8-9 notes 37-41, 78-80, 84-87. In point of fact, the issue is far more complex. Since the beraita's statement is a negative one, we may regard it—if not as advice—as a *gezerah* rather than a *takanah*. (On the definition of a *gezerah* as a negative enactment, see *Entziklopedia Talmudit*, vol. 5 [Jerusalem: 1963], 529-530.) Schepansky, at ibid., 8, points out that according to the Rosh, though one may not cancel a *takanah* the reason for which is no longer relevant, a *gezerah* whose reason is no longer valid may be annulled (*Teshuvot haRosh*, *Klal Beit* sect. 8 ad fin., cited in the *Beit Yosef* to *Orah Hayyim* 9, and *Magen Avraham*, ibid., sect. 7, *Mahtzit*

haShekel ibid). Schepansky (ibid., note 38), discusses the view of the *Mahtzit haShekel*, and concludes decisively that the Rosh made this clear distinction between a *gezerah* and a *takanah*. See also *Entziklopedia Talmudit*, ibid., 539, on the limitations of a *gezerah* when there is no "*hashash*". See also Menachem Elon, *Ha-Mishpat ha-Ivri: Toldotav, Mekorotav, Ekronotav* (Jerusalem: 1973), 445, and especially note 201.

23. This is a point of cardinal importance, and really deserves a more detailed exposition. Here, suffice it to say that the fact that the majority may hold that giving an opinion does not necessarily mean that that opinion is truly the correct one. See, for example, the well-known Mishnah in *Eduyot* 1:5, which asks:

> And why do we record [in the Mishnah] the opinion of the individual alongside that of the many (i.e. majority), since the halakhah is only in accordance with the majority? So that, if a court sees the [validity of] the opinion of the individual, it may rely upon it. . . .

See commentators ad loc. who explain that the rejected opinion could become the correct halakhic approach. Thus, R. Menashe of Ilya (Lithuania 1767-1831) clarifies the *Eduyot* statement as follows:

> We thus learn that a court may rely on some individual and, at its discretion, change a law from the one that had bound their ancestors. . . . (*Alfei Menasheh* vol. 1 [Jerusalem: 1979], 44).

Indeed, it could well be that both dissenting views are actually correct. So we read in *b. Eruvin* 13b and *b. Gittin 6b* that:

> R. Abba stated in the name of Samuel: For three years there was a dispute between Beit Shamai and Beit Hillel, with these claiming "the halakhah is as we say," and these countering "the halakhah is as we say," then a heavenly voice declared, "these and these are the words of the living God, but the halakhah follows the rulings of Beit Hillel". . . .

And, perhaps similarly, we read in *b. Hagigah* 3b:

> "The masters of the assemblies" (*Ecclesiastes* 12:11): these are the scholars who gather together in assemblies and study Torah, some ruling pure and other ruling impure, some prohibiting and others permitting, some rejecting and others accepting. Were one to say, "how, then, can I learn Torah from now on?" The Scripture says, "they are given from our Shepherd" (*Ecclesiastes* 12:11). One God gave them, and one Leader uttered them.

See on this whole subject the comprehensive and penetrating analytical study of Avi Sagi, *The Open Canon: On the Meaning of Halakhic Discourse* (New York: Bloomsbury, 2007), passim; Eliezer Berkovits, *Not in Heaven: The Nature and Function of Halakha* (New York: KTAV, 1983), 50-53. See further Yitzhak Yosef, *Maarechet haShulhan* vol. 2 (Jerusalem: 2010), on the rationale for ruling according to a minority opinion where there is great loss [*hefsed merubeh*], or in special circumstances [*shaat hadehak*], and ibid., 642, as to whether the rulings in the *Shulhan Aruch* are final and certain or remain in the area of uncertainty [*mikoah safek*] (citing as examples, Hayyim David Hazan, *Responsa Nediv Lev* (Salonica–Jerusalem: 1862-1866), *Hoshen Mishpat* sect. 50, and his father Rephael Yosef Hazan, in his *Hikrei Lev* vol. 3 (Salonica: 1787), *Yoreh Deah* sect. 127, and others). And see, most recently, my article entitled "On How to Lean towards Leniency: Halakhic Methodology for the *Posek*," *Conversations*, Autumn 2015, issue 23, pp.1-28.

24. See *Entziklopedia Talmudit* vol.26 (Jerusalem: 2004), 563-565, for a full discussion on this issue. And for an interesting partly parallel issue, see N.E. Rabinowitz, *Shut Siah Nachum* (Maaleh Adumim: 2008), no.7, 20-21.
25. *Otzar Michtavim* 1, 454; cf. Marc B. Shapiro, *Conversations* 7 (2010), 101.
26. See his son, Abraham's response at the beginning of *Maaseh Rokeah*, (and in the Freimann edition of Rambam's Responsa nos. 35 and 36, Blau ed. 256, 258, cited by David Yosef, ibid., note 13; see also the additional references he cites, ibid.) David Yosef explains that this does not contradict his basic position on not annulling *takanot*, because he too would agree to such annulment when the *takanah* itself has negative effects, referring us to *Hilchot Mumrim* 2:4, and yet another of his responsum, in ed. Freimann no.38, ed. Blau 291. (And even if it did, there is an opinion that when there is a contradiction between the Rambam's rulings in *Mishneh Torah* and those in his responsa, we follow the responsa. See Yitzhak Yosef, *Ein Yitzhak* vol. 1, [Jerusalem: 2009], 407-408. However, this seems to be a minority view; ibid., 206-208.)
27. *Yehaveh Daat* vol.5, no. 12 (Jerusalem: 1983).
28. For an explanation of this reasoning, see Amiram Domovitz, *Ha-Halachah ve-ha-Olam ha-Moderni* (Gush Etzion: n.d.), 153.
29. Ibid.
30. *Responsa, Klal* 2:8.
31. See Yitzhak Yosef, *Ein Yitzhak* vol. 2 (Jerusalem: 2009), 281-352, and especially 301-307, section 15-17, and also 287, where a triple *safek* is always a path to leniency, and vol. 3, 309-311. See also Reuven David Nawi, *Yehi Reuven* (Jerusalem: 1983), 83 n.16, who argues that we may use a *sfek sfeka* to contradict a clear ruling of the *Shulhan Arukh*.
32. Ibid., 116:1.
33. ad loc.
34. *Pinhas*, sect. 9.
35. And for further references to the Rabbis of North Africa, who follow the original Talmudic ruling, see Mosheh Suissa, *Ateret Avot*, vol.3, Israel (no date, but c. 2013), p. 295, note 20; but R. Yosef Messas, in his *Otzar ha-Michtavim* no. 1884, vol. 3, Jerusalem, p. 211, clearly states that nowadays this decree no longer applies.
36. Ibid., 86.
37. And see the additional example cited by Schepansky, ibid. p. 87 note 22, and *Entziklopedia Talmudit* vol. 26, Jerusalem 2004, 669, on looking in a mirror.
38. The sources in full can be found in *Entzikopedia Talmudit* vol. 26 (Jerusalem: 2004), s.v. *Kevod ha-beriot*, 477-542.
39. Ibid., 495-496.
40. And note ibid., 159.
41. Ibid., 511 n.295, and again 534-535 notes 493 et seq.; and see also N. Rakover, *Gadol Kevod ha-Briyot* (Jerusalem: 1998), 937, referring to R. Meir Arik, *Tal Torah*, vol. 1 (Vienna: 1921), to *b. Berakhot* 19b).
42. Also taking into account the position that *Koah deheteira adif*, i.e., the primacy of lenient ruling; see E. Shochetman, "The Power to Render a Lenient Ruling: *Koah Deheteira Adif*, *Jewish Law Association* vol. 1 (1922), 126-155; my *Darkah Shel Torah* (Jerusalem: 2007), 111-113, 138-139; and Yitzhak Yosef, *Ein Yitzhak* vol. 1

(Jerusalem: 2009), 414-420, on the parameters of this principle.

43. Some responses to this criticism were also expressed in blogs, etc. (see above).
44. For the *Pri Megadim*, *Seder Hanhagot haShoel in haNishal beIssur veHeter*, 1:2, (*Shulhan Arukh*, ed. Machon Yerushalayim, *Orah Hayyim* vol. 1 [Jerusalem: 1984], 395) states that a brilliant youngster, thirteen years old, who has not yet signs of maturity (*simanei bagrut*), and who is therefore not qualified to give evidence, may nonetheless give rulings (*Hoshen Mishpat* 7:3, and see *Sefer Meirat Einayim* [*Sma*] sect. 9).
45. See *Sheelot uTeshuvot haRivash*, by R. Yitchak ben Sheshet, no. 271, ed. David Metzger, vol.1 (Jerusalem: 2013), 356, basing himself on *b. Sanhedrin* 5a; and similarly *Lehem Mishneh* on Rambam, *Hilkhot Sanhedrin* 4:8.
46. *Darkhei Mosheh*, Yoreh Deah 242:2.
47. See, most recently, Moshe Walter, *The Making of a Halachic Decision: A Comprehensive Analysis & Guide to Halachic Rulings* (Brooklyn: Menucha, 2013), 116-117, with additional references.
48. This notion of *kabbalah mahania* may be related to the very basic principle of *Kiblu alaihu*, discussed in detail in Abraham Hirsch Rabinowitz, *The Jewish Mind in its Halachic Talmudic Expression* (Jerusalem: Hillel, 1978), 209-225.
49. See *Sheelot uTeshuvot Shvut Yaakov*, by R. Yaakov Reischer, vol.2 (Offenbach: 1719), sect. 64.
50. (Jerusalem: 1959), sect. 114 (fol. 17ab).
51. See Avi Sagi, apur *Rabbanut: Ha-Etgar* (Jerusalem: 2011), vol. 2, 716, and n. 24, ibid., for additional material on this issue. And see *Entziklopedia Talmudit* vol. 8, s.v. *Horaah*, 489-490, on the various opinions on ruling from books; but there is a consensus that one may rule in accordance with the *Shulhan Arukh*, and its supercommentaries; see *Pithei Teshuvah* to *Yoreh Deah* 242:8. And see *Entziklopedia*, ibid., 491-494, and especially ibid., n. 109, that women may give rulings if they are sufficiently well educated (*ishah hakhamah*).

    The importance of books is already mentioned in mediaeval rabbinic sources. See, for example, the statement of the Tosafist, R. Mosheh of Evreux, who stated that:

    > From the time the Jewish people was exiled from its land, when our Temple was destroyed . . . the law that reverence for a teacher must be like reverence for God no longer applies, and all the rules regarding the relationship between disciple and master are abrogated. This is because the books, the treatises, and the commentaries are our masters, and everything depends on intelligence and logic.

    See further R. Ovadiah Yosef, *Yabia Omer* vol. 4, *Hoshen Mishpat* 1:6, that this phrase "the books . . . are our masters" mandates that all books must be examined prior to rendering a *psak*. See A. Yehudah Warburg, *Rabbinic Authority: The Vision and the Reality* (Jerusalem-New York: Urim, 2013), 34 (especially n. 63), 47-49, on *sifrei psak*. On the importance of *sevara*, see Rabinowitz, *The Jewish Mind*, 149-165. However, in ibid., 151-161, one finds a discussion of the limitation of ruling from codices without a true understanding of the underlying sources and principles involved, i.e., *sevara*.
52. See Yitzhak Yosef, *Shulhan ha-Maarechet*, vol. 2 (Jerusalem: 2010), 412-420. See further, ibid., 425-427, on the minimum age for writing books of halakhic rulings, citing, inter alia, the *Noda biYehudah* and *Yabia Omer* vol. 4, *Hoshen Mishpat* 1:7.
53. It has been argued that there is also an issue of lack of modesty. In actual fact, the

issue of modesty is largely irrelevant. For R. Yehuda Henkin, in his *Understanding Tzniut: Modern Controversies in the Jewish Community* (Jerusalem-New York: Urim, 2008), 72-84, has convincingly demonstrated that because we are so used to seeing women in a broad variety of roles and situations, this no longer causes sexual distraction [*hirhur*]. Thus, for example, among the several sources he cites, we read that the Levush, at the end of his *Minhagim*, writes:

> We do not take care about [avoiding] mixed seating, because nowadays women are very common among men, and there are relatively few sinful thoughts about them. . . (ibid., 81-82).

Indeed, this was the basis of R. Yosef Messas' remarkable ruling permitting married women to appear in public without hair covering. At the end of his responsum, he writes:

> It is certainly understood . . . that since nowadays all women uncover all their hair . . . this being so usual, it is not considered immodesty (peritzut) . . . and any man is personally aware that in seeing thousands of women day by day passing before him with an uncovered head, he does not even notice them, and certainly has no *hirhur*, for uncovered hair [no longer] excites sexual distraction. (*Otzar ha-Michtavim* no. 1484, vol. 3 [Jerusalem: 1975], 211).

More recently, R. Mosheh Lichtenstein, in his article entitled *Shirat Nashim le-Lo Kiruv ha-Daat, Tehumin* 32 (2002), 291-299, reached much the same conclusion with regard to listening to a woman's singing, that where there is no likelihood of sexual distraction (*hashash hirhur*) there is no reason to forbid it, and in the reality of our social situation, this indeed is the case.

54. ed. Finkelstein, 208.
55. In my *Congregational Dignity* study, 103-104 n. 89, I brought copious evidence as to the fact that in classical antiquity women held leadership positions in synagogues, and that we have inscriptions from the Roman and Byzantine period referring to women as *archisynagogos* or *presbytera*. To that material I should like to add the following data. See further J. Reynolds and R. Tannenbaum, *Jews and Godfearers at Aphrodisias* (Cambridge: 1984) (Cambridge Philological Society, Supplementary Vol. 12), 41 note to p. 5 line 9: *Iael prostates* (Greek): "Jael may be a woman's name (as in Judges 4:18 f), but [certainly is a woman's name, D.S.]: the title is no obstacle to its being so here, since women are often given titles of high synagogue or community office in the diaspora. . . ." See further the n. 130 to p. 71: "Philo normally employs *prostates* and *prostasia* in the sense of the title or office of the 'president' of a community." However, on 101 no. 34, they think Yael is masculine, which I think is highly unlikely.
56. Elsewhere, in *Darkah shel Halachah* (Jerusalem: 2007), 139, I quoted The *Taz* (*Turei Zahav*) to *Yoreh Deah* 141:2, who wrote:

> It would appear to me that even with regards to uncertain (safek) idolatry [where normally we rule] stringently, nonetheless, wherever there is a reason (sevara) to rule either leniently or stringently, we should rule leniently. For in all cases we do not establish a prohibition on the basis of a point of uncertainty (*misafek*), and we do not rule stringently on a point of uncertainty, except where there is already an assumption of it being forbidden.

And there is a well-known rabbinic statement:

> Just as it is forbidden to permit that which is forbidden, so it is forbidden to forbid that which is permitted. (Shach, *Kitzur Hanhagot Issur veHeter*, 9, Yoreh Deah 245. And cf. R. Nehuniah ben haKanah's prayer on entering the Beit Midrash in *b. Berachot* 28b: ". . . that I do not declare the impure pure, neither the pure impure. . . .")

This position is already reflected in the statement in *y. Sotah* 8:2, that "just as it is prohibited to decree as pure something that is impure, so too it is forbidden to decree as impure that which is pure". Cf. *b. Berachot* 28b, and *Rokeah* sect. 28, who wrote: "The sin of permitting things that are prohibited is just like the sin of prohibiting things that are permitted." And see further R. Ovadiah miBartinoro LeAvot 5:8, and Yitzhak Yosef, *Shulhan haMaarechet* vol.2 (Jerusalem: 2010), 409-411.

See further Y. *Terumot* 5 ad fin., statement of R. [E]liezer; parallels in *y. Hagigah* 1:8; *y. Sotah* 8:2; cited in *Semag Asin* 111; *Hagahot Maimoniyot Mamrin* 1:5. See further *Teshuvot Maimoniyot* to *Ma'achalot Asurot* 15, in name of Yerushalmi, etc. (Of course, this principle also has its parameters, and the Rabbis frequently imposed prohibitions to distance and prevent people from sinning. However, this subject is beyond the scope of this study.)

In our essay on *Congregational Dignity*, 97, we also cited Rav Kook's words (in *Orah Mishpat* [Jerusalem: 1985], sect. 112):

> Heaven forbid that we should think that, by permitting that which is permitted—because it did not exist in reality, so that the custom of prohibiting it should apply to it [he refers here to the use of sesame oil made from dry seeds]—we are giving an opening to those who wish to breach [the Torah]. Heaven forbid. On the contrary, when the people see that we permit that which is permitted, then they will believe more strongly that that which we prohibit is done because such is indeed the law of Torah. . . . But if we prohibit even those things that have come about by means of a new invention which never existed before, they will say that the rabbis wish to be strict on their own whim, and don't care for or take pity on the public—and thereby we will allow room for greater breaches, may God protect us.

This should not be confused with the statement found in *b. Nedarim* 81b (and cf. *b. Pesahim* 50b-51a):

> *Tania*: Those practices which are permitted and others regarded them as forbidden (*nahagu bahem issur*), one is not permitted to see them as permissible in order to annul them, for it is stated, "[If a man vow a vow unto the Lord, or swear an oath to bind his soul with a bond;] he shall not break his word. . . ." (Number 30:3).

(And cf. *y. Pesachim* 4:1)

This sees the prohibition as having been somehow enacted (*nahagu bahem issur*), and as such has something of the status of an oath, taken by a community (*neder shehudar berabbim*) which may not be annulled. (See also G. Student and R. Singer, "Values, Halakhah and Psak. . . ." *The Edah Journal* 3:2, 2003.) However, in our case there was no such "prohibitive enactment", merely the absence of a certain practice, due primarily to sociological circumstances.

See further on this principle *Igrot haRambam*, ed. Y. Shilat, vol.1 (Jerusalem: 1987), 278-279; Yitzhak Yosef, *Ein Yitzhak*, vol. 3 (Jerusalem: 2009), 611-612.

On the status of *minhag* as relating to oaths or vows, see what I wrote in my *Minhagei Yisrael* vol. 2 (Jerusalem: 1991), 17-22.

And as to the effects of societal change on the halakhah, see ibid., 92-93, where we cited R. Hayyim David Halevy's remarks in "On the Flexibility of the Halakhah" [Hebrew], *Shanah be Shanah* 5749 (1988), 185-186:

> As it is extremely clear that no law or edict can maintain its position over a long period of time due to the changes in the conditions of life, and that laws which were good in their time are no longer suitable after a generation or more but require correction or change, how is it that our Holy Torah gave us righteous and upright laws and edicts thousands of years ago and we continue to act in accordance with them to this very day (and will even continue to do so to the end of all generations)? How is it that these same laws were good in their time and are good to this very day as well? (ibid., 183). . . . Such a thing was only possible because the Sages of Israel were given permission in every generation to innovate in matters of Halakhah in accordance with the changing times and situations. And it is only by virtue of this that the existence of Torah has been possible in Israel, and that they were able to follow in the way of Torah and mitzvot. . . . Anybody who thinks that the Halakhah is frozen and that one is not permitted to deviate from it right or left is very much mistaken. On the contrary, there is nothing as flexible as the Halakhah, for a teacher of Halakhah can rule regarding the very same question and at the very same time to two different enquirers and to declare something treif to the one and kosher to the other—a thing that is well-known to those who give rulings on what is permitted and forbidden. . . . And it is only by virtue of the flexibility of the Halakhah that the Jewish people have been able, by virtue of the numerous and useful innovations that were introduced by Jewish Sages over the generations to follow in the way of the Torah and mitzvot for thousands of years.

Similarly, R. Ben-Zion Meir Hai Uziel, in his introduction to his *Mishpetei Uziel*, vol. 1 (Tel Aviv: 1935), ix-x, writes:

> In each generation the conditions of life, the changes in values, the discoveries of technology and science, bring about new questions and problems that require solutions. We cannot close our eyes to these questions and say that "innovation is forbidden by the Torah", that is, that anything not explicitly mentioned by our forebears is to be considered as prohibited.

Such quotations could be greatly increased, but these should suffice to make our point.

57. See also n. 8, ad loc. in *Otzar Mefarshim* in the Machon Yerushalayim (Friedman) ed. of the *Shulhan Arukh*. And see Yitzhak Yosef, *Maarechet haShulkhan* vol.2 (Jerusalem: 2010), 462-466.

DOV WEISS

The Rabbinic Doctrine of "The Righteous Decrees and God Fulfills"

FROM ALL OF MY FATHER'S AMAZING ATTRIBUTES, two of them stand out, at least for me. The first is his abiding *compassion* as evidenced in his abiding pastoral care and love for the most vulnerable and disadvantaged in our midst. The second is his unflinching *courage* to speak "truth to power" as evidenced in his years of political activism for the Jewish people and beyond. These two components of my father's stellar character—compassion and courage—are nowhere found more starkly than in the bold rabbinic doctrine of the "*righteous decrees and God fulfills.*" The following essay is thus dedicated to my father—my teacher, role model, spiritual guide, and closest of friends.

• • •

Confrontations with God in rabbinic literature most often take the form of critique or challenge.[1] But there is another significant type of confrontation that has received lesser attention: making demands of God. The sages in a dozen or so texts declare: "[whatever] the righteous decrees [of God], God fulfills (צדיק גוזר והקב"ה מקיים)." Alternatively, the righteous are also

DOV WEISS is currently an Assistant Professor of Jewish Studies in the Department of Religion at the University of Illinois at Urbana-Champaign. He completed his Ph.D. at the University of Chicago as a Martin Meyer Fellow in 2011 and was the Alan M. Stock Fellow at Harvard University's Center for Jewish Studies in 2012. After receiving rabbinic ordination from RIETS (Yeshiva University) in 1999 as a Wexner Graduate Fellow, Dov helped found Yeshivat Chovevei Torah (YCT) Rabbinic School, where he served as Director of Operations and instructor of Talmud and Jewish Law. Specializing in the history of Jewish biblical interpretation and rabbinic theology, Dov's most recent article, "Divine Concessions in the Tanhuma Midrashim," appeared in *Harvard Theological Review* (108:1). His recently completed monograph, *Pious Irreverence: Confronting God in Rabbinic Judaism*, was published by University of Pennsylvania Press in 2016.

described as being able to "nullify" (מבטל) the "decrees" (גזירות) of God (with their own decrees). This theological dictum, in either formulation, inverts the typical Jewish view—one that has become so central in contemporary Haredi discourse—that positions God as the one who decrees (גוזר) and Israel as the one who always submits. But in this bold ancient Jewish maxim, the sages position the righteous in the more dominant position in relation to God. It is God who submits Himself to the human will. While most of these rabbinic texts grant this privilege to *all* righteous people, some limit it to Moshe.

This essay examines this bold rabbinic theology, what I call "the righteous decree" doctrine, from a number of vantage points:

1) What is its exegetical basis? Does Scripture itself evince this sort of theology? If so, in what ways do the rabbis transform it? If the doctrine does not appear in the Hebrew Bible, how do the rabbis read this doctrine back into the Hebrew Bible? Do different proof texts emerge in different rabbinic strata, and, if so, why? (*The exegetical dimension.*)

2) What is the doctrine's conceptual basis and justification? Why would the rabbis imagine God conceding to the demands of the righteous? What does this communicate about the rabbinic conception of God? In this regard, the essay highlights the various relational metaphors used by the rabbis to concretize this theology (such as parent-child, lovers, husband-wife, etc.) As Moshe Halbertal has argued, the particular relational metaphor appropriated by the rabbis reflects a particular rabbinic theological orientation.[2] (*The conceptual dimension.*)

3) Can we detect differences between early rabbinic formulations and later rabbinic ones (amoraic or post-amoraic)? In what ways do post-tannaitic texts radicalize the doctrine as it appears in earlier strata (the *inner-rabbinic dimension*)?[3]

4) Do the rabbis generate this doctrine in principle only or do they apply this doctrine to shed light on specific biblical or early rabbinic stories? Here, I will show that in late rabbinic literature, the sages have a tendency to use the "righteous decree doctrine" as an interpretive tool. (*The hermeneutical dimension.*)

I. Hebrew Bible: "You will decree and it will be fulfilled for you" (Iyov 22:8)

After telling Job at the start of chapter 22 that all suffering is the result of sin, Job's friend Eliphaz promises Job that, should Job follow the "Torah" (v.22) and "delight in God" (v. 26), then God "*would shine light*" [נגה אור] on Job and fulfill his decrees (v. 28): "*You will decree and it will be fulfilled for you*" [ותגזר אומר ויקם לך] (Job 22:8). Eliphaz then provides Job with some examples: via Job's demands, Job could uplift the downcast (v. 29) and save the guilty (v. 30).[4] To Eliphaz's suggestions, Job offers no response. However, as is well-known, God, at the close of the book, rebukes Eliphaz "for not speaking the truth" (42:7). It is not clear, though, how much of Eliphaz' speech, according to God, is false.

II. Tannaitic Literature—Sifre Bamidbar

The rabbinic notion that God fulfills the decrees of the righteous first appears in *Sifre Bamidbar* (ca. third-century).[5] In Numbers 20, God tells Moshe that he would not be allowed to enter the Promised Land because Moshe—after denouncing the Israelite rebels—failed to sanctify God during the rock-striking episode at Merivah. Sefer Bamidbar does not record any protest from Moshe who, in Sefer Devarim 3:17, only requests that he be allowed to enter the land. As we all know, God refuses his pleas (v. 26), declaring "*Enough! Never speak to Me of this matter again!*"

An anonymous teaching recorded in *Sifre Bamidbar* (ca. third-century CE) reads the word "*this*" [הזה] from God's response as an exclusionary demonstrative, rather than, as a simple reading would suggest, a neutral demonstrative. Based on this interpretation, *Sifre* has God signal to Moshe that, while he should no longer request entry into the Land, [*Never speak to Me of THIS matter again!*"] God would accede to any *other* of his wishes.

> *The LORD said to me [Moshe], "Enough! Never speak to Me of this matter again!* (Deut. 3:26) He [God] said: Moshe, On *this* matter do not ask me [תבקש ממני], but concerning another matter, make your demand upon me [גזור עלי] and I will fulfill it [ואני אעשה]. To what can this be compared? To a king who decrees upon his son a harsh decree [after turning down his son's request]. He [the king] said: on this matter do not ask me [any further], but on another matter, make your demand, and I will fulfill it. So did the Holy One, blessed be He, say to Moshe: Moshe, but concerning another matter, make your demand upon me [גזור עלי] and I will fulfill it, [as it says] "You will decree and it will be fulfilled for you" [ותגזר אומר ויקם לך] [Job 22:28]. . . . Moshe said "show it to me. . . ."[6]

According to *Sifre*, God's reaction to Moshe' supplication was not all negative. Feeling bad about rejecting Moshe's ultimate wish to *enter* the Land, God grants Moshe a consolation prize: his second wish would be fulfilled.

And so it was. Moshe, at least, *saw* the Promised Land.

To concretize the teaching, the tannaitic Midrash, as it often does, employs a *mashal* (parable): God is likened to a king/father, who, feeling sorry for his dejected son, offers him a consolation prize. The midrashic employment of the parent-child model is significant. It underscores that, although God announces that He would accede to any request Moshe had (excluding one), God continues to occupy the dominant position in the relationship. God is depicted as parent, and Moshe as a child. God's concession here, according to *Sifre*, should not be taken as a sign of weakness; the opposite is the case: God's offer of a "blank check" to Moshe is depicted as a one-time event fueled by God's compassion for His disappointed "child." It does not, in any way, represent a universal principle that God perforce submits to the commands of the righteous.

To exegetically anchor its reading of Devarim 3:26, the *Sifre* cites the aforementioned words of Eliphaz to Job: "*You will decree and it will be fulfilled for you.*" [Iyov 22:28] By linking these two sections, Devarim 3:26 and Iyov 22:28, the *Sifre* seems to suggest that Eliphaz's assertion (to Job) that "*you will decree and it will be fulfilled*" applied to Moshe at the moment God denied him entry into the Land. While God, at the close of the book, rebukes Eliphaz "for not speaking the truth . . . as did My servant Job," (42:7) the *Sifre*, it seems, nevertheless affirms that Eliphaz, at least on this issue, got it right: God fulfilled Moshe's decree that he *see* the Promised Land.

III. *Amoraic Literature*—Talmud Yerushalmi

As noted above, Eliphaz promises Job that Job has the power, should he commit to the Torah and God, to demand that God lift the spirits of the downtrodden (22:29) and save the guilty (22:30). And, according to *Sifre Bamidbar*, God promises to accede to any wish Moshe has, excluding his desire to *enter* the Land. Notably, these "decree" examples—from Iyov and *Sifre*—are mild: they do not contravene the direct decree of God. We can call them "neutral" as there is no divine counter-pressure. By stark contrast, the *Talmud Yerushalmi* (ca. fifth-century CE) radicalizes the principle of "the righteous decrees" by extending it to cases where the decree clashes head-on with God's direct will:

> Shimon ben Shetach said. . . The Holy One, blessed be He, nullifies His decree when it conflicts with the decree of a righteous person [הקב"ה מבטל גזירתו של צדיק בפני גזירתו].[7]

Attributing the doctrine to Simeon b. Shetach, the first-century BCE Nasi of the Sanhedrin, the *Yerushalmi* posits that God not only follows the decrees of the righteous in neutral cases (such as Moshe seeing Eretz Yisrael), but even in situations where the human decree opposes the divine decree. In short, according to the *Yerushalmi*, righteous people can overrule God's decisions.

Following the *Sifre*, the *Yerushalmi* cites Iyov 22:28 as a proof text: "*You will decree and it will be fulfilled for you* [ותגזר אומר ויקם לך]." But given the *Yerushalmi*'s maximalist reading, it produces, contra *Sifre*, an added exegetical teaching:

> R. Berekhyah, R. Abba bar Kahana, [and] Rabbi Zeurah ...[remarked]: *You will decree and it will be fulfilled for you* [Iyov 22:8]—why does Scripture say "*for you*" [rather than just "*it will be fulfilled*" without the add-on "*for you*"]? [God said:] Even if I [God] say this, and you say that, your [words] will be fulfilled, and My words will not be fulfilled [ודידי לא קיימא].[8]

The *Yerushalmi* cites a number of amoraim (R. Berekhyah, R. Abba bar Kahana, [and] Rabbi Zeurah) who read the seemingly redundant words "*for you*" from the phrase "*you will decree and it will be fulfilled <u>for you</u>*" in its maximalist sense. That is, not only will God accede to *your* [the righteous] decrees (when there is no opposition), but also even in cases where it is <u>only *your* decree</u>, i.e., where God has decreed to the contrary. Moreover, note how the *Yerushalmi* has *God*—not Eliphaz—proclaim the dictum in Iyov 22:28. This act of replacement not only sanctions the doctrine, but it also undermines any counter-reservations about having the error-prone Eliphaz as its author (as per Iyov 42:7).

To reflect its radical extension of the "righteous decree" principle, the *Yerushalmi* rewrites the examples given in Iyov 22:29 and 22:30. Whereas, according to a simple reading, Eliphaz tells Job that he could—by simple decree—lift the spirits of the downtrodden and rescue the sinful, the *Yerushalmi* presents an actual debate between God and Job:

> a) *When people are brought low and you say 'Lift them up!' (lit. 'it is pride')* [Job 22:29]: I [God] said: They shall be brought down, but you said: to lift them up (lit. to make them proud). [God says:] Your view shall be fulfilled, and mine shall not be fulfilled.
>
> b) *Then he will save the downcast.* [Job 22:29]—I [God] said: their eyes shall be bent for suffering [or evil], but you said: to save them. Your view shall be fulfilled, and mine shall not be fulfilled.

> c) I [God] said: he shall be rescued, [but only] if he is innocent [Job 22:30], but you said: he shall be rescued even if he is not innocent. Your view shall be fulfilled, and mine shall not be fulfilled.[9]

Without getting into the exegetical details, suffice it to say that here the *Yerushalmi* transforms mere factual realities of Iyov 22:29 and 22:30 into divine decrees. For instance, the righteous do not merely demand that God lift the spirits of the downtrodden (a fact on the ground), as a simple reading suggests, but, more radically, that another's spirits be lifted *even when God demands the opposite—that a person's spirits shall be lowered*! The same transformation occurs in regard to Iyov 22:30. Instead of simply having the righteous saving the guilty by their declaration, the *Yerushalmi* presents a human-divine clash: God wills to only save the innocent, but the righteous person demands that even the guilty shall be saved. Markedly, in each of them, the *Yerushalmi* has God declare the human will triumphant.[10]

IV. Post-Amoraic Literature I—Retelling Torah Stories in Tanhuma-Yelammedenu (TY)

In post-*amoraic* literature, most notably in the Midrashim of *Tanhuma-Yelammedenu* (TY), the notion that God concedes to the demands of the righteous is further developed, and radicalized. The doctrine is no longer just a hypothetical principle, but becomes a hermeneutical tool to illuminate a number of biblical narratives. Moreover, TY literature produces bolder proof texts, new parables, and new formulations that all highlight the distinctive humanism of late rabbinic culture.

Because texts from the *Tanhuma-Yelammedenu* (TY) literature are less known even to scholars of Midrash who tend to focus on the earlier tannaitic and amoraic strata of rabbinic literature, an introduction to this literary family is in order. According to Marc Bregman, the vast majority of the *Tanhuma-Yelammedenu* Midrashim developed towards the end of Byzantine rule in Palestine (sixth and early seventh century CE).[11] In their final form, they generally postdate the tannaitic works, such as *Mishnah*, *Tosefta*, *Mekhilta de-Rabbi Ishmael*, *Sifre Numbers*, *Sifre Deuteronomy* (edited ca. third century), and also generally postdate the amoraic texts, such as *Jerusalem Talmud*, *Genesis Rabbah*, *Leviticus Rabbah* and *Pesiqta de-Rav Kahana* (redacted ca. fifth century). Texts from this *TY* group can be found in the following midrashic works: 1) *Midrash Tanhuma*—both the standard and Buber editions; 2) *Exodus Rabbah* II—chapters 15-52; 3) *Numbers Rabbah* II—chapters 15-23[12]; 4) *Deuteronomy Rabbah*—both the standard and Lieberman editions;

5) *Pesiqta Rabbati*—chapters 1-14, 19, 25, 29, 31, 33, 38-45, 47, and supplements 1 and 2; and 6) hundreds of *TY* fragments found at the Cairo Genizah.[13]

In what follows, three examples where *TY* authors insert the "righteous decree" doctrine back into biblical narratives are examined. In the process, new formulations and conceptions of the doctrine emerge.

1. Generation of the Spies: "Whose [Word] Will Be Victorious [מי נוצח]"?

In the Torah, Moshe dispatches twelve spies to gather information about the soon-to-be-conquered Land of Canaan and its inhabitants. To the dismay of Moshe, upon the spies' return, ten of them advocate abandoning the idea of conquering Canaan altogether. They claim that the Israelites are militarily weaker than the natives (Num. 13:31) and, even should Israel emerge victorious in war, the Land of Canaan "devours its inhabitants" (Num. 13:32). Affected by the ominous report, the Israelites complained to Moshe and Aharon:

> "If only we had died in the land of Egypt . . . or if only we might die in this wilderness! Why is the LORD taking us to that land to fall by the sword? Our wives and children will be carried off! It would be better for us to go back to Egypt!" And they said to one another, "Let us head back for Egypt."(Num 14:2-4)

Interpreting the Israelites' response as a lack of faith (14:11), God threatens to destroy all of the Israelites, telling Moshe: "I will strike them with pestilence [בדבר] and disown them, and I will make of you a nation far more numerous than they!" (Num 14:12)

Defending Israel, however, Moshe seeks to change God's mind by making two arguments. First, God's reputation would be damaged in the eyes of nations if He were to destroy Israel. The nations would argue, says Moshe, that, despite God's closeness with His people ("God *is among this people, you, God, are seen face to face*" Num. 14:14), God "was not able to bring this people into the land that He swore to them, He (thus) killed them in the wilderness" (Num. 14:16). Second, Moshe invokes God's attributes of mercy: "*The LORD is slow to anger and abounding in loyal love forgiving iniquity and transgression…*" (14:18). Notably, to save Israel, Moshe does not critique God or make demands of God, but rather pleads with God to change His mind, twice using the submissive "please" ["נא"] (14:17, 19). Immediately after that, God declares: "I have forgiven them as you asked [סלחתי כדברך]."

While in the biblical narrative God forgives the nation in response to Moshe's submissive supplications, *Deuteronomy Rabbah*—a Midrash associated with the *Tanhuma-Yelammedenu* literature—presents a very different correspondence:

> "*You will decree and it will be fulfilled for you.*" (Job 22:28). Rav say: This verse alludes to the time when God was wroth with Israel concerning the Spies. God said [to Moshe]: 'They think that I need swords and spears with which to destroy them? As I created the world with a word (בדבר), as it is said, "*By the word* [בדבר] *of the Lord were the heavens made; [and all the host of them by the breath of His mouth]*" (Ps. 33:6), so Will I do unto them; I will let a word go forth from My mouth and it will slay them.' This is the meaning of "*I will smite them with word/pestilence* [בדבר], *and disinherit them.*" [Num. 14:12]
>
> And what did Moshe say at this hour? [He said:] *You YHWH are seen face to face* (Num. 14:14). [What does it mean?] "*You YHWH* [אתה ה]"—R. Aha said in the name of R. Simeon b. Lakish: Moshe said to Him: Master of the World, the Attribute of Justice and the balancing scales [on the nation's fate] are even"—and still You [God] say, "*I will smite them with pestilence* [בדבר]" (Num. 14:12) and I say, "Please, forgive" (Num. 14:19).
>
> He [Moshe] said [further]: [with regard to] the "word [דבר]" [14:12] we will see [נראה]," [14:14] i.e., whose [word] will prevail [מי נוצח]? "Yours, God [אתה ה]," or mine?'
>
> R. Berekya said: God said to him: 'By your life, you have nullified My [word] [שלי בטלת] and yours prevails.' How do we know this? For it is said, And the Lord said: "*I have forgiven according to your word* (ib. 20)". Hence [the force] of "you will decree and it will be fulfilled for you" [Iyov 22:28].[14]

Based on the biblical reinterpretations of three amoraim—Rav, Shimon ben Lakish and R. Berekya—*Deuteronomy Rabbah* posits that Moshe did not *supplicate* for forgiveness, but rather Moshe *decreed* that God forgive the nation after the episode of the Spies. God, in the spirit of Iyov 22:28, immediately announces that His genocidal intentions have been nullified [בטל].

To support this bold re-reading, *Deuteronomy Rabbah* (DR) embarks on a number of counter-intuitive exegetical moves. First, *Deuteronomy Rabbah* reads the word "דבר" in אכנו בדבר [Num. 14:12] as "I will smite them with a *word [davar]*" rather than, as the context requires, "I will smite them with *pestilence* [*dever*]."[15] Then, in response to God's intention to commit verbal genocide, Moshe declares that his own word—favoring clemency—will prevail. Seemingly aware of the Iyov dictum, Moshe audaciously, if not rhetorically, asks: "[with regard to] the word [Ha-DAVAR]—we will see who will be victorious [נראה מי נוצח]: "Yours YHWH [אתה ה]" or mine?" To produce this bold encounter, *Deuteronomy Rabbah* re-reads the phrase: "*You, YHWH, are seen face to face* (literally "*eye to eye*") [אשר עין בעין נראה אתה ה']" [Num. 12:14]. Rather than reading it as Moshe communicating how close the Israelites are to God [God can be seen!], as a straightforward reading requires, *Deuteronomy Rabbah* reads it as highlighting the distance between God and Moshe. "Eye to eye" [עין בעין] signals not only that the scales of the Israelites are balanced [מעויין], but also to a confrontation of *view*points, between God's and Moshe's [eye against eye!]: God desires tipping the scales to guilt, Moshe to innocence. *Deuteronomy Rabbah* then reinterprets Moshe's words "נראה אתה ה':" it does not mean You are seen [נראה] by Israel, but rather: "we will see [נראה] [who will be victorious]: You YHWH [אתה ה'] [or me, Moshe]."[16] According to the Midrash, God then concedes "defeat," announcing in conformity with the Iyov principle: "you have nullified My [word] and your [word] prevails [שלי בטלת ושלך קיימת]." Further exegetical support for this concession is found in the scriptural phrase: "I [God] have forgiven them according to your [Moshe's] word [Num. 14:20] [סלחתי כדברך]," reading "your" word to the exclusion of "My" [God's] word.

2. Decree via Defiance: The War against Sihon

Immediately after the aforementioned teaching, *Deuteronomy Rabbah* cites Rabbi Joshua who, in the name of Rabbi Joshua ben Levi, argues that the Iyov principle applied to Moshe: "Whatever Moshe decreed [שגזר], God agreed to [הכסים הקב"ה]. . . ." While this formulation is relatively moderate—it does not explicitly state that Moshe's decree counters the divine will, nor is the bold language of "nullification" used—the primary example provided by Rabbi Joshua is quite radical. Before explicating it, however, we need some background in regard to the Israelite war against Sihon.

The Torah presents two different accounts of the Israelite conquest of the Amorite Kingdom in Transjordan. In Bamidbar 21:21-35, the Israelites conquer the Amorite territory as an act of self-defense when Sihon, the Amorite king, refuses to let Israel pass through his land (v. 23).[17] In Devarim 2:24-37, however, the picture is more complex. As in the Bamidbar account, Sihon refuses to let Israel pass peacefully through his country (v. 26–30), but, unlike the Bamidbar account, his refusal is orchestrated by God who "stiffened his [Sihon's] heart in order to deliver him [Sihon] into [Israel's] power" (v. 30). In addition, before Moshe makes his request for peaceful passage (v. 26-29), God commands him: "Set out across the wadi Arnon! See, I give you into your power Sihon the Amorite, king of Heshbon, and his land. Begin the occupation; engage him in battle" (v. 24). In this passage, the occupation of Sihon's territory is described not as the result of a war of self-defense but as part of an offensive conquest of the Land of Canaan. Finally, in contrast to the Bamidbar account, Devarim applies the principle of *herem* (חרם), or annihilation of the entire population, to Sihon's kingdom; all their men, women, and children are killed, "leaving no survivor" (v. 34).

Academic Bible scholars solve these conflicting accounts by arguing that they reflect two different traditions on the status of Transjordan, an area that included Sihon's territory.[18] The older tradition, represented by Numbers, treats this area as outside of the Promised Land. As a result, Israel's conquering of Sihon's kingdom could only be justified as an act of self-defense, rather than as part of the rightful occupation of their given lands. By contrast, the later tradition (represented in part by Deuteronomy) views Transjordan as an integral part of the Promised Land.[19] Accordingly, like the other territories within the Land of Canaan, this area falls under the divine command of occupation.[20] However, given that the Numbers narrative had already emerged as an established tradition, the deuteronomic author attempted to retain it alongside the new tradition. Both traditions are thus reflected in Devarim, albeit with some tension and inconsistency. On the one hand, echoing the older Numbers view, Moshe sends "messengers of peace" to request that Sihon allow Israel to pass (Deut. 2:26). On the other hand, representing the newer view, God commands Moshe to wage an offensive war to occupy Sihon's territory (2:24), to conquer this integral part of the Promised Land. Bible scholars also argue that the deuteronomic author attempted to integrate the inconsistent accounts by claiming that the request for peaceful passage through Sihon's area merely served as a pretext for the ultimate war of conquest. Because God had already intended to harden Sihon's heart (v. 30), Moshe's request for a safe passageway would inevitably fail, although it did provide Israel with justification for their military offensive. Finally, since the newer tradition sees Sihon's territory as part of the Promised Land, the deuteronomic laws of *herem*, annihilation of the entire population apply.[21]

In many *Tanhuma-Yelammedenu* texts, this textual inconsistency is resolved by generating a confrontation between Moshe and God. These post-amoraic texts claim that by sending messengers of peace, Moshe defied God's wishes.[22] Thus, the inconsistency in the various biblical verses reflects two different points of view and an initial dispute between God and Moshe: God commands war, yet Moshe seeks peace. Significantly, many *Tanhuma-Yelammedenu* texts have God concede to Moshe's approach and affirm a new policy of "negotiation first" for any future war. This new ethical approach to battle, codified in the biblical passage "when you come to a city to fight against it, you shall call forth peace" (Deut. 20:10), reflects a divinely sanctioned Mosaic revision of God's earlier decree that mandated war *without* first seeking peace (Deut. 2:24).

Our *Deuteronomy Rabbah* text adopts the general approach of other *Tanhuma-Yelammedenu* Midrashim (scholars designate *Deuteronomy Rabbah* as a TY text), but uniquely uses the formulation of "whatever Moshe decree, God confirms" to explain God's concession:

> R. Joshua said in the name of R. Joshua son of Levi: Whatever Moshe decreed [שגזר], God agreed to [הכסים הקב"ה] . . . . God told him [Moshe] to make war on Sihon and Og, as it is said, *And contend with him in battle* (Deut. II, 24), [but] he did not do so, but [as Scripture has it], *And I sent messengers, etc.* (ib. 26). God said to him: 'I told you to make war with him [Sihon], but instead you began with peace. By your life, *I will affirm your decree* [אני מקיים גזרתך]; every war upon which Israel enter, they shall begin with [a declaration of] peace,' as it is said, "*when you draw near unto a city to fight against it, then proclaim peace unto it.*"[23]

In this Midrash, Moshe's act of defiance carries with it an implicit demand that God revise His war code. This Mosaic decree is not communicated *verbally*, as most demands are, but *demonstratively* via Moshe's active transgression. Moreover, Moshe's "decree" [גזרה] explicitly counters a divine command, not merely the divine will.

3. The Golden Calf and a New Rationale

A final example: *Tanhuma-Yelammedenu* literature also applies the "righteous decree, God fulfills" doctrine to Moshe's conversation with God after the Israelites worshipped the Golden Calf. God tells Moshe: "Let Me be, that My anger may blaze forth against them and that I may destroy them (ואכלם), and make of you a great nation" (Exod. 32:11). As He would do forty years later with the Generation of the Spies, here too God wants to destroy the entire Israelite nation and produce a new one through Moshe alone. Defending Israel, Moshe seeks to change God's mind by making two arguments. First,

God's reputation would be damaged in the eyes of the Egyptians if He were to destroy Israel (v. 12). They would argue, says Moshe, that God knowingly took Israel out of Egypt only to maliciously destroy them in the desert.[24] Second, God should remember His own promise to the patriarchs that He would make their offspring as numerous as the stars of heaven (v. 13). Notably, neither of Moshe's arguments defends the Israelites on substantive grounds. They do not challenge the notion that Israel willfully performed a heinous crime. Moshe, however, argues that it would be in God's best interest not to destroy Israel; either it would ruin God's reputation among the Egyptians, or through their destruction, God would be reneging on certain promises made to the patriarchs.

While most amoraic texts reread Exodus 32:11-14 as an attempt by Moshe to exonerate Israel from all legal wrongdoing, virtually none of them have Moshe make demands of God.[25] In *Tanhuma-Yelammedenu* literature, on the other hand, we witness a revolutionary rereading and re-imagining of this God-Moshe encounter. Rather than have Moshe occupy the role of defense attorney and plead for divine mercy on extra-judicial grounds (as the biblical text records), or plead for divine justice by positing legal loopholes (as many classical rabbinic texts maintain), they have Moshe mandate that God forgive Israel:

> "*You will decree and it will be fulfilled <u>for you</u>*" (Iyov 22:28)—Rabbi Berekhyah HaKohen[26] said: What does it mean "*for you*"? I [God] say a word [davar] and you say a word [davar], as if to say: I will nullify My [word] [מבטל את שלי] and establish yours [ואקיים שלך], that is [what it means] "*for you.*"
>
> The matter [דבר] was [found to be] true when [the Israelites] did the deed [i.e. worshipped the Golden Calf]. What did God do? He said to Moshe: "*Go quickly, descend, because your people have acted corruptly.*" [Ex. 32:7] What is written next? "*So now, leave Me alone [so that my anger can burn against them and I can destroy them, and I will make from you a great nation]*." [Ex. 32:10]
>
> Immediately Moshe stood up in prayer and supplication as it says: "*But Moshe sought [the favor of the LORD his God]*." (Ex. 32:11). . . . Immediately "*Then the LORD relented over the evil that he had said he would do to his people*" [Ex. 32:14]. [This is in fulfillment of]: "*You will decree and it will be fulfilled for you*" (Job 22:28)."[27]

And, interestingly, right before applying the doctrine of "the righteous decree and God fulfills" to Moshe's encounter with God after the Golden Calf episode, the *Tanhuma (Buber)* provides a new rationale as to why God established this principle in the first place:

> "*You will decree and it will be fulfilled for you*" (Job 22:28)—The holy one, Blessed be He, said to the righteous person: if you performed My will, so too I will perform Your will more than Mine.[28]

Unlike *Sifre Bamidbar* (above) which based the dictum on compassion and pity for a dejected Moshe, in *Tanhuma (Buber)*, the animating principle is equality and reciprocity: God reasons that if the righteous submit to His demands, then, according to the rules of fairness, God should act similarly to them. Here, strikingly, God positions Himself on equal footing with the righteous. Otherwise, God would have never entertained such a premise, maintaining that He is the ruler of the world, and the righteous, His mere subjects. In other words, the *Tanhuma* posits a divine-human interaction where the relational axis is no longer vertical, but horizontal.

Interestingly, in all three of the aforementioned cases: 1) Generation of Spies, 2) War against Sihon, and 3) Golden Calf Incident, God wills destruction and death, while Moshe seeks to save human life. Also, in these Midrashim, God does not change His mind in response to Moshe's critiques (as per other TY texts[29]); God continues to assert that His view is correct. Nonetheless, God agrees to adopt Moshe's position in practice. This is the ultimate expression of submission: agreeing to abide by the "others'" position even while you maintain the correctness of your own view.

V. *Post-Amoraic Literature II—Exegetical Inversions in* Tanhuma-Yelammedenu *(and* Bavli*)*

While the *Sifre Bamidbar* and *Talmud Yerushalmi* base the "righteous decree" doctrine on Iyov 22:28-30, *TY* texts and the *Talmud Bavli* generate new biblical proof texts. These additional "sources" reflect not only a theological extension of the "righteous decree" dictum (contra *Sifre*), but also a remarkable boldness of the exegetes themselves.

1. Ecclesiastes 8—Is God's Word Authoritative [שלטון] for the *Shomer Mitzvah* (observant)?

Ecclesiastes 8:4 rhetorically asks: "*Surely the king's word [דבר] is authoritative [שלטון]; who can say to him, 'What are you doing [מה תעשה]?'* The answer, of course, is no one! The king's authority is absolute. The next verse (Eccl. 8:5) begins a new point: *Whoever obeys [the king's] mitzvah [command] will not experience harm.*" *Midrash Tanhuma*, however, cites R. Hiyya, who ignores the natural breaks between vv. 4 and 5 and reads v. 4 as a genuine question, rather than a rhetorical one. And the answer is supplied by v.5:

> R. Hiyya bar Abba said: How brazen [מתחטאין] are those who perform mitzvoth in front of God. For God issues a decree [גוזר גזירה] and the righteous nullify it [with their counter decree], as it says: "*Surely the king's word* [דבר] *is authoritative* [שלטון]; *who can say to him, 'What are you doing* [מה תעשה]*?'* [Ecclesiastes 8:4] *Whoever obeys* [*his*] *mitzvah*" [*Ecclesiastes* 8:5]—[he] can protest [ממחה] the Holy One Blessed be He.[30]

According to R. Hiyya, the answer to verse 4's question is found at the start of v. 5: "those who obey the king's command." By reading the verses in this way, R. Hiyya boldly inverses the force of v. 4: instead of it underscoring the King's unchecked sovereignty (i.e., in rabbinic culture the "king" in Ecclesiastes is God), it now points to the fact that those "*who keep God's command*" (v. 5) i.e., the righteous, can challenge God with the question "what are you doing?" Thus, R. Hiyya's teaching is doubly bold: not only does it produce a theological inversion whereby God follows the dictates of the righteous (even against His own will), but in order to produce this teaching, R. Hiyya generates an exegetical inversion whereby Ecclesiastes 8:4 no longer emphasizes the unlimited control of God; it now communicates appropriate checks on divine power![31]

2. 2 Samuel 23—The Righteous "Rule" [מושל] God

R. Hiyya then adduces a second proof text from 2 Samuel 23:3

> And so did [King David] say: "*The God of Israel spoke, the protector of Israel spoke to me. The one who rules righteously among men is the one who rules with the fear of God* [מושל באדם צדיק מושל יראת אלהים]" [2 Samuel 23:3].[32]

Here, too, R. Hiyya reverses the force of the passage. According to a simple reading, God the Protector of Israel tells King David that the king who rules "righteously" is the one who rules <u>with</u> the fear of God. No one, not even the king, should see himself as superior to the Creator of the World. R. Hiyya, however, interprets the verse as *God* declaring: "When a righteous person rules, he [the righteous ruler] rules *over* [the fear] of God."[33] In other words, in some sense, a righteous ruler has power even over God; this occurs when he nullifies the demands of God. The *Bavli* (*Moed Katan* 16b) records a similar exegetical inversion of 2 Samuel 23:3, this time in the name of R. Abahu: "God says I rule man [אני מושל באדם]; who *rules* Me [מי מושל בי]? [It is] the righteous [צדיק]: for I make a decree and he [may] annul it."[34]

One central difference emerges between R. Hiyya bar Abba's two proof texts: whereas the Ecclesiastes 8 passage has King Solomon (the purported "author" of Ecclesiastes[35]) announce the "righteous decree" dictum, 2 Samuel 23 has God Himself proclaiming it.

3. Deuteronomy 32—Moshe as God's Demanding "Husband"

TY literature also derives the "righteous decree" doctrine from Deuteronomy 33:1 where Moshe is described as a "man [איש] of God." As a "man of God," Moshe of course would submit to all of God's dictates. Veering from the plain sense of the biblical phrase, however, a *TY* text preserved in our editions of *Pesikta de-Rav Kahana* cites Reish Lakish who reads the word "*ish*" to mean not "man of"—as the context clearly suggests—but "husband of."[36] As a result, the force of the passage shifts dramatically:

> "*The man of God*" [איש אלהים] [Deut.33:1]: Reish Lakish said: Were it not written in Scripture, it would be impossible to say such a thing [אלמלא מקרא כתוב אי אפשר לאומרו]—as a man makes decrees on his wife and she does them, so too Moshe decrees [גוזר] on the Holy One, blessed be He, and He does [them].[37]

According to this counter-intuitive reading, Scripture declares that, as God's "husband," Moshe could make demands of God, his "wife."[38] Unlike the other Midrashim, the author of this teaching is aware of its radical nature. It, thus, introduces the exegesis with the disclaimer "were it not written in Scripture, it would be impossible to say such a thing." And, as Moshe Halbertal has noted, this phrase is invoked when the rabbis seek interpretive shelter for their radical descriptions of God.[39] Of course, Scripture only "says it" when read midrashically! He further notes that this is one of many instances in which the Rabbinic God assumes a weaker position in the human-divine metaphor: "The singular contribution that the midrash makes to textual anthropomorphic theology is through the depiction of social spaces in which the accepted biblical authority relationships are reversed and in which God takes the place expected of man. God is the slave, the student, the judged, *the wife*, and the one who is redeemed from suffering" [emphasis mine].[40] Conversely, Halbertal argues, humans assume, at times, the more powerful role of husband, parent, creditor, judge, and master. In these moments, the sages boldly invert the traditional and standard biblical analogy between God and humanity in which God assumes the superior position in the relational hierarchy. I would merely add to Halbertal's point that, in the above text, not only does Reish Lakish produce a *theological* inversion, but he does so by employing an *exegetical* inversion. A plain reading of Deut. 33 emphasizes that Moshe follows God, not God following Moshe.

4. Numbers 36:2—Moshe issues "commands" [מצוה] before God

A final set of *TY* proof texts for the "righteous decree" theology can be found in *Shemot Rabbah II* (also associated with *Tanhuma Yelammedenu* literature). As in the previous three instances, a *TY* text employs an exegetical inversion, this time citing the amora R. Levi:

> "*The LORD said to Moshe, 'Why do you cry out to me? Tell the Israelites* [דבר אל בני ישראל] *to move on . . .* '" [Exodus 14:15]. As it is written, "*You will decree and it will be fulfilled for you*" [ותגזר אומר ויקם לך] [Job 22:28] *R. Levi* said: Just as God commanded Moshe and spoke with him, as it were, so did Moshe command God [מצוה לפני הקב"ה].
>
> Thus the sons of Joseph said to him: "*The Lord commanded my lord*" (Num. 36:2), and later, "*And my lord commanded the Lord*" (ibid.). And just as the Lord called unto Moshe and spoke with him [ומדבר עמו], so did Moshe call God and speak with Him [ומדבר עמו]; for it says [often in the Bible], And the Lord spoke unto Moshe and also, "*And Moshe spoke unto the Lord, saying: 'Let the Lord, the God of the spirits of all flesh* [*appoint a man over this community*]'" (Numbers 27:15, 16).
>
> See what control [שולט] he [Moshe] wielded! Yet when he beheld Pharaoh pursuing the Israelites, he began to cry, as it says, "*The LORD said to Moshe, 'Why do you cry out to me?'*" [Exodus 14:15]. God said to [Moshe]: Why are you distressed [מצטער]?
>
> *R. Joshua the son of Levi* said: It is like a king's friend who was concerned about a matter and came crying unto the king. The king said: Why do you cry? You have only to decree and I will perform it [גזור ואני אעשה]. God said the same to Moshe: "*Why do you cry out to me?*" [Exodus 14:15]. Decree [גזור], and I will perform [your word].[41]

According to R. Levi, the "righteous decree" doctrine is located in two biblical sections. The first, Exodus 14, records when the Egyptians regretted letting the Israelites leave, and were now pursuing them. In v. 15 of that chapter,

God tells Moshe "'*Why do you cry out* [תצעק] *to me? Tell the Israelites* [דבר אל בני ישראל] *to move on*." Though Scripture makes no mention of it, R. Levi assumes, given God's response, that Moshe had been distressfully crying out to God to save Israel. According to a straightforward reading, God tells Moshe to stop praying, but "*tell the Israelites to move on*." R. Levi, however, reads this verse through the lens of the "righteous decree" doctrine. To do so, he shifts the recipient of God's command (דבר "tell" or "speak").

Ignoring the continuation of the passage which has the recipient of "דבר" as the Israelites, R. Levi now has God position Himself as the recipient. Thus, R. Levi has God telling Moshe that Moshe should stop nervously begging for salvation, but rather, given the "righteous decree" doctrine," simply "tell" i.e., command, that God bring salvation. In other words, *Shemot Rabbah*'s Levi reads "דבר" in v. 15 as "גזר"—*where God is the one being commanded.* It is also possible that R. Levi discovers a hint for this radical new reading with the word "אל" that immediately follows "דבר". Rather than interpreting it, as the context requires, as a preposition "towards" [the Israelites], R. Levi might be reading "אל" as "God." In other words, "דבר אל" is no longer "speak to [Israel]," but "speak to (command) God."

R. Levi's second main proof text is even more daring. In Numbers 36:2, the elders from the tribe of Manasseh remind Moshe that "my lord [Moshe] was commanded by the LORD [ואדני צוה יהוה) to give the inheritance of our brother Zelophehad to his daughters." Here, the elders from Manasseh's tribe allude to God's decree (recorded in Numbers 27:2) that the complaint of the daughters of Zelophehad had merit: even though their deceased father had no male heirs, the daughter's of Zelophehad would stand to inherit their father's share in the Land. Again inverting the obvious contextual reading, R. Levi replaces the Masoretic passive (*pual*) vowels under the word צוה, "was commanded," and reads it instead with active vowels (*piel*) as if it read, "my lord (Moshe) commanded at God [ואדני צוה יהוה]." Accordingly, the verse now has the elders of the tribe of Manasseh, son of Joseph, remind Moshe that *Moshe commanded God* to grant the daughters of Zelophehad an inheritance in the Land. Remarkably, R. Levi embarks on an exegetical inversion to produce a theological inversion. Rather than the passage emphasizing God's ability to issue commands towards Moshe, it now reveals, on a deeper level, that Moshe issued forth commands towards God!

The Midrash concludes with R. Levi's son, R. Joshua, offering a parable. "It is like a king's friend [אוהבו] who was concerned about a matter and came crying unto the king. The king said: Why do you cry? You have only to decree and I will perform it [גזור ואני אעשה]." This parable provides us with yet another rationale and relational metaphor to understand the "righteous decree" doctrine. Rather than viewing Moshe or the righteous as a submissive and dejected *child* (as in *Sifre*), or a domineering *husband* (as in *Pesikta de-Rav Kahana*), R. Joshua ben Levi depicts Moshe as God's close confidant [אוהבו]. Accordingly, God's desire to submit to Moshe's commands is grounded in friendship: lovers always seek to fulfill the wishes of the other. Here, Moshe and God are depicted as equals on a horizontal axis (rather than standing in a vertical relationship of husband-wife or parent-child). This model fits well with R. Levi's teaching that "just as the Lord called unto Moshe and spoke [strongly] with him [ומדבר עמו], so did Moshe call God and speak [strongly] with Him [ומדבר עמו]." This conceptual model contrasts, albeit slightly, with the one we saw in *Tanhuma (Buber) Vayishlach.*[42] While both ground the "righteous decree" doctrine on the assumption of a non-hierarchical relational model, there is one key difference. In *Tanhuma (Buber)*, God agrees to submit to the decrees of the righteous out of a sense of judicial fairness or reciprocity (because the righteous fulfill God's commands); it's an act of formal gratitude. In *Shemot Rabbah*, more ambitiously, God's decision to affirm the commands of Moshe, the righteous, is driven by love and friendship—not fairness. Simply put, Moshe' relationship with God is not depicted as citizen and king, but a relationship of lovers.

VI. Summary and Conclusion

In the Hebrew Bible, Job's friend Eliphaz posits that God fulfills the wishes of those who follow God and His Torah (Iyov 22). The early rabbinic Midrash, *Sifre Bamidbar*, has God confirming Eliphaz's claim, and then applying the doctrine to Moshe's demand that he see the Promised Land. The *Yerushalmi* radicalizes the doctrine by extending its scope to cases where the decrees of the righteous *counter God's own decrees*. Subsequently, *Tanhuma-Yelammedenu* Midrashim use the *Yerushalmi*'s radical formulation as a hermeneutical tool to illuminate a number of biblical narratives. In them, Moshe courageously and compassionately demands that God spare the lives of thousands of people; God, in line with the doctrine, obliges.

The *Tanhuma-Yelammedenu* also generates new proof texts. Remarkably, as I have tried to show, these proof texts not only *produce* the theology of "righteous decree and God fulfills," but they are themselves *a product* of this very theology. The exegetical process here is circular. On a straightforward reading, these verses declare the very opposite: the will of God should always reign supreme. Ignoring context and grammar, however, the rabbis invert the force of these passages. Their exegetical moves are in themselves "decrees of the righteous"; and thus, their readings of Scripture are victorious even over the Author's original intent. In short, the rabbinic doctrine of "righteous decree, God fulfills" not only reflects a revolutionary hierarchical inversion between commander and the one commanded, but an exegetical inversion between *p'shat* and *derash*. Put otherwise, this bold rabbinic theology is fueled by a bold rabbinic exegesis that relies on the very theology it generates.

The exegetical theology of the "righteous decree" doctrine reflects the distinctive humanism of rabbinic culture: the sages grant immense power to righteous people, power that far surpasses anything we encounter in the Hebrew Bible.[43] On the flip side, the doctrine also illustrates a certain degree of divine disempowerment; this coheres with the scholarly claim that rabbinic literature intensifies the anthropomorphic descriptions of God.[44] I would argue that this divine "disempowerment" should not be understand, primarily, as antagonism to the Creator of the World, but rather as an attempt by the rabbis to communicate the intimate bond God continues to have with His people. Despite what it looks like, Israel has not been abandoned.[45] This Jewish yearning for divine closeness and love in late antiquity Palestine makes sense in the aftermath of two recent painful defeats: first, politically—the Roman usurpation of sovereignty, and, soon after, religiously—the Christianization of the Roman Empire.[46]

BIBLIOGRAPHY

Anisfeld, Rachel A. *Sustain Me with Raisin-Cakes: Pesiqta Derav Kahana and the Popularization of Rabbinic Judaism*, Supplements to the Journal for the Study of Judaism. Leiden: Brill, 2009.

Bregman, Marc. *Sifrut Tanhuma-Yelammedenu: Te'ur Nusheha We-'iyunim Be-Darke Hithawutam*. Piscataway, NJ: Gorgias Press, 2003.

———. "Tanhuma Yelammedenu." In *Encyclopaedia Judaica* edited by Fred Skolnik, 503-04. Detroit: Keter, 2007.

Ehrman, Bart D. *After the New Testament: A Reader in Early Christianity*. New York: Oxford University Press, 1999.

Feldman, Louis H. *"Remember Amalek!": Vengeance, Zealotry, and Group Destruction in the Bible According to Philo, Pseudo-Philo, and Josephus*. Cincinnati [Ohio]; Detroit, MI: Hebrew Union College Press, 2004.

Fisch, Menachem. "Judaism and the Religious Crisis of Modern Science." In *Nature and Scripture in the Abrahamic Religions, 1700-Present: Brill's Series in Church History*, edited by Jitse M. Meer and S. Mandelbrote, 525-67. Leiden and Boston: Brill, 2009.

Fishbane, Michael A. *Biblical Interpretation in Ancient Israel.* Oxford: Clarendon Press, 1985.

Garb, Yoni. "Kinds of Power: Rabbinic Texts and the Kabbalah." *Kabbalah: Journal for the Study of Jewish Mystical Texts* 6, (2001): 45-71.

Green, Arthur. "The Children in Egypt and the Theophany at the Sea." *Judaism* 24, (1975): 446-56.

Halbertal, Moshe. "If the Text Had Not Been Written, It Could Not Be Said." In *Scriptural Exegesis: The Shapes of Culture and the Religious Imagination*, edited by Deborah A. Green and Laura Suzanne Lieber, 146-65. Oxford: Oxford University Press, 2009.

———. "Ilmale' Miqra' Katub Iy Epsar Le'omro." *Tarbiz* 68, no. 1 (1998): 39-59.

Harris, Jay M. *Nachman Krochmal: Guiding the Perplexed of the Modern Age*, Modern Jewish Masters Series 4. New York: New York University Press, 1991.

Hartman, David. *A Living Covenant: The Innovative Spirit in Traditional Judaism.* New York, London: Free Press, 1985.

Idel, Moshe. *Kabbalah and Eros.* New Haven: Yale University Press, 2005.

Kahana, Menahem. "The Halakhic Midrashim." In *The Literature of the Sages*, edited by Shemuel Safrai. Assen, Netherlands: Fortress Press, 1987.

Mandelbaum, Irving. "Tannaitic Exegesis of the Golden Calf Incident." In *Journal for the Study of the Old Testament. Supplement Series 100*, edited by Philip R. Davies and Richard T. White, 207-22. Sheffield, England: JSOT Press, 1990.

Marmorstein, Arthur. *Studies in Jewish Theology.* London: Oxford University Press, 1950.

Nirenberg, David. *Anti-Judaism: The Western Tradition.* 1st ed. New York: W. W. Norton & Co., 2013.

Roberts, Alexander, and James Donaldson. *The Ante-Nicene Fathers: Translations of the Writings of the Fathers Down to A. D. 325.* Edinburgh: T&T Clark, 1989.

Schremer, Adiel. "Between Radical Interpretation and Explicit Rejection." In *Renewing Jewish Committment: The Work and Thought of David Hartman*, edited by A. Sagi and Z. Zohar. Jerusalem: Machon Shalom Hartman, 2001.

Smolar, Leivy, and Moshe Aberbach. "The Golden Calf Episode in Postbiblical Literature." *Hebrew Union College Annual* 39, (1968): 91-116.

Stern, David. "Imitatio Hominis: Anthropomorphism and the Characters of God in Rabbinic Literature." *Prooftexts* 12 (1992): 151-74.

Van Seters, John. "The Conquest of Sihon's Kingdom: A Literary Examination." *Journal of Biblical Literature* 91, no. 2 (1972): 182-97.

Weinfeld, Moshe. *Deuteronomy 1-11: A New Translation with Introduction and Commentary.* 1st ed, The Anchor Bible. New York: Doubleday, 1991.

Weiss, Dov. "Confrontations with God in Late Rabbinic Literature." Ph.D. diss., University of Chicago, 2011.

———. "Divine Concessions in the Tanhuma Midrashim." *Harvard Theological Review* 108, no. 1 (2015): 70-97.

Wolfson, Elliot R. *Through a Speculum That Shines: Vision and Imagination in Medieval Jewish Mysticism*. Princeton, N.J.: Princeton University Press, 1994.

NOTES

1. Dov Weiss, "Confrontations with God in Late Rabbinic Literature" (Ph.D. diss., University of Chicago, 2011).
2. Lecture notes from Moshe Halbertal's course on the Rabbinic Conception of God, Hebrew University (ca. 2009).
3. I have dealt with another type of theological transformation in late rabbinic texts in Dov Weiss, "Divine Concessions in the Tanhuma Midrashim," *Harvard Theological Review* 108:1 (2015).
4. The Hebrew phrase "אי נקי" (22:30) is ambiguous. Here, I follow Rashi (s.v. ימלט) who renders it "not innocent." For other interpretations, see Ibn Ezra s.v. גם ימלט.
5. For background information on *Sifre Bamidbar*, see Menahem Kahana, "The Halakhic Midrashim," in *The Literature of the Sages*, ed. Shemuel Safrai (Assen, Netherlands: Fortress Press, 1987), 87-91.
6. *Sifre Numbers* according to MS Oxford 135. I have obtained rabbinic manuscripts for this article from the Historical Dictionary Project of the Academy of the Hebrew Language. These manuscripts can be found online here (now free of charge): http://maagarim.hebrewacademy.org.il/Pages/PMain.aspx
7. *Jerusalem Talmud* 3:8 according to MS Leiden.
8. *Ibid.*
9. *Ibid.*
10. By contrast, *Bavli Ta'anit* 23a does not have the same transformations of Job 22:29 and 30.
11. Marc Bregman, "Tanhuma Yelammedenu," in *Encyclopaedia Judaica* ed. Fred Skolnik (Detroit: Keter, 2007), 503, 04.
12. Excluding *Numbers Rabbah* 18:15-18 and 20: 5, 6, which is post-*Tanhuma-Yelammedenu*.
13. There is even some *TY* material that has been deposited in *Genesis Rabbah* and *Pesiqta de-Rav Kahana*. For a listing of all extant *TY* texts and manuscripts, see Marc Bregman, *Sifrut Tan uma-Yelammedenu: Te'ur Nusheha We-'iyunim Be-Darke Hithawutam* (Piscataway, NJ: Gorgias Press, 2003), 20-96.
14. *Deuteronomy Rabbah, Shoftim* 13 according to MS Oxford 147.
15. The Septuagint has "death" [θανατος] instead of "pestilence."
16. A similar phrase is employed by Moshe according to *Exodus Rabbah* II 32:8 "we will see whose words will stand? [נראה דברי מי עומדים]." There, Moshe and God debate who will escort the Israelites to Israel. Ultimately, God accedes to Moshe's demand that God Himself lead the Israelites to the Promised Land.
17. On the ethically-driven reading of the Sihon war in the writings of Philo and Josephus, see Louis H. Feldman, *"Remember Amalek!": Vengeance, Zealotry, and Group Destruction in the Bible According to Philo, Pseudo-Philo, and Josephus* (Cincinnati [Ohio]; Detroit, MI: Hebrew Union College Press, 2004), 173-83.
18. See Moshe Weinfeld, *Deuteronomy 1-11: A New Translation with Introduction and Commentary*, 1st ed., The Anchor Bible (New York: Doubleday, 1991), 173-78.
19. This scholarly approach follows those Bible scholars who see the deuteronomic account as later than the Numbers account. For the opposite view, see John Van

Seters, "The Conquest of Sihon's Kingdom: A Literary Examination," *Journal of Biblical Literature* 91, no. 2 (1972): 182-97.

20. Weinfeld argues that this new tradition was established sometime during the reign of Hezekiah or Josiah. Weinfeld, *Deuteronomy 1-11*, 177. On the status of Transjordan in the tannaitic period, see *Sifre Numbers* 159.
21. The laws of *herem* are delineated in Deut. 7:2, 7:26, and 20:17. For more on *herem* as a distinctly deuteronomic legal doctrine, see Michael A. Fishbane, *Biblical Interpretation in Ancient Israel* (Oxford: Clarendon Press, 1985), 200-01.
22. For other treatments of this *Tanhuma* text and its parallels, see Menachem Fisch, "Judaism and the Religious Crisis of Modern Science," in *Nature and Scripture in the Abrahamic Religions, 1700-Present: Brill's Series in Church History*, ed. Jitse M. Meer and S. Mandelbrote (Leiden and Boston: Brill, 2009), 549-51, Adiel Schremer, "Between Radical Interpretation and Explicit Rejection," in *Renewing Jewish Committment: The Work and Thought of David Hartman*, ed. A. Sagi and Z. Zohar (Jerusalem: Machon Shalom Hartman, 2001), 759-63.
23. *Deuteronomy Rabbah, Shoftim* 13 according to MS Oxford 147.
24. Compare with Devarim 9:28.
25. According to Levi Smolar and Moshe Aberbach, the ubiquitous theological exploitation of the Golden Calf incident by early anti-Jewish Christians (claiming that God had rejected Israel for its worship) drove many rabbinic texts to "apologetically" and "polemically" have Moshe pleading for Israel's innocence. On the Christian side, see The Letter of Barnabas" 4:6-8 and chapter three of Tertullian's "Answer to the Jews," which can be found in Bart D. Ehrman, *After the New Testament: A Reader in Early Christianity* (New York: Oxford University Press, 1999), 100, 30. Also see "Irenaeus Against Heresies" 15:1, in Alexander Roberts and James Donaldson, *The Ante-Nicene Fathers: Translations of the Writings of the Fathers Down to A. D. 325* (Edinburgh: T&T Clark, 1989), 479. On the rabbinic side, see most prominently *Exodus Rabbah II* 43:1, 43:5, and other sources cited in Leivy Smolar and Moshe Aberbach, "The Golden Calf Episode in Postbiblical Literature," *Hebrew Union College Annual* 39 (1968): 91-116. While Smolar and Aberbach merely argue that there existed conflicting rabbinic approaches to the Golden Calf incident—some seeing Israel as fundamentally guilty and others not—both Irving Mandelbaum, "Tannaitic Exegesis of the Golden Calf Incident," in *Journal for the Study of the Old Testament. Supplement Series 100*, ed. Philip R. Davies and Richard T. White (Sheffield, England: JSOT Press, 1990), 207-23, and Arthur Marmorstein, *Studies in Jewish Theology* (London: Oxford University Press, 1950), 198-206, have correctly noted that these differing opinions line up historically. While the tannaim (with one exception) understood the Golden Calf incident as a narrative of sin and punishment, the amoraim attempted to exonerate Israel of all misdoings (see especially the statement of R. Joshua b. Levi in *b. Avodah Zarah* 4b).
26. This is the third instance in which the dictum of "righteous decree, God fulfills" is cited in the name of Rabbi Berekyah.
27. *Tanhuma, Buber, Vayishlach* 6. See also *Tanhuma, Vayera*, 19.
28. Ibid.
29. See Weiss, "Divine Concessions in the Tanhuma Midrashim," 88-91.
30. *Midrash Tanhuma Ki Tavo* 1 according to MS Cambridge 1212.
31. This reading of Ecclesiastes 8:4 is made explicit by an anonymous teaching in *Tanhuma Vayera* 19 [according to MS Cambridge 1212]. The proof text is also

recorded in *b Shabbat* 63a (MS Munich 95) in the name of Rav Yossi or R. Hanina bar Papa. See also *Exodus Rabbah* II 32:8, which has the Holy Spirit call out the Ecclesiastes' verses to explain how Moshe "defeated" God in a debate.

32. *Midrash Tanhuma Ki Tavo* 1 according to MS Cambridge 1212.
33. It is not clear to me if or how R. Hiyya reads the words "fear of" [יראת] before "God."
34. The teaching is also recorded in *Exodus Rabbah* 15:20.
35. Numerous rabbinic sources see Solomon as the author of Ecclesiastes. For a history of rabbinic approaches to the authorship of Ecclesiastes, see Jay M. Harris, *Nachman Krochmal: Guiding the Perplexed of the Modern Age*, Modern Jewish Masters Series 4 (New York: New York University Press, 1991), 172-78.
36. For the claim that this section of *Pesiqta de-Rav Kahana* is a TY Midrash, See Bregman, *Siprut Tan uma-Yelammedenu*, 60.
37. *Pesiqta de-Rav Kahana Ve-zo t ha-Berakha* supp. 1 (TY)
38. On the concept of Moshe or other humans as God's "husband" in kabbalistic literature, see Elliot R. Wolfson, *Through a Speculum That Shines: Vision and Imagination in Medieval Jewish Mysticism* (Princeton, N.J.: Princeton University Press, 1994), 388; Moshe Idel, *Kabbalah and Eros* (New Haven: Yale University Press, 2005), 161. Other rabbinic texts use the typical metaphor of God as husband when describing the demands of the prophet. See, for example, *Song of Songs Rabbah* 1:7:2 "Rabbi Yosi the son of Jeremiah said: Why are the prophets compared to women? To tell you: just as a wife is not embarrassed to demand [לתבוע] needs for the house from her husband, so too the prophets are not embarrassed to demand needs of Israel from their Father in heaven." [cf. *Midrash Proverbs* 31.]
39. Moshe Halbertal, "If the Text Had Not Been Written, It Could Not Be Said," in *Scriptural Exegesis: The Shapes of Culture and the Religious Imagination*, ed. Deborah A. Green and Laura Suzanne Lieber (Oxford: Oxford University Press, 2009), 146-65. The original Hebrew to Halbertal's article can be found here: Halbertal, "Ilmale' Miqra' Katub Iy Epsar Le'omro," *Tarbiz* 68, no. 1 (1998).
40. Halbertal, "Text Had Not Been Written," 157.
41. *Exodus Rabbah* II according to MS Jerusalem 24 5977.
42. See above p. 12,13.
43. See Yoni Garb, "Kinds of Power: Rabbinic Texts and the Kabbalah," *Kabbalah: Journal for the Study of Jewish Mystical Texts* 6 (2001): 45-71; David Hartman, A *Living Covenant: The Innovative Spirit in Traditional Judaism* (New York, London: Free Press, 1985).
44. See David Stern, "Imitatio Hominis: Anthropomorphism and the Characters of God in Rabbinic Literature," *Prooftexts* 12 (1992): 151-74; Arthur Green, "The Children in Egypt and the Theophany at the Sea," *Judaism* 24 (1975): 446-56, Wolfson, *Through a Speculum*, 33.
45. See Rachel A. Anisfeld, *Sustain Me with Raisin-Cakes: Pesiqta Derav Kahana and the Popularization of Rabbinic Judaism*, Supplements to the Journal for the Study of Judaism, (Leiden: Brill, 2009).
46. David Nirenberg calls this the "twice-defeated people." David Nirenberg, *Anti-Judaism: The Western Tradition*, 1st ed. (New York: W. W. Norton & Co., 2013), 86.

DOV S. ZAKHEIM

Seven Who Matriculated: Orthodox Rabbis and the Universities They Attended

WRITING TO HIS DEVOTED DISCIPLE and translator Rabbi Samuel Ben Judah Ibn Tibbon some eight hundred years ago, Maimonides provided a "course guide" for the study of Aristotle's works. His list of approved authors included some well-known to modern students, such as Ibn Rushd (Averroes), and some far less well known, such as Alexander of Aphrodisius, Themistius, Abubakr ibn al-Caig and Abu Nasr al Farani (Farabi). Among those he thought were not worth his students' time were al Razi, Isaac Yisraeli, and the works of Pythagorus, Hermes, and Porphidius.[1]

No modern university student would consider the advice remarkable in itself; it is what every professor offers to those attending his or her classes. But Maimonides was no ordinary professor; he was perhaps the greatest Jewish scholar, legislator and codifier since Talmudic times. For modern-day Haredim, who venerate the man they call the Rambam, and for whom secular studies are a necessary evil that preferably should be avoided altogether, the less said about the letter to Ibn Tibbon, the better.

Yet it was not, and has never been, the case that great Orthodox rabbis, respected by the Haredi scholars and laymen alike, have avoided secular studies. More to the point, ever since secular—indeed, Christian—universities were open to Jews, men who later became prominent scholars and decisors accepted by what is now called the Haredi world attended them. This fact contrasts wildly with the position of contemporary Haredi leaders, who not only condemn university study in the strongest possible terms, but tolerate and in many cases applaud, efforts to avoid giving even school children the basic educational tools for coping with modern life.

DOV S. ZAKHEIM served as United States Deputy Under Secretary of Defense (1985-87) and Under Secretary of Defense (2001-2004). He earned his doctorate from the University of Oxford and semikhah from HaGaon Rav Shmuel Walkin.

The following pages present brief sketches of seven rabbis who attended universities and of the environments in which they pursued their studies, including the hardships they faced while engaged in those studies. The time frame for this essay stretches from the sixteenth century, when some universities first opened their doors to Jewish students, through the modern era. Like the universities they attended, these rabbis hailed from a variety of European locales, ranging from Poland to Germany to Italy. Their secular studies enabled them to relate to the wider world around them, including to Jews with whom they differed on religious grounds. Accepted and respected by the Haredim of their time (the term is of recent vintage), they were nevertheless the forerunners of what is today called Modern Orthodoxy.

Rabbi Ovadiah ben Jacob Sforno

Ovadiah Ben Jacob Sforno was born in 1475 in Cesena, a town in the Emilia-Romagna region of northern Italy, on the Savio River, near Ravenna and Rimini. Sforno left Cesena for Rome in the 1490s; by then he had become proficient not only in Hebrew and rabbinic literature, but also in mathematics and philosophy.

At the University of Rome, Sforno studied philosophy, mathematics, philology, and, in particular, medicine.

Like all other European universities of that era, the University of Rome, better known as La Sapienza, was a Catholic institution. It differed from the others in that it was a pontifical university, the first ever of its kind. It had been founded in 1303 by Pope Boniface VIII specifically as an ecclesiastical university under his direct control, in particular contrast to the older Italian universities of Padua and Bologna. In 1431, Pope Eugene IV reorganized the university's curriculum to include the four faculties that were common to other universities, namely: law, philosophy, theology and medicine; Sforno was admitted to the last.

That a Jew would be accepted at a papal university during the Middle Ages was less surprising than might be imagined. While European universities generally were reluctant to admit Jewish students, just two years before Eugene VI had reorganized La Sapienza, his predecessor Martin V specifically included attendance at universities as an activity permitted to Jews. Moreover, Italian universities of the time generally were lax about admitting Jews.[2] No doubt this was the case at matriculation, as well as upon graduation and the conferral of the doctoral degree, from which, because of its equivalent to knighthood, Jews were officially barred.

Like other students, Sforno wore a special academic gown—still the norm for students at the ancient universities such as Oxford and Cambridge. That Sforno could do so without violating the ban against wearing *beged Akum*—non-Jewish garb—was no doubt the result of a ruling to that effect by Rabbi Joseph Colon of Mantua (popularly known by the acronym *Maharik*) several decades earlier. *Maharik* rejected the claims of those who thought otherwise and stated unequivocally "there is no prohibition in the matter" (*eyn issur badavar*).[3] On the other hand, in a separate, later ruling *Maharik* asserted that a cape required *tzitzit* (ritual fringes worn at the four corners of a garment). It is not clear whether Sforno followed this ruling of the Maharik's as well; others had issued lenient rulings in this regard.[4] Like other Jewish university students, Sforno would have been exempt from wearing the distinctive cap that marked out Jews.

As he attended his lectures, Sforno must have been conscious of the crucifixes that looked down upon him from the walls of the lecture hall. Most, if not all, of his professors would have been priests wearing their vestments. Sforno could not eat any food that may have been served to his fellow students in the university dining hall. And he would have had to find ways of circumventing any requirements to take examinations on Shabbat and Jewish holidays.

Upon his graduation, it is likely that Sforno had to give the university authorities and students gifts of various kinds, possibly to include inviting all his fellow students to dinner. His graduation fees would have been higher than those of his non-Jewish colleagues. In sum, the cost of his university education may have been twice as that of his fellows. On the other hand, he probably received the same lavish diploma that was awarded to all other university graduates.

From 1498 to 1500, on the recommendation of Cardinal Domenico Grimani, himself a graduate of the University of Padua, Sforno was hired to teach Hebrew to the Christian humanist Johannes Reuchlin. Upon receiving his degree at the University of Rome sometime shortly before 1500, Sforno began to earn his living as a doctor. However, he went on to become one of Judaism's greatest biblical commentators.

Sforno's commentary on the Torah has become a mainstay of the genre; it has been incorporated in the various versions of classic *Mikraot Gedolot* anthologies. Sforno also wrote commentaries on several of the books of Prophets—Jonah, Habakkuk, and Zechariah, and on Psalms, the Song of Songs, Job, and Ecclesiastes, dedicating the last of these to King Henry II of France, who had expanded the rights of Jews living in Guyenne and its main towns, Bayonne and Bordeaux.[5] Sforno also served as an halakhic decisor, receiving and responding to questions put to him by various Italian rabbis. His rulings were quoted by Rabbi Meir Katzenellenbogen of Padua (*Maharam Padua*), perhaps the leading halakhic decisor of his time.

Sforno resided in Bologna during the latter years of his life—he died in 1550—and established a yeshiva there. His duties as Rosh Yeshiva did not prevent him from continuing to publish, however; in 1548, he issued a critique of Aristotle entitled *Or Ammim*. Not only did he publish this work in Hebrew, he also personally translated it into Latin—hardly the language of the yeshiva study hall—and sent it to King Henry II. Clearly, Sforno's university education, and secular studies generally, remained an important part of every phase of his varied and accomplished life

Haham David Nieto

David Nieto was born in Venice in 1654, probably the son of Marranos who had escaped from Portugal. Nieto graduated from the University of Padua's faculty of medicine, where he likely earned a doctorate in medicine and not the lower degree of magister (i.e., Master's).

The University of Padua was Italy's second oldest university, founded in 1222. Some three decades later, in 1250, the university established a faculty of medicine that came to be recognized as one of the leading institutions of its kind in all of Europe. The university was the first to grant a doctorate to a Jew, conferring the degree in medicine on Leone Benaiah of Imola in 1409. Nevertheless, Nieto no doubt encountered many of the same indignities that confronted Sforno at Rome. These included special fines or levies, as well as the requirement at graduation to "provide the beadle of the university a quantity of sweet-meats for the academic attendants and for each of the many 'nations' into which the student body was divided."[6]

Despite his medical training, Nieto gravitated toward rabbinics and astronomy. His first work, *Pascalogia*, was written in Italian, and dealt with the astronomy that determined the dates of Passover and Easter. It was dedicated to Cardinal Francesco Maria de' Medici.[7] The book was written in Livorno, where Nieto served as *dayan* (religious judge) and preacher, as well as a doctor. It was not published until after Nieto had moved to London in 1701, however, where he became rabbi of the community's oldest congregation, Shaarei Shamayim, the Spanish and Portuguese Synagogue. Nieto's sermons regarding Divine providence, which he argued worked through nature, sparked considerable controversy; he was called a devotee of Spinoza, at best a pantheist, at worst an atheist.

Nieto defended his views in a volume written in Italian, *Della Divina Providencia*. The book did not quell his critics, however, and the leaders of Shaarei Shamayim turned to Rabbi Zvi Ashkenazi, popularly known as the *Hakham Zvi*, head of the yeshiva in Altona, now a suburb of Hamburg. Ashkenazi upheld Nieto, stating that "we must be grateful to the Chief Rabbi, his excellency our rabbi David Nieto for his sermon," and concluded his responsum by stating that, together with two other accomplished scholars in Altona, "after deliberation we the three agreed that all the statements made above [in the responsum] are true and just."[8] The ruling finally put the controversy to rest.

Nieto's major work, which brought him fame and reverence that continues until today even in the Haredi world, was *Matteh Dan* (The Rod of Dan), which was published in 1714 in both Spanish and Hebrew, and was a spirited defense of the Oral Law. At the same time, by making the case in *Matteh Dan* that the rabbis of the Talmud were experts in geography, medicine, science and astronomy, Nieto underscored the importance of secular studies, not only for shaping his own career, but for those of his religious compatriots as well. He died in 1728, succeeded by his son as rabbi of Shaarei Shamayim.

Rabbi Jacob Ettlinger: The Arukh LaNer

The works of some rabbis are so famous that they become their authors' monikers, overshadowing their actual names. Such is the case with Jacob Ettlinger, for nearly forty years Chief Rabbi of Altona and the leader of German Orthodox Jewry, whose *Arukh LaNer* was and remains a major commentary on the Talmud. Born in Karlsruhe in 1798, when the Enlightenment was at its height and Jewish Emancipation was rapidly spreading throughout much of Europe, Ettlinger pursued a dual curriculum, studying under Rabbi Abraham Bing of Wurzburg, in Bavaria, a noted scholar, while attending the university in the same town.

The University of Würzburg was founded in 1402; it was the sixth oldest university in the German states, which included what is now Germany, Austria, Hungary and Czechia. Officially known as the Julius Maximilian University of Würzburg, it was refounded and permanently endowed and established in 1582 on the initiative of Prince Bishop Julius Echter von Mespelbrunn. Like all universities in Europe, Wurzburg was closely tied to the church; Jews were not permitted to study at any of the universities in the German regions until 1678. As in Italy, the first faculties to admit Jewish students were those of medicine and philosophy.

However, the universities bitterly objected to the governments' policies mandating the admission of Jews. Many universities raised tuition for Jews to twice the amount charged to their non-Jewish counterparts. There were frequent attacks on Jewish students, and frequent pogroms as well. One such pogrom took place at the University of Würzburg in August 1819, while Ettlinger was a student there. The attacks on students were part of a wider pogrom that took place throughout the city when crowds attacked Jewish shops, homes and passers-by.

It was because of the riots that Ettlinger left the university, and he therefore never received a degree. A contemporary of his at the yeshiva of Würzburg, David Seligmann, writing in 1872, tried to minimize the importance of Ettlinger's attendance at the university by recalling that he only attended classes "for a few hours a day, a few days a week." Seligmann had not attended university, and may not have realized that lectures were not always given daily, and nor did the lecture hall consume a student's entire day.[9]

In any event, it became clear that Ettlinger attached considerable importance to secular education. The religious school that he opened in Altona in 1839 was Orthodox in outlook, and had a program of Jewish studies taught by Orthodox Jews. Nevertheless, Jewish studies accounted for only thirty percent of student class time. The remaining hours were devoted to a secular curriculum, including the study of Danish (Altona was part of Denmark at the time). Ettlinger's more worldly experience at the university may also have been a reason for his permitting girls to attend his school, something unheard of in Eastern Europe for another half century.[10]

Finally, his university education may have made him the realist that he was. Though he was a bitter opponent of the Reform Movement, organizing the protest against the 1844 conference of Reform rabbis at Brunschweig, and then founding the first Orthodox Jewish journal (in German) a year later, he refused to go as far as the many Hungarian rabbis, notably Rabbi Solomon Eger of Posen, who sought to exclude Reform from Judaism. He was of the view that "to have done so would have reduced Judaism to a confession of faith alone—and Ettlinger, like most other Orthodox leaders, refused to do this."[11] Thus, while describing a Reform Jew who, for example, did not circumcise his son as an "apostate and heretic" ("*Kofer beDat Yisrael v'hu apikores*"), Ettlinger refused to cut such a person off from the community, instead stating that "we wish to pray to the Holy One Blessed be He, that he will open the eyes of these erroneous ones and will bring them back into the lap of Torah and belief."[12] Ettlinger thus realized that

> Reform had established itself, at least for the foreseeable future, as a permanent fixture within German Jewish society. This by no means implies that he extended it legitimacy. But as opposed to those of the previous generation who felt that they still had a chance to destroy Reform before it spread to the masses, he lived in an age in which nonobservance was becoming the norm. In such an environment, he felt that his main goal should be to develop vehicles for strengthening the endangered observant minority.[13]

His views anticipated by more than a century and a half the reality that Orthodoxy faces in contemporary America, where some eighty percent of the population is non-Orthodox—a circumstance that Open Orthodoxy has sought to address in a positive manner.

Ettlinger's yeshiva in Altona was attended by many students who later led German Orthodoxy; his followers included Samson Raphael Hirsch in Mannheim, and Israel (Esriel) Hildesheimer in Altona. Ettlinger presided over the Altona Beit Din, which also had jurisdiction in civil matters. His position was abolished by the Danish Government in 1863 when the civil authority of the Beit Din was revoked. It was restored by Prussia when, after Denmark ceded Schleswig-Holstein to it the following year, Ettlinger made an extremely favorable impression on King William I of Prussia during his visit to Altona in 1865. He died in Altona six years later.

Rabbi Esriel Hildesheimer

A student and disciple of Rabbi Jacob Ettlinger, Esriel Hildesheimer became the leader of German moderate Orthodoxy during the latter half of the nineteenth century. Born in 1820 in Halberstadt, Prussia, the son of Rabbi Lev Galia, a dayan (rabbinical judge) and teacher of Talmud, Hildesheimer attended that town's Hasharat Zvi school, the first Orthodox elementary school in Germany to add secular subjects to its curriculum. He entered Rabbi Ettlinger's yeshiva in Altona in 1837; Haham Isaac Bernays was one of his teachers there. By all accounts Hildesheimer was a prize student, devoted to his Talmudic studies. Both rabbis encouraged him to continue his secular education while studying in yeshiva, and he studied classical languages while at the yeshiva. In 1840, he returned to Halberstadt to take his diploma at the Gymnasium and then entered the University of Berlin, where he studied Semitic languages and mathematics even as he continued his Talmudic education. He then went on to study at the University of Halle, where he earned his doctorate in 1846 writing his thesis on the proper mode of biblical interpretation.

The universities of Berlin and Halle were considered to be the finest in Germany at that time. The University of Berlin was founded as an independent university by a group that included Friedrich Wilhelm von Humboldt, who in 1812, as Minister of Education, opened all Prussian universities to Jewish students. In 1949, the university was renamed Humboldt University at Berlin in his honor. Humboldt and his colleagues envisioned the integration of the natural sciences, social sciences, and humanities; such an approach would have been especially congenial to the young Hildesheimer, who was already comfortable with the blending of religious and secular studies.

The University of Halle, whose actual name is the Martin Luther University of Halle-Wittenberg, was created through the merger of the University of Wittenberg, which was founded in 1502, and the University of Halle, which was founded in 1691. It was in 1517 at Wittenberg where Luther, then a professor at the university, promulgated the ninety-five theses that led to the founding of Protestantism. Though Luther himself had become increasingly hostile to Jews when they refused to convert to his reformed version of Christianity, within about a century the university that bore his name "became the central point of approach of Jewish students of medicine."[14] By the end of the century, more than 60 doctorate diplomas were given to Jewish candidates by the Faculty of Medicine of Halle University. By 1784, restrictions on Jewish students were further loosened when they were able to undergo the same examination process as their Christian counterparts. As the nature of Hildesheimer's doctorate indicated, by the mid-1840s, Jews were pursuing a variety of subjects at the university.

Upon becoming rabbi of Eisenstadt, Hungary, Hildesheimer's background and strong belief in the importance of secular studies led him to found a school that offered students both secular and Jewish subjects, with increasing emphasis on the former, particularly mathematics—which he felt was an important tool for studying Talmud—as students moved to higher grades. All courses were taught in German, rather than the usual Yiddish. Hildesheimer then established a Yeshiva that, like Yeshivat Chovevei Torah which Rabbi Avi Weiss established over a century later, required students to have a serious secular education as a condition of admission. Hildesheimer's yeshiva also taught Hebrew and Tanakh, neither of which were part of the traditional yeshiva curriculum and came to be (and still are) frowned upon by the Haredim by virtue of being subjects that were emphasized by the Reform movement.

Not surprisingly, Hildesheimer came in for considerable criticism from much of the highly conservative Hungarian Orthodox rabbinate; the fact that he dressed in modern European clothing did not help matters. He broke with them on numerous issues, most notably when he rejected nine resolutions that the right wing rabbis, reacting to the growth of Neologism[15] in Hungary, approved at an assembly that was held in Mihalowitz early in 1866. Among the resolutions was one that banned preaching in a non-Jewish language, which particularly irked Hidlesheimer, who spoke German at home, and whose teachers, Rabbi Ettlinger and Haham Bernays, had both preached in German. In 1869 he seized upon the offer to become leader of Berlin's independent Adas Yisroel Orthodox community. Four years later, Hildesheimer again established a yeshiva, *Rabbinerseminar für das orthodoxe Judentum* in Berlin, which, like the one he had opened in Hungary, offered studies beyond the classic yeshiva curriculum and indeed became a focal point for the Orthodox approach to *Wissenschaft des Judentums* (the scientific study of Judaism).

Hildesheimer, like his teacher Rabbi Ettlinger and his contemporary Rabbi Samson Raphael Hirsch, was a strong opponent of Reform. He supported Hirsch's successful attempt to win official recognition for the separatist Orthodox community in Germany, which passed into law in 1875. He differed from Hirsch in that he was far more prolific in his Hebrew writings, notably in his responsa, which were addressed to rabbis all over Germany and beyond. He also wrote commentaries on the Torah and selected portions of other books of the Scriptures.

Despite, or perhaps because of, his opposition to Reform, Hildesheimer was sufficiently realistic to recognize that he could not impose exceedingly heavy restrictions on his own Orthodox community if he wished to keep them within the Orthodox fold. A prime example of his attitude was his reluctant acceptance of the reality that Orthodox children were attending secular schools on Shabbat: he instituted a change in the service by having the reading of the Torah and the Musaf prayer both take place in the afternoon, after the children had returned home from school.[16]

By the time Hildesheimer passed away in 1899, he was recognized as Germany's leading Orthodox rabbi, and was respected by many rabbinic leaders in Eastern Europe as well. The yeshiva he founded survived until it was shut down by the Nazis in 1939. But before then, however, it produced numerous great rabbis, who, like Hildesheimer, came to be respected by the Haredi community; notably, rabbis Dovid Zvi Hoffmann and Yaakov Yechiel Weinberg, both of whom are treated below.

Rabbi Dovid Zvi Hoffmann

Unlike Hildesheimer and Hirsch, Dovid Zvi Hoffmann was not born in Germany, though it was there that he made his reputation as a scholar and leader. Born in Verbo in 1843, in what is now Slovakia, his father was a *dayan*, but the boy was orphaned at the age of four. His mother initially enrolled him in the yeshiva of Rabbi Moshe Schick (the *Maharam Schick*), a student of the acknowledged leader of Hungarian ultra-Orthodoxy Rabbi Moshe Sofer (the *Hatam Sofer*). Schick was perhaps the greatest Hungarian Jewish Talmudist of his time; he was also a bitter enemy of Reform who ruled that Reform Jews should be treated as Karaites and issued a public proclamation condemning the 1844 Reform Brunschweig conference.[17] Hoffmann then went on to study at the yeshiva of another leader of Hungarian Jewry, Rabbi Abraham Sofer, popularly known as the *Ktav Sofer*, and son of the *Hatam Sofer*. Hoffmann subsequently studied at Esriel Hildesheimer's Seminary in Eisenstadt, where he obtained sufficient secular knowledge to enable him to enroll in German-speaking universities—initially Vienna and then Berlin, where he studied philosophy, history and oriental languages, and then at Tubingen, where he earned his doctorate in 1871. His dissertation subject was the Amoraic sage Mar Samuel (published in 1873), who, in addition to his vast knowledge of the law and his many legal rulings, was a leading astronomer and doctor—the ideal prototype for the modern Orthodox Jew.[18]

Although Austria had only emancipated its Jewish residents less than three years before Hoffmann studied at the University of Vienna, Jews not only flocked to the capital, but also to the university. The university had a liberal reputation that stemmed from the Revolution of 1848, when its faculty and students formed a major part of the Academic Legion that "had been at the heart of revolutionary Vienna's organized fighting force."[19] The University of Tübingen, in southern Germany, where Hoffmann earned his doctorate, was founded in 1477 by Count Eberhard V, later the first Duke of Württemberg, a civic and ecclesiastic reformer. By the time Hoffmann studied there, it had been renamed Eberhard Karls University, Tübingen in 1769 after Duke Karl Eugen. In 1828, a new law in what was now the Principality of Wurttemberg placed the rabbinate under the civil bureaucracy and required that all rabbinical candidates obtain a university degree.[20] Thus, by the time Hoffmann entered the university to write his doctoral thesis, Jews, and especially those intending to enter the rabbinate, had long been a presence on the university campus.

Upon obtaining his doctorate, Hoffmann spent a brief spell teaching in one of the schools established by Rabbi Samson Raphael Hirsch, at which Hirsch told him to remove his head covering at his school, since non-Jewish teachers would view his wearing a hat as a sign of disrespect for the school director.[21] In 1873, Hoffmann joined the faculty of Hildesheimer's newly established Rabbinical Seminary in Berlin. There he initially taught Talmud, Codes and *Poskim*, and later Bible as well. In 1899, he succeeded Hildesheimer as rector of the Seminary upon the latter's death.

Hoffmann was a member of the Adass Yisroel Orthodox Bet Din in Berlin, and later became its *Av Bet Din*, or chairman of the rabbinical court. By the beginning of the twentieth century he was recognized as Germany's leading halakhic decisor. During his lifetime, he issued over 400 responsa—that is, over four times as many as Samson Raphael Hirsch; indeed, his responsa on *Orah Haim* alone were more numerous than all Hirsch ever produced. His responsa were published in a volume entitled *Melamed Le'ho'il*.

Alongside his rabbinic endeavors, Hoffmann vigorously pursued what he formulated as an Orthodox version of *Wissenschaft des Judentums*; "in fact he is the only *gadol beYisrael* who has ever been recognized as an outstanding practictioner" of that discipline.[22] His *Die Erste Misschna und die Controversen der Tannaim* ("The First Mishna and the Tannaitic Controversies") won him widespread recognition in the field when it appeared in 1882. He translated and commented on the Mishnaic orders of *Nezikin* and *Taharot*. He wrote commentaries on Genesis, Leviticus and Deuteronomy. He published a major investigation of halakhic Midrashim. From 1876 to 1893, he co-edited the *Magazin fur die Wissenschaft des Judentums*. Hoffmann's long list of other publications, among them hundreds of articles, also included a major refutation of higher Biblical criticism made popular by the Protestant scholar (and anti-Semite)[23] Julius Wellhausen. Entitled *Die wichtigsten Instanzen gegen die Graf-Wellhausensche Hypothese* "The Major Examples Contradicting the Graf-Wellhausen Hypothesis"; it was published in two volumes, in 1903 and 1916.

Hoffmann was unique in his time for being willing in his investigations of the history of rabbinics to study the evolution of the Oral Law, and to cite scholars such as Frankel, Geiger and Graetz—whom he otherwise considered to be heretics—even as he insisted on the divinity of both the Scriptures and the Oral Law.[24] In so doing, and in undertaking Talmudic criticism, he earned the ire of many of his more traditionalist colleagues, even including Rabbi Samson Raphael Hirsch. Nevertheless, by the time of his passing in 1921, no one could, or would, challenge him as German Jewry's pre-eminent scholar, educator, rabbi and halakhic decisor.

Rabbi Isaac Halevi Herzog

Born in 1888 in Lomza, in what was then Russia but actually in the area of what Jews called Lita and had been Poland before its final partition, Isaac Herzog moved with his family to Leeds, in northeast England, when he was ten years old. Herzog was initially educated by his father, Rabbi Joel Herzog, who served as a community rabbi, and ultimately earned his *semikhah* from Rabbi David Wilkowsky (known as the *Ridbaz*) without attending a yeshiva. Herzog's first publication, when he was twenty-one, was an appendix to his father's book, *Imrei Yo'el*.[25] The younger Herzog's piece, *Divrei Yitzhak*, actually consisted of two essays. The first addressed the issues relating to the question of whether an extant ban could be further circumscribed by a rabbinical prohibition (*gezeirah l'g'zeirah*).[26] The second, addressed to the *Ridbaz*, was an analysis relating to labor not required for itself (*melakhah sh'ein tz'rikhah legufah*).[27]

When his family moved to Paris in 1910, Herzog enrolled at the Sorbonne, formally known as the University of Paris. Founded in 1257, the Sorbonne, like all French universities, was not open to Jews until after the revolution of 1789. Indeed, until the eighteenth century, Jews could not openly live in most of France.[28] The Napoleonic decrees of 1808 opened the universities to Jews throughout the lands France had conquered;[27] nevertheless, Jews began to attend French universities in numbers "only after the demise of Napoleon."[30]

After pursuing his initial studies in Paris, Herzog soon moved to the University of London to earn his doctorate. Sephardic Jews such as Isaac Lyon Goldsmid had played a prominent role in establishing the university as a secular seat of higher learning in 1827; the so-called "ancient" universities—Oxford and Cambridge—would not grant degrees to Jews until 1871.[31]

Herzog never published his 1913 dissertation, entitled "Hebrew Porphyrology," which earned him a D. Litt. in marine biology.[32] Nevertheless, the thesis was a ground-breaking study of the Biblical *tekhelet*, the blue dye derived from the murex snail that had been part of *tzitzit* since ancient times.[31] Herzog argued that the art of dyeing to achieve *tekhelet* had come to an end off the eastern shores of Israel in the late Byzantine period, but that the snail had now been identified. Contemporary scientists still cite his findings.[34]

Herzog's thesis, on the heels of his essays, established him as a young expert in halakhah. Within three years of its completion, he became rabbi of Belfast, Northern Ireland. Three years later, he became rabbi in Dublin, where about two-thirds of all Irish Jews, many of them Litvaks like himself, resided.[33] There, he became close to Eamon de Valera, leader of Sinn Fein and later first prime minister of Ireland, and reportedly often hid de Valera from the British police.[36] In 1922, upon the creation of the Irish Free State, Herzog became its chief rabbi. The small Irish Jewish community, especially its Litvak element, was a stronghold of Zionism, which Herzog actively supported, and which permeated his household;[37] during his tenure, Hatikvah was sung at the end of synagogue services.[38] It was therefore no surprise that in 1936 he immigrated to Palestine, accepting the offer to succeed Rabbi Abraham Isaac Kook as Ashkenazi Chief Rabbi.

Herzog played an active political role during the Mandate years leading up to the creation of the State of Israel in 1948. In addition to his role as a major halakhic decisor—he was recognized as such by Rabbi Issar Zalman Meltzer, one of the most prominent Haredi yeshiva leaders[39]—Herzog, and his Sephardi counterpart Rabbi Ben Zion Uziel, "concerned themselves with secular matters." Unlike their present day successors, whose hostility to the non-Orthodox has been palpable, Herzog and Uziel were "involved with the leadership of the Yishuv in the full range of its needs." In particular, Herzog

> perceived his function not just as a spiritual authority but as a politician representing the nation in external affairs. . . . Rabbi Herzog was especially qualified for contacts with the British. . . . This was caused by his broad education, his fluency in English, his urbanity and western cultural background, his knowledge of the British people, and his acquaintance with religious and political figures in Britain.[40]

In this regard, Rabbi Herzog was chosen as a representative of the *Yishuv* to the ill-fated 1939 London Round Table Conference that the British Government convened to find a solution to the future status of Palestine, though he, together with the Mizrachi delegation, subsequently withdrew from the conference.

Herzog interacted with two American presidents. His meeting with Franklin Roosevelt, which he obtained after a dangerous crossing of the Atlantic, and in which he pleaded for assistance to the endangered Jews of Europe, produced nothing but the president's smiles. His telephonic conversation with Harry Truman was notably different. Congratulating Truman for recognizing the state of Israel, Herzog brought the president to tears when he told him: "God put you in your mother's womb so you would be the instrument to bring the rebirth of Israel after two thousand years."[41]

Herzog's ability to work with Israelis of all stripes, as well as his experience in the turbulent formative years of independent Ireland, stood him in good stead when he became the State of Israel's first Ashkenazi Chief Rabbi. He addressed issues that had not been relevant to the Jewish experience for two thousand years: these included the place of religious law in the operations of the Israel Defense Forces;[42] the sale of the land during the sabbatical *Shemitah* year now that Israel was an independent state;[41] the reciting of *Hallel* on *Yom Ha'atzmaut*;[44] and the status of the Bene Israel of India.[45] Herzog's scholarship extended well beyond halakhah. He continued to maintain his interest in science, which he considered authoritative, writing about medicine and evolutionary theory (which he did not oppose), as well as Jewish philosophy.[46]

Herzog's legacies included his son Yaakov, a rabbi and scholar in his own right, who served as Ambassador to Canada and was a long time Director-General of the Prime Minister's office. Another son, Chaim, was a general in the Israeli Defense Forces and a noted military historian, and served as Ambassador to the United Nations and President of the State of Israel. And Isaac Herzog's grandson and namesake served as a Minister in several Israeli governments and in 2013 was elected leader of the Israel's venerable Labor Party.

Rabbi Zvi Hirsh Zakheim

Zvi Zakheim, my father, was born in 1910 in Ruzhany (*Rozhenoi* in Yiddish), a part of Lita in Czarist Poland.As a young child, Zakheim's parents sent him to study at the Zionist *Tarbut* school in Vilna. There, he studied most subjects in Hebrew, including Shakespearean plays; he also joined the Zionist scout movement.

Zakheim then attended the Ramailes yeshiva, under the leadership of his near contemporary, the brilliant Rabbi Yisroel Gustman, who became the youngest member of the Vilna *beit din* and earned his semikhah there.[47] In 1930, Zakheim was admitted to the faculty of law at Vilna's Stefan Batory University; he earned his Master's diploma in 1934.

The University's history, and name, reflected the political vicissitudes that befell Vilna over the centuries. Founded in 1579 as the Jesuit Academy of Vilnius (the city's Lithuanian name) by Stefan Batory, King of Poland and Grand Duke of Lithuania, it came under Czarist control after the Third Partition of Poland in 1795. When the university's students joined the 1830-31 November uprising against Russia, the authorities shut it down, and it remained closed until 1919, when Vilnius, called Vilno in Polish, was incorporated into the newly independent Polish state.[48]

Jews were permitted to attend the university once it reopened its doors after World War I. They were, however, marked out for discrimination, with only a small number accepted under a quota called *numerous clausus*. Once admitted, Jewish students were subjected to a variety of indignities, such as having to stand at the back of classrooms.

Upon earning his law degree, Zakheim became legal counsel for the governing body of the Jewish Community of Vilna, which supported and funded all aspects of the community's Jewish life: rabbinical salaries, religious and secular Jewish schools, hospitals, old age homes, and cemeteries. The Community leadership role was critical, as Jews suffered from increasing discrimination, notably in the economic sphere. As a result, poverty was endemic: fully four-fifths of Vilna's Jewish children were diagnosed as anemic.[49]

The religious leadership of the community fell to Rabbi Yosef Rubenstein, a member of the Polish Senate, and Rabbi Haim Ozer Grodzinski, the acknowledged leader of eastern European Orthodox Jewry.[50] Zakheim also served as legal advisor and secretary to Rabbi Grodzinski. In his dual role as counsel to both the Community and its leading rabbi, Zakheim employed his links with both Polish and, after 1939, Lithuanian officials to address a host of issues that confronted not only Orthodox Jewry, but Jewry in general, as another war loomed in Europe. In one case, he employed his connections to obtain the release from jail of a family of "illegal" Czech Jewish immigrants, arrange for their legal entry into Poland, and enable their emigration to Sweden, where they survived the war.[51]

The Nazi invasion of Poland led Rabbi Grodzinski to encourage hundreds of yeshiva students and their rabbis to flee to Vilna, which, in the aftermath of the Ribbentrop-Molotov pact had become capital of neutral Lithuania. In fact, virtually every leading Haredi rabbi of the post-war era was saved by virtue of their escape to Vilna in 1939.[52] Zakheim ensured the care and feeding of these rabbis and their students, among whom was his brother Yaakov Isser, a student in Mir. In one instance, responding to direct and personal pleas for help from all the *roshei yeshiva,* including Rabbis Aharon Kotler, Avrohom Yaffen, and Reuven Grozovsky, he arranged for all the yeshiva students and their *roshei yeshiva* to receive identity cards, which they had been unable to obtain, and which were valid only with his signature.[53] The following year, in 1940, with yeshiva students starving due to food shortages in Vilna that had materialized in the aftermath of the Soviet annexation of Lithuania, Zakheim successfully convinced Vilna's economic commissar, himself the son of a rabbi, to release sufficient flour not only for the yeshiva students, but for outlying Jewish communities in Lithuania as well.

In yet another matter, Zakheim was confronted by pleas from anguished parents whose sons had been drafted into the Polish Army and had been captured by the Nazis. Zakheim formulated the argument that since Vilna and its environs had been conquered by Poland in 1920 and had only recently returned to Lithuania, the soldiers were actually Lithuanian neutrals, and deserved special treatment. Together with the president of the Jewish community, Dr. Vigodski, Zakheim persuaded the Lithuanian leadership to forward a long list of these Jewish prisoners to the Nazis. As a result, the Jewish soldiers were transferred to special camps for captured neutrals, from which many escaped and survived the war.[54]

Zakheim himself escaped Vilna in March 1941 after learning of his imminent arrest by the NKVD, the Soviet secret police. After working with the Japanese consul, Chiune Sugihara, to obtain visas for the yeshiva students and their *rabbonim*, he traveled with them to Vladivostok via the trans-Siberian railroad, again acting for the yeshiva leaders as an intermediary with the outside world. Arriving in Shanghai in 1941, Zakheim obtained a law certificate at Aurora University and acted as legal representative of the yeshiva refugees to the Japanese authorities.

Upon his arrival in the United States, Zakheim obtained another law degree from New York Law School, and served as rabbi for the Rozehnoi *landsmannschaft*. He also remained active in communal politics, advocating for the absorption of the Ethiopian Falashas into Israel, much to the annoyance of his Agudah colleagues, who refused to recognize them as Jews. He began his five-volume work on Tractate *Sanhedrin*, *Zvi Hasanhedrin*, at the age of seventy-four, and completed it a decade later, eight years before his passing.

Conclusion

The seven rabbis of this essay who "matriculated"—that is, formally registered at a university, were deliberately chosen to highlight the role and challenges of university life for Jews across the centuries and in all parts of Europe: western Europe (the universities of London and Paris), central Europe (the German universities), eastern Europe (Stefan Batory), and southern Europe (Rome and Padua). Many more rabbis than those whose lives have been outlined above attended university and engaged with the secular world around them. Not all were accepted by most of the Haredi world during their lifetimes. Indeed, even the great Rabbi Joseph Ber Soloveitchik, the acknowledged leader of American Modern Orthodoxy throughout much of the second half of the twentieth century, and teacher to hundreds of rabbis at Yeshiva University, including Avi Weiss, only came to be respected by much of the Haredi community after his passing.

Attending university, obtaining a degree, interacting with the secular world—or, for that matter, with non-Orthodox streams of Judaism, which is the watchword of the Open Orthodoxy that Rabbi Weiss has advocated—thus has a long pedigree. Moreover, the very fact that it was not only in past centuries that one could be a recognized by the Haredim as a *Talmid Hakham* and still be an educated individual—and interact with the modern era as well—is of no small significance. For those who wish to excel in both the world of Torah, regardless of the branch of Orthodoxy with which they identify, as well as the in non-religious (and non-Jewish) world around them, the lives and accomplishments of the seven rabbis who are the subject of this essay should be an example and an inspiration.

NOTES

1. Rabbi Moshe ben Maimon, *Sh"ut HaRambam: "Pe'er Hador"* No. 143 (ed. David Yosef; Jerusalem: Machon Yerushalayim, 5744/1983), 278.
2. See Cecil Roth, *The Jews in the Renaissance* (Philadelphia: Jewish Publication Society, 1977), 37.
3. *Sh"ut Maharik Hayeshanot LeRabeinu Rabbi Yosef Colon* (ed. Rabbi Shmuel Baruch HaKohen Deutsch and Rabbi Elyakim Schlesinger; Jerusalem: Oraysoh, 5748/1988), *Shoresh* 88, 168-71.
4. For a discussion see ibid., *Shoresh* 149, 298-301.
5. Jacques Attali, *Les Jufs, le Monde et L'Argent: Histoire Economique du people Juif* (Paris: Fayard, 2002), 350.
6. Roth, *Jews in the Renaissance*, 37.
7. For a discussion of Nieto's writings and views on astronomy, see Jeremy Brown, *New Heavens and a New Earth: The Jewish Reception of Copernican Thought* (Oxford: Oxford University Press, 2013), 106-116.
8. Zvi Ashenazi, *She'eylot U'Teshuvot Haham Zvi* vol. 1 (Jerusalem: Mifal Haham Zvi, 5758/1998), no. 18, 58-60.
9. David Seligmann, *Kina LeDavid* ("David's Lament") *Halevanon*, vol 8. no. 16, (5632/1872), 125, cited in Yehuda Aharon Horowitz, "From the Biography of the Author," cited in Yaakov Yukob Ettlinger, *Binyan Tzion Hashalem*, vol. I (ed. Yehuda Aharon Horowitz; Jerusalem: Devar Yerushalayim, 5749/1989), 13. Reflecting the current Haredi outlook, Horowitz goes to even greater pains to demonstrate that reports of Ettlinger's attendance at the university "was not without some exaggeration." (Ibid., 12).
10. See David Ellenson, *Rabbi Esriel Hildesheimer and the Creation of Modern Jewish Orthodoxy* (Tuscaloosa, AL and London: University of Alabama Press, 1990), 118.
11. David Ellenson, *After Emancipation: Jewish Religious Responses to Modernity* (Cincinnati: Hebrew Union College Press, 2004), 171.

12. Ettlinger, *Binyan Tzion Hashalem*, vol. I, No. 59 (trans. from German to Hebrew), 74.
13. W. Kaiser and A. Volker, "The History of the Halle Ars Medica Judaica II: The beginnings of Jewish medical education," *Zeitschrift für die gesamte Innere Medizin* 44 (January 1989), 25 abstract (in English), www.ncbi.nlm.nih.gov/pubmed/2652895.
14. Adam S. Ferziger, *Exclusion and Hierarchy: Orthodoxy, Nonobservance, and the Emergence of Modern Jewish Identity* (Philadelphia: University of Pennsylvania Press, 2005), 95.
15. The Neologues were Hungary's equivalent of Reform, though in practice they were closer to early variants of American Conservative Judaism.
16. Cited in Dovid Zvi Hoffmann, *She'aylot U'Teshuvot Melamed Le'ho'il*, no. 51, 101.
17. Moshe Schick, *Sh'eylot U'teshuvot Maharam Schick, Chelek Yoreh De'ah VeChoshen Mishpat* (Jerusalem: n.p., n.d.), *Yoreh De'ah* no. 331
18. Not surprisingly, in his brief biographical sketch of Hoffmann, his Haredi great-grandson and namesake mentions neither his studies under Hildesheimer nor at university; see Dovid Zvi Hoffmann, "*Pesach Davar*," in Hoffmann, *Melamed Le'ho'il.*
19. Carl E. Schorske, *Fin-de-Siecle Vienna: Politics and Culture* (New York: Vintage, 1981), 39.
20. Daniel B. Schwartz, *The First Modern Jew: Spinoza and the History of an Image* (Princeton, NJ: Princeton University Press, 2012), 66.
21. Hoffmann, *Melamed Le'ho'il, Yoreh De'ah*, no. 54, 235.
22. Marc B. Shapiro, "Rabbi David Zevi Hoffmann on Torah and Wissenschaft," *The Torah U'Madda Journal* 6 (1995-96), 129.
23. Wellhausen's anti-Semitism, which was a contributing factor to his biblical criticism, was also a motivator for Hoffman's rebuttal.
24. David Ellenson and Richard Jacobs, "Scholarship and Faith: David Hoffmann and His Relationship to *Wissenschaft des Judentums*,"*Modern Judaism* 8 (February 1988), 35.
25. Shlomo Shapira, "Preface," Harav Yitzchak Isaac Halevy Herzog, *Pesakim U'Ketavim: Sh'eylot U'Teshuvot B'dinei Orach Chaim*, vol. 1 (ed. *Shlomo Shapira*; Jerusalem: Mossad Harav Kook, 1989), 11-12.
26. *Ibid.*, vol. 2, no. 68, 314-16.
27. *Ibid.*, no. 69, 317-23.
28. The exception was Bordeaux, and its surrounding area, as noted above. See S. Ettinger, "The Modern Period," in *A History of the Jewish People* (ed. H.H. Ben-Sasson; Cambridge, MA: Harvard University Press, 1976), 734. See also Jacques Attali, *Les Juifs, le Monde et l'Argent*, 420-21.
29. Ibid., 429.
30. Jay R. Berkovitz, "The French Revolution and the Jews: Assessing the Cultural Impact," *AJS Review* 20:1 (1995), 74.
31. Lipman, *A History of the Jews in Britain*, 30.
32. Though Herzog did not publish his thesis, he did review many of its arguments in his halakhic writings. See Herzog, *Pesakim U'Ketavim* vol. 1, nos. 5-9, 38-64
33. Roald Hoffman, "Marginalia: Blue as the Sea," *American Scientist* 78 (July-August 1990), 308-309.
34. As Z.C. Koren states, "Jewish sources, as noted by Herzog, also indicate that the dyeing of blue or violet *tekhelet*—purple's relative—ceased to exist at the shores of

ancient Israel at about that period (i.e. of the early Muslim conquests of the seventh century). Hence, it is a safe conjecture to conclude that murex dyeing died out along the shores of present day Israel and environs about 1,350 years ago." See Zvi C. Koren, "The First Optimal All-Murex All-Natural Purple Dyeing in the Eastern Mediterranean in a Millennium and a Half," *Dyes in History and Archaeology* 20 (1995), 136-49, at 138.

35. Cormac O' Grada, "Settling In: Dublin's Jewish Immigrants of a Century Ago," *Field Day Review* 1 (2005), 87. See also Rory Miller, "The Look of the Irish: Irish Jews and the Zionist Project 1900-1948," in *Jewish Historical Studies* 43 (2011), 189-211, at 202-20.
36. Reported to the author on a visit to Dublin.
37. Miller, 195, 202-204, *passim*.
38. Ibid., 205-206.
39. Rabbi Issar Zalman Meltzer, father-in-law of Rabbi Aharon Kotler, had headed the yeshiva in Slutzk, Poland, which he moved to Palestine. When responding to a question by Rabbi Hananiah Gavriel, the head of Jerusalem's Sephardi *beit din*, regarding a particular thorny matter of erroneous matrimony by means of a messenger (*kidushei ta'ut al yedei shaliah*). Rabbi Meltzer asked that before any action was taken his ruling receive the support of the Haredi chief rabbi of Jerusalem, Zvi Pesach Frank, and of Rabbi Herzog, both of whom he described as the "*geonim* of the holy land." He specifically called Rabbi Herzog "my friend, the great *Gaon* . . . the chief rabbi of Eretz Yisrael." Reproduced in Hananiah Gavriel, *Minchat Hach"ag*, vol. 1, *Even Ha'ezer* (Jerusalem: Yehuda Amram Nitah, 5702/1942), no. 8, 59a.
40. Shulamit Eliash, "The Political Role of the Chief Rabbinate of Palestine during the Mandate: Its Character and Nature," *Jewish Social Studies* 47 (Winter 1985), 39-40.
41. David McCullough, *Truman* (New York: Simon & Schuster, 1992), 620.
42. See, e.g., his ruling requiring an eiruv on military bases; Herzog, *Pesakim U'Ketavim* vol. 2: *Sh'eylot U'Teshuvot B'dinei Orach Chaim*, no. 73, 342-48.
43. Herzog, *Pesakim U'Ketavim* vol. 3: *Sh'eylot U'Teshuvot B'mitzvot Hateluyot Ba'aretz*, no. 50, 212-13.
44. Ibid., vol. 2, no. 105, 473-89.
45. He ruled that every case needed to be evaluated on its merits. See ibid., vol.6: *Sh'eylot U'Teshuvot B'Dinei Even Ha'ezer*, no. 15, 54-65. For a discussion, see Dov S. Zakheim, "What Happened to the Ten Lost Tribes," in *Mishpetei Shalom: A Jubilee Volume in Honor of Rabbi Saul (Shalom) Berman* (ed. Yamin Levy; New York: Yeshivat Chovevei Torah, n.d.), 642-45.
46. For a discussion and analysis of Herzog's views on science, see Raphael Shuchat, "Rabbi Isaac Halevi Herzog's Attitude to Evolution and His Correspondence with Immanuel Velikovsky," *The Torah U-Madda Journal* 15 (2008-2009). The quote is from page 144.
47. Gustman, who escaped the Nazis though the sewers of Vilna, became a lifelong friend; Zakheim was on the yeshiva's Board of Directors when it relocated to Brooklyn after the war. The yeshiva, founded in 1831, was noteworthy in that students had considerable free time; some pursued secular studies while in attendance there. Regarding the yeshiva and secular studies, see Yaffa Eliach, *Once There was a World: A 900-Year Chronicle of the Shtetl of Eishyshok* (Boston and New York: Little, Brown, 1998), 199-200.
48. The university retained its name after Vilno, now Vilnius, became Lithuania's cap-

ital after a 1938 plebiscite, but was renamed Vilnius State University after the Soviets annexed Lithuania in 1940. Following Lithuania's independence in 1990, it was renamed the University of Vilnius.

49. Howard M. Sachar, *Dreamland: Europeans and Jews in the Aftermath of the Great War* (New York: Knopf, 2002), 60.
50. Zvi Hirsh Zakheim, "Kuntres Vilna Lifnei Hashoah," in *Zvi Hasanhedrin v'Kuntres Vilna Lifnei Hashoah* (ed. Zvi Hirsh Zakheim; Brooklyn, NY: Simcha Graphic, 1988), 17. Grodzinsky was known in the yeshiva world as "Rashkbehag," an acronym for *Rabbon Shel Kol B'nei Hagolah* ["the rabbi of all the Diaspora"].
51. Zakheim, *Kuntres Vilna*, 19.
52. The list of rabbis is a long one: Yosef Zeev Soloveichik of Brisk; Eliezer Yehuda Finkel and Chaim Shmuelevich of Mir; Aharon Kotler of Kletzk; Avrohom Yaffen of Novardok; Reuven Grozovski of Kamenetz; Shabsai Yogel of Slonim; Isaac Shor of Sloboka; Yechezkel Levenstein of Kelm; Eliezer Menachem Shach; Dovid Lifshitz of Suvalk; the Amshinover Rebbe; and many others. Ibid., 19.
53. The events in this and the following paragraphs are recounted in ibid., 19-21.
54. In one case, a former student of Rabbi Kotler met Zakheim in Kotler's home in 1947 and related that the Nazis, armed with the list that Zakheim had compiled, released him from his POW camp to the special camp from which he escaped. Ibid., 21-22.

ההיסטורי או התודעתי באה החוויה, היהודי המאמין חווה את החג ומסיק ממנו לגבי נוהגו בעולם.

נדגים זאת באמצעות תודעת יציאת מצרים, שעליה נאמר בליל הסדר כי בכל דור ודור חייב אדם להראות את עצמו כאילו הוא יצא ממצרים. בראש עשרת הדיברות מופיע התוכן היסודי המפגיש את האומה הישראלית עם ההיבט ההיסטורי של הא־לוהות. מכאן ואילך מדגישות מצוות רבות ונבואות את מעמד ריבונו של עולם כמנהיג ההיסטוריה, שבחר בעם ישראל וכדומה. כל אלה הם תכנים הנובעים מיציאת מצרים. רבי יהודה הלוי הדגיש את ההיבט ההיסטורי כעיקר המפגש שבין א־לוהים לאדם, וביאר מפני מה לא העמידה התורה את המפגש על בסיס היות הא־לוהים בורא העולם. מערכת החגים שעיקרה זכר ליציאת מצרים משחזרת את חוויית היציאה ממצרים, לצד חוויות נוספות; דוגמה בולטת לדבר היא היבטים מסוימים של חג הסוכות. חג זה נועד לשחזר את חוויית ההליכה במדבר. היושב בסוכה חווה בצורה בלתי אמצעית את ההליכה במדבר ומסיק ממנה מסקנות רבות, הראשונה שבהן היא אמונית, מכוח היות ריבונו של עולם מוליך את עמו במדבר. אך נודעת לחוויה משמעות גם מבחינת אתגרי ההווה. זיכרון המסע במדבר נחווה דווקא על רקע חג האסיף, והוא מזכיר לאדם החוגג את הצלחתו החקלאית את התקופה שבה נדד במדבר והיה תלוי בחסדי שמיים. כך מכוננות ומעצבות חוויה זו ואחרות הדומות לה יחס מתוקן יותר של האדם להצלחתו החומרית, ומסייעות לו להפנימו.

שימוש נוסף של הזיכרון ההיסטורי לא זכה לתשומת לב ראויה. לצד החובה לזכור את יציאת מצרים מצווה עלינו התורה לזכור גם את חוויית העבדות שקדמה לה. גם מצווה זו אינה מחדשת ואין היא הצהרה ותו לא. אלא, בכל מקום בתורה שבו אנו מצווים לזכור את העבדות אנו מוצאים את החובה לתרגם את זיכרון חוויית העבדות למסקנות בתחום הצדק החברתי.

הזכרנו לעיל כי התורה מנמקת את יום השבת ביציאת מצרים ומצווה עלינו לזכור את היותנו עבדים שם ולהסיק מחוויות העבדות את מחויבויותינו כלפי ה"אחר". עיקרו של יום השבת הוא "למען ינוח עבדך ואמתך כמוך". מצוות השבת אפוא מזכירה את יציאת מצרים, אך בהקשר חברתי.

עיון מדוקדק יותר במצוות הקשורות בזיכרון יציאת מצרים יגלה כי אין מצוות השבת חריגה, וזיכרון גלות מצרים ויציאתה מהווה יסוד מהותי של מצוות חברתיות רבות, כגון איסור אונאת גר, חובת הענקה לעבד המשתחרר, חובת שחרור עבד ביובל ועוד. הזיכרון ההיסטורי אינו עוסק אפוא ביחסי א־לוהים ואדם בלבד, כי אם גם בטיפוח חובת הסדרת החיים עלי אדמות. חווית החגים אינה מצמצמת עצמה בארבע אמות של תודעה לאומית אמונית, כי אם מכוונת גם לתיקון פני החברה.

אלה דוגמאות בלבד ליכולת לקשר בין החוויה הדתית ובין התיקון החברתי. אפשר אפוא שהחוויה הרוחנית הדתית לא תנתק את האדם מעולם המחויבות המוסרית כי אם להפך – תעצים אותו, וכחלק מחיפוש החוויה הדתית המרוממת תופנה האנרגיה הפנימית לתיקון פני עולם. מקורו של תיקון זה יהיה החיפוש אחר חוויה דתית שאינה מטפסת רק לגובהי מרומים כי אם פונה גם אל המציאות בארץ ומקדמת את פני העולם.

על דמו בשעת במצוקה. כל אלה הן מצוות דתיות. הן עצמן עשויות להיות חלק מחוויה דתית של צמצום העצמי מול הא־לוהים וקבלת עולם המצוות.

העולם המיסטי:

> מיסטיקה עוינת תמיד כל קוד של מוסריות, לא בגלל הנטייה שבה לאי מוסריות אלא פשוט משום שחוק וסדר מנסים לכבול במקום שאין בו עוד מבחינתה משהו שיש להגבילו (ואן דר לאו, הדת, עמ' 505).

שאלת היחס שבין המיסטיקה לתיקון העולם בתחום החברתי שנויה במחלוקת שבה מעורבות הבחנות מחקריות בהנחות אידיאולוגיות. חוקרים הסבורים שמיסטיקה ומוסר אינם עולים בקנה אחד נימקו זאת באופנים שונים: הסתירה המהותית שבין עמדה הנוטה לחוק ולמוסר ובין האנרכיה שהיא חלק בלתי נפרד מהחוויה המיסטית; הסתירה שבנפש המיסטיקן – הוא מבקש להתנתק מהעולם הזה ורואה את המציאות כלבוש חיצוני של מהות פנימית שהיא מרכז עולמו, ואילו המוסר מתייחס אל העולם הקונקרטי; המיסטיקן מתמקד בדרך אל הא־לוהים, וחברת בני אדם, התובעת מהלך מתמיד של תיקון, לא זו בלבד שאינה מסייעת לו אלא שהיא מעיקה עליו; מכל מקום, כל עיסוק בסוגיה זו מחייב הבחנה בין תודעות מיסטיות שונות ויסודות מוסר שונים, ורוב הדיון המחקרי התמקד במוסר בדפוסו הנוצרי – הפרוטסטנטי או הקתולי.

למרות הנאמר לעיל אין להתכחש לאפשרות קיומה של חוויה מיסטית הפונה דווקא אל העולם הזה, ותובעת מתוכה את תיקונו. דרך משל החסידות, שחלקים ממנו ינקו מתורת הדרוש והמוסר שקדמה לה, ויש בה יסודות מיסטיים בסיסיים שחלקם פונים לתיקון העולם. הקשר בין החסידות למיסטיקה הוא נושא כבד משקל השנוי במחלוקת בין החוקרים, אולם בוודאי שיש יסודות מיסטיים בחסידות, ובוודאי שיש בחלק מהחסידויות פירורים מעולם התיקון החברתי. שורש התיקון החוויתי המיסטי הוא בראיית העולם הזה כלבוש של מקום, ובראיית כל אדם בכלל וכל יהודי בפרט כמי שמגלם את בחייו את ההופעה הא־לוהית, ועל כן כל פעולה למענו ולמימוש זכויותיו היא למעשה התקשרות מיוחדת בא־לוהות. תיקון העולם מסוגל לחולל אפוא חוויה מיסטית עמוקה ביותר, הנטועה ברום עולם הספירות הא־לוהיות ובד בבד חותרת לממש אותן במציאות.

מערכת חגי זכר ליציאת מצרים:

מערכת החגים ההיסטוריים היא חלק בלתי נפרד מהחוויה הדתית הממוסדת, והיא פונה הן אל התודעה, הן אל החוויה. בתחום התודעה אנו פוגשים לדוגמה שני נימוקים למצוות השבת: "כי ששת ימים עשה ד' את השמים ואת הארץ את הים ואת כל אשר בם, וינח ביום השביעי..." (שמות כ, יא); "וזכרת כי עבד היית בארץ מצרים ויוציאך ד' א־להיך משם ביד חזקה ובזרוע נטויה, על כן ציווך ד' א־להיך לעשות את יום השבת" (דברים ה, טו). לצידם אנו מוצאים פסוקים רבים שעניינם בחוויה. כיוונם הפוך, על מקום הנימוק

לשמים ולהידבק בשכינה? אותו שכתוב בו כי ד' א-להיך אש אוכלה, וכתיב כורסיה שביבין דינור וכתי' נהר דינור נגד ונפק מן קדמוהי, ואתה אומר ובו תדבקון?

אלא מתחילת ברייתו של עולם לא נתעסק הקב"ה אלא במטע תחלה. הדא הוא דכתיב ויטע ד' א-להים גן בעדן,

אף אתם כשנכנסין לארץ לא תתעסקו אלא במטע תחלה, הדא הוא דכתיב כי תבואו אל הארץ.

ההשוואה בין א-לוהים לאדם נוגעת למעשיו של האדם ולפעולותיו בעולם בתחום ממוקד. ריבונו של עולם מתואר כאן כמי שפעולותיו בעולם הן פעולות של בניין ויצירה, בין יצירה חומרית ובין יצירה של כוחות חסד וצדק בעולמנו. האדם המבקש להידבק בו עושה זאת במעשה תיקון העולם.

קיום המצוות כחוויה דתית:

מאז ומתמיד עסקו חכמים וחוקרי מדעי היהדות בניסיון להגדיר את מקומן של המצוות במערכת הדתית. עיקר הדיון ספרות הענפה נגע למטרת המצוות ולמשימה שהן משרתות.

במקביל לדיון הפילוסופי וכחלק מהשינוי התרבותי הכולל בשנים האחרונות נידונה סוגיה זו לא רק במישור הפילוסופי אלא מזווית החוויה הדתית. השאלה אינה מקומן של המצוות במערכת הערכים של הדת היהודית, אלא מה מקומו של קיום מצוות בחוויית האדם המאמין. קריאה מחודשת במקורות הקדומים, ובמשנתם של חכמי דורנו, מלמד ששאלה זו לא היתה זרה להם, אף שמקומה בעולמם אינו מרכזי כבעולמנו. בשפת הקבלה נשאלת שאלה זו במישורי התיקון – מהו התיקון שאותו מבקש אדם לעשות בשעה שהוא מקיים מצוות, וכיצד תיקון זה נוגע בתודעתו הדתית. יש שראו את החוויה כשותפות לתיקון העולמות העליונים; והיו שראו במצוות את הביטוי המעשי לעולמו הפנימי של האדם. אדם המורכב מגוף ונשמה מבקש לממש את אהבתו הגדולה לא-לוהים, והוא עושה זאת במעש: במצוות מעשיות, בהקרבת קורבנות, או בכל עניין ממשי אחר. משניות אחרות הדגישו את חוויית קיום המצוות בענווה הגדולה, ותיארו אדם המפנה חלל בעולמו, מקטין את עצמו ואת רצונו הפרטי ופועל. השוואות רבות ניתן לעשות בין השפה הקיומית של המצוות ובין שפת האהבה. גם האהבה הופכת את עולמנו לטוב יותר, ומתקנת אותו בפועל; גם האהבה חותרת לצאת מגרעינה האפלטוני ולהתממש בקשרים ממשיים בין איש לאישה; גם האהבה מחייבת פינוי חלל עצמי, ענווה ונסיגה כדי שהנאהב והנחשק יוכלו להיכנס לתוכו ועוד ועוד.

ראיית המצוות בעולם היהדות כחלק מחוויותיו של האדם מאפשרת להעצים את החוויה הדתית ולהעמיקה. כאמור לעיל, עניינים שבין אדם לחברו לא נותרו לשיח הוולונטרי ולאלטרואיזם, כי אם נוסחו כחובות דתיות שחלקן אף משפטיות. הקוצר את שדהו נתבע להניח לקט שכחה ופאה ולשתף ביבולו את הכהן הלוי והעני שאין להם נחלה. חובות דתיות אחרות מחייבות להיות רגיש למצוקתו של הזולת ואוסרת לעמוד

אם כך מקור שעליו ניתן לבסס אחריות חברתית לתיקון עולם כחלק מחווייתו הדתית של האדם. בשעה שהוא עוסק בתיקון העולם במובן החברתי הוא מממש את המפגש המיוחד שלו עם ריבונו של עולם בצלמו ובדמותו.

ולדבקה בו:

אחרי ד' א-להיכם תלכו ואותו תיראו ואת מצוותיו תשמרו ובקולו תשמעו ואותו תעבדו ובו תדבקון (דברים יג, ה).

קשה מאוד להגדיר את טיבה של דבקות בא-לוהים. היא שייכת למערכת מושגית המתארת יחס שבין אדם לא-לוהיו, אולם היא בלתי אפשרית במושגי העולם – כיצד ניתן לדבר על "דבקות" בין ישות סופית ובין זו האין סופית, בין ישות מוגבלת במושגי זמן ובין ישות על זמנית, בין ישות רציונלית לישות על מושגית. יש לזכור כי המונח דבקות נתייחד בתורה גם לקשר שבין איש ואישה – "ודבק באשתו והיו לבשר אחד". דווקא השוואה זו מלמדת על הקושי להחיל אותה על יחסי א-להים ואדם.

רוב העיסוק בשאלת הדבקות ובמימושה נוגע בדבקות התודעתית. מה שאין השכל הרציונלי הכבול במסגרותיו מסוגל לעשות מתאפשר ביכולת המופשטת של התודעה האנושית, באינטואיציה, בחיי הרגש וברצונו של האדם. מה שאינו נתפש בהגדרות מושגיות פילוסופיות אפשר שיוכל במאפייני נפשו של האדם. שמות רבים הוענקו למאפייני הנפש: נשמה, רוח ודומיהם. בעולם החסידות דיברו על הדבקות לאור הפסוק "מבשרי אחזה א-לוה", וראו ב"בשר" כינוי למכלול אישיות האדם המהווה מקור לידיעת הא-לוהות ולביטוי הדבקות בו.

כל העמדות הדתיות האלה מנתקות את האדם מהמערכת המושגית שבה הוא חי את חייו הרגילים, כתנאי הכרחי לדבקות בישות עילאית וזרה. הדבקות מחייבת נטישת החיים השגרתיים לצד התעלות תודעתית. על כן ניכרת בה לרוב תביעה לפרישות ולהתבודדות, לסיגוף פנימי ולהתפנות מוחלטת משאר עיסוקי העולם. אחת מחוויות הדבקות השגרתית היא התפילה, וככזו נוסחו הלכותיה בדרך המחייבת את האדם לפרוש מכל ענייניו ולהתרכז במעשה התפילה. ריטואל זה הוא מבוא לחוויות דבקות עשירות בהרבה מבחינת אורכן ועוצמתן. כאמור לעיל, המקום הגיאוגרפי המתאים ביותר לחוויית דבקות זו הוא המדבר, ואנו מוצאים את המדבר כמקום מועדף למבקשי הדבקות בא-לוהים. משנתו של רבי נחמן מברסלב, שעסקה רבות בחווית הדבקות, צירפה אליה את ההתבודדות ואת הפרישה מכל ענייני העולם.

לעומת זאת, בבואם לתאר את הדבקות נקטו חז"ל בשיח שונה לחלוטין. בסגנונות שונים ועל פסוקים שונים הם אמרו כי הדבקות הא-לוהית משמעה הליכה בדרכיו. הליכה בדרכיו היא סוג מסוים של חיקוי מעשיו של בורא עולם במציאות:

ר"י ב"ר סימון פתח: אחרי ה' א-להיכם תלכו,
וכי אפשר לבשר ודם להלוך אחר הקב"ה? אותו שכתוב בו בים דרכך ושבילך במים רבים, ואתה אומר אחרי ה' תלכו ובו תדבקון? וכי אפשר לבשר ודם לעלות

לוהים ברא את העולם מתוך התוהו – "והארץ היתה תוהו ובוהו וחושך על פני תהום" – כך מופקד האדם על הפיכת התוהו ובוהו הכללי למסד מאורגן המסדר את העולם על פי עקרונות היכולת האנושית. למעשה מדובר במימוש צלם הא־לוהים באדם. האדם פוגש בנשמתו את כוחות הבריאה והיצירה, ואת עצמיותו הממשיכה את ההתגלות הא־לוהית עלי אדמות. זו חוויית הקיום העמוקה ביותר שבאפשר – ההכרה בזהות העצמית של צלם א־לוהים. הרב סולובייצ'יק תיאר את עוצמת החוויה בשפת הפילוסופיה הקיומית. הוא לא בחן אותה בשאלות הפילוסופיות של חכמי ימי הביניים, ולא ניסה להשיב על שאלות הנוגעות לעצם האפשרות של חיבור בין האדם ובין הא־לוהים, כי אם תיאר אותה בפסוקי שירת ספר תהילים:

> ותחסרהו מעט מא־לוהים וכבוד והדר תעטרהו.
> תמשילהו במעשי ידיך כל שתה תחת רגליו (תהילים ח, ו־ז).

אמת שאין הכרח שחווית קיום זו תהיה דתית, היא עשויה להיות חוויה ניטשיאנית שאין לה דבר עם הא־לוהים. ברם, אפשר שהיא תהיה חוויה דתית עמוקה ביותר, ויש חידוש של ממש בקישורה בעולם הדתי. בדרך כלל מתוארת חוויית הדת ככזו שמחייבת את האדם לצמצם את עצמו, להכיר את האופי המוגבל של כוחותיו ושל מהות קיומו, ולחיות בענווה פנימית שאינה מייחסת את הישגיו לכוחו ולעוצם ידיו, אלא מובילה להכרה העמוקה שכל הישגיו הם תוצאה של השגב הא־לוהי. הרב סולובייצ'יק לא חלק על כך שזהו אחד הרגשות המעצבים את דמות האדם. הוא חלק על בלעדיותו, ומצא במקורות ישראל שורש לחוויית קיום מקבילה המיוסדת על העוצמה והשגב של דמות האדם. המשמעות הדתית של חוויה זו היא ההכרה המתמדת כי כוחו של האדם נובע מבריאתו כצלם א־לוהים, ואת בורא העולם הוא מכיר בתוך עולמו הפנימי. האדם פוגש את הא־לוהים דווקא כמקור העוצמה והכוח שהוא נהנה מהם.

הרב הרחיב במשנתו את ייעודו של האדם ואפשרויותיו גם למבנה החברתי, ולמושגי הצדק והמשפט. אין מדובר בהישגים טכנולוגיים בלבד, ואף לא רק ביצירה התרבותית הפלסטית, כי אם גם ביכולתו להפוך את התוהו ובוהו החברתי לעולם מאורגן ובנוי. לו היה העולם ניתן לשלטון כוחות הטבע בלבד הוא היה מתנהל על פי היכולת הכוחנית, והחזק היה שולט בו. צלם א־לוהים שבאדם הוא הגורם לו להעדיף את המוסר על פני הכוח, וליצור חברה שומרת חוק והגינות. לסוגייה זו אין קשר הכרחי לשאלה האם האדם ביסודו טוב או רע, מפני שבמלחמת הקיום היה החזק שורד בין כך ובין כך. לעומת זאת, האדם הרואה עצמו כמבטא את "צלם א־לוהים" מבסס את היחסים בין בני האדם על עקרונות הצדק והמוסר. לא זו בלבד, אלא שהוא מחדש את יסודות החסד והצדקה, המוציאים את האדם ממעגל מצומצם אגואיסטי ומחדשים בו אחריות לחלש ול"אחר".

מכיוון שמדובר בחוויית קיום עמוקה, היא יכולה להיות בסיס להעצמת הצדק החברתי. ככל שפוגש האדם את דמות הא־לוהים במקביל לעולמו הפנימי, ושומע בה את הציווי ליטול אחריות על דמות העולם ותיקונו, כך הופכת חוויתו הדתית לחוויית האחריות. מה שמוטל עליו אינו לנטוש את העולם כדי להיפגש במלכות שמיים, כי אם לפתח את העולם ולהכניסו בעולם של חוקים – חוקי הצדק והמשפט וחוקי החסד. לפנינו

מתמקד בצדק חברתי ותו לא, ויש לעדן את האמירה הזו: אף שאין החוויה הדתית החדשה תנועה החותרת לפתרון כולל, יש בה מענה חברתי לתחומים אחרים של התיקון. דווקא בעידן המודרני נודעת חשיבות עילאית לטיפול בחסכים אחרים: בדידות האדם, מאור פנים, הקצאת מקום לפרט, קבלת הזולת כמות שהוא, הכרה בדרכים שונות לחיים וכדו'. התייחסויות לאלה מצויות בשפע בשפה הדתית החדשה; היא אף מעצימה אותן בדומה לדרכן של החצרות החסידיות, ואין לכפור במשקלו החברתי הגדול של עניין זה. על כן, למרות הסתירה שבין החוויה הדתית לתיקון העולם, לא יהיה זה נכון לראות את התיקון החברתי בהיבטי המשפט והמדינה לבדם, אלא יש להרחיב את היריעה גם לתחום הדת.

במאמר זה אני מבקש להציע ראשי פרקים לתיקון חברתי עמוק על בסיס חוויה דתית שתהיה מנת חלקם של העוסקים בצדק החברתי, זאת מהנחות היסוד של החוויה עצמה. כפי שראינו כשלו מסריה החברתיים של הנבואה מפני שעולם המצוות שבין האדם לחברו דוחה מפניו את החוויה הדתית. על כן יש לפתוח את תיקונה של מציאות זו בעיגון המצוות בחוויה דתית עמוקה. לכאורה קיימת סתירה בין שני המרכיבים, שכן החוויה הדתית יונקת מהמפגש שבין אדם לא־לוהים, ואילו צדק חברתי הוא מפגש בין אדם לאדם. למרות זאת אפשר לגלות בעולם הדתי עקרונות שיענו לבקשה הפנימית העמוקה, וייתכן שדרכם יתחולל איחוד משמעותי בין התחומים.

חווית האדם כ"צלם א־להים":

> האדם הראשון אינו תיאורטיקן יוצר בלבד. הוא גם אסתטיקן יוצר. בשכלו הוא מעצב אידיאות ובליבו הוא יוצר את היופי. הוא נהנה מיצירותיו השכליות והאסתיטיות והוא גאה בהן. הוא מגלה כוח יצירה גם בתחום החוק: הוא מחוקק לעצמו חוקים ונימוסים מפני שהקיום הנהדר מחייב סדר. אנארכיה והדר אינן דרות בכפיפה אחת... (איש האמונה עמ' 17).

במילים אלה משרטט הרב סולובייצ'יק את מה שהוא מכנה דמותו של ה"אדם הראשון". משנתו מבוססת על הסיפור הכפול של בריאת האדם: זה המופיע בפרק א' של ספר בראשית, ומתאר את האדם כצלם אלוקים שייעודו הוא "פרו ורבו ומלאו את הארץ וכבשוה", וזה המופיע בפרק ב', המתאר את האדם השני. דמותו של האדם הראשון מכונה במשנתו "איש ההוד וההדר", ומאפיינה המרכזי הוא חוויית הקיום של האדם כאחראי לכינונו של העולם. המילים המקראיות "ורדו בדגת הים ובעוף השמיים ובכל חיה הרומשת על הארץ" נתבארו על ידי הרב סולובייצ'יק בהיקף רחב בהרבה מהמקופל בפשוטן – אין מדובר בשליטה פיזית בלבד, כי אם במיצוי כל הכשרונות שבאדם, והעצמת הפוטנציאל הגנוז בעולמן. חלק בלתי נפרד מפוטנציאל זה אינו קשור במדעי הטבע בלבד – גם האומנות, התרבות, המדע וכישורים אחרים הם חלק בלתי נפרד מעולמו הרוחני של האדם ומייעודו.

חוויית הקיום העיקרית של אדם זה היא ההוצאה מהכוח אל הפועל של אחריות זו. הוא מודע לעצמו באופן מתמיד, ומסתער על המציאות המציבה לו אתגר. כשם שהא־

לא תיתכן סתירה בין זכויות הפרט ובין מצוות שבין אדם לחברו, שהרי אף הנפגע הוא חלק ממערכת הציות לצו הא-לוהי. מובן מאליו כי גם בשפה הדתית ניתן לטעון את ההפך, היינו שא-לוהים מעדיף את טובת היחיד או את מבנה החברה על פני המצוות שבין אדם למקום. ברם, עמדה זו, אף שאנו מוצאים אותה כאמור רבות במישור הדקלרטיבי לא באה לידי ביטוי ממשי בספרות השאלות והתשובות.

לאמור, המציאות שתיארו הנביאים ופעלו בתוכה לא השתנתה, והיא המשיכה לאפיין את החיים הדתיים ואת עולמה של ההלכה שהיא המעצבת המובהקת של חיים אלה. ראיית האמונה הדתית כפותחת שערי שמיים גברה על ראיית האמונה הדתית כמתקנת עולם. אמנם, לאורך הדורות היו שהתריעו מפני תפיסה שגויה זו. במישור הדקלרטיבי ניתן למצוא עמדות על גבול הרדיקליות. רבי יהודה הלוי דרך משל תיאר בספר הכוזרי סדר שבו יש לקיים את המצוות: "...התורה הא-לוהית לא תשלם כי אם לאחר שלמות החוקה החברתית והשכלית, ובחוקה זו כבר נכללו מעשי הצדק וההודאה על חסד הא-לוה, ואיש החסר כל אלה מה לו כי יביא קורבנות או יקיים מצוות השבת והמילה ודומיהן אשר השכל אינו מחייבן ואף לא דוחן..." (ספר הכוזרי מאמר שני, מח). רבי ישראל ליפקין, אבי תנועת המוסר, כתב על כך רבות, ואף נהג בפועל זהירות מרובה, והעתיק את משקלן הראוי של מצוות שבין אדם לחברו מהעולם התיאורטי לעולם המעשי. אך אלו לרוב חריגים שהעידו על הכלל, או שהיו חלק מסוגיה אחרת (כמו בתנועת המוסר) שלא התמקדה בתיקון העולם החברתי כי אם בתיקון מידותיו של האדם. ועוד זאת, דמויות מופת רבות הקפידו בצורה מעוררת התפעלות על דקדוקי עניינים שבין אדם לחברו, וייסדו תנועות לשינוי מציאות זו, אך לא הצליחו לשנות את התפישה העמוקה הרווחת בחברה.

כאמור לעיל, כישלון מגמת השינוי נבע משני כיוונים שונים. ראשון בהם הוא המישור הפילוסופי – קשה לנמק מפני מה קודמות מצוות שבין אדם לחברו לאלה שבין אדם למקום. הקושי גובר מפני שבחלק מהתפישות האמוניות מקור סמכותן של מצוות שבין אדם לחברו הוא צו הא-לוהים, ובלעדיו כלל לא היתה חובה מוסרית לנהוג במצוות אלה ואחרות, ועל כן ברור כי חובת כבוד הא-לוהים קודמת לחובות האחרות. השני הוא המישור החווייתי: מבקשי הא-לוהים לא מצאו בעולם החברתי את המענה לקשר האין-סופי. לא לחינם מקומם של המחפשים את שער השמיים הוא המדבר, ואליו נמלטים המבקשים את הבשורה ואת ההתגלות. המדבר מאפשר לאדם לברוח מחברת בני אדם ולמצוא שם את אשר לבו מחפש.

גם הספרות המחקרית העוסקת בחוויה הדתית מתעלמת כמעט לחלוטין מההיבט הקושר בין החוויה הדתית ובין תיקון העולם ומוסריות החברה. עיון ברשימת ראשי הפרקים של ספר כמו "החוויה הדתית לסוגיה" מאת ויליאם ג'יימס מלמד על נתק מוחלט מהיבט זה של החוויה הדתית.

בעידן החדש מציאות זו מחריפה. אחד ממאפייני העידן הוא המשקל הגדול של החוויה לרבות הדתית. השפה הפילוסופית הדתית מפנה את מקומה לשפת ההתחברות, והמגע עם הא-לוהות מתקיים יותר ויותר במישור החוויה האישית. מוחרפת איפה התופעה של חוויה דתית נקייה מיעדי תיקון העולם ותיקון החברה. אלא שתיקון אינו

את רגישותם המוסרית. בשל כך, אין מאבק זה מעניק לעוסקים בו את אותו עולם פנימי עליון שמעניק המקדש.

דומה אפוא כי מאבקם של הנביאים נדון מראש לכישלון – לא רק בשל החולשה הפילוסופית של טיעונם כי יש להקדים את עבודת הא-לוהים לעשיית חסד וצדק עם האדם, כי אם, ואולי בעיקר, מפני שאין בתיקון מוסרי של העולם החברתי משום מענה למה שמבקש האדם בחיפושו אחר הנשגב והעילאי. זאת ועוד, הבעיה מחריפה כאשר דווקא כהני ד' הם המושחתים, ועל כן מאבק נגדם מתפרש כסתירת השראת השכינה.

המחסום שבפניו ניצבו הנביאים לא נפרץ במשך הדורות. קיים פער עצום בין העמדה הדקלרטיבית של מקורות היהדות ובין הפסיקה האופרטיבית במציאות. אמנם האגדה, שרעיונותיה העיקריים שאובים מהנבואה, המשיכה את הקו הבולט בדברי הנביאים, והאדירה את מעמד המצוות שבין אדם לחברו. הלל הזקן תמצת את התורה כולה על מה ששנוא עליך אל תעשה לחברך; רבי עקיבא קבע כי ואהבת לרעך כמוך הוא כלל גדול בתורה, ודבריו נקבעו לדורות בתור אחד האתוסים הבסיסיים ביותר של תורת ישראל; ההלכה קבעה כי על עברות שבין אדם לחברו אין יום הכיפורים מכפר עד שירצה אותו, ואף הרחיבה חובה זו לעניינים הקשורים בגזל; מדרשי אגדה העצימו את מעמדה של החברה היהודית המאוחדת אף שעבדה עבודה זרה, ודיברו בשבח היחסים שבין אדם לחברו מול עבודת המשכן; אפילו דמויות בעייתיות ביותר מבחינה השיפוט הנבואי זכו למעמד מיוחד (כגון אחאב בן עמרי מלך ישראל) מפני שלא פגעו פגיעה פנימית בעם ישראל ועוד ועוד. לעומת זאת, בשעה שאנו בוחנים את פסקי ההלכה שהם המעצבים את החיים היהודיים בפועל, ולמעשה משקלם גבוה יותר מכל עמדה פילוסופית או חווייתית אחרת, אין אנו מוצאים מעמד כה גבוה לעניינים שבין אדם לחברו, והדבר בולט בשני תחומים: התחום ראשון הוא הספרות ההלכתית. הספרות העוסקת בתחומים שבין אדם לחברו במישור ההלכתי דלה יחסית. בנוגע למערכת המשפטית ממונית אנו מוצאים מסכתות רבות בתלמוד, אך הדיון ביחסי איש ורעהו מצומצם מאוד. אין בידינו ספרות הלכתית קדומה על רובן המוחלט של המצוות שבין אדם לחברו, ולמעשה עד היום קיימות עשרות מצוות שאינן מעצבות בפועל את החיים הדתיים. די לנו אם נציין את העובדה כי על אף העמדה הדקלרטיבית הרואה בלשון הרע את העוון החמור ביותר הממיט הרס טוטאלי על החברה, לא נכתבה ספרות הלכתית מסודרת הנוגעת להלכות לשון הרע עד לתחילת המאה העשרים. השוואה למספר הספרים שנכתבו על דיני שבת לדוגמה תעיד כמאה עדים על המשקל הנמוך שניתן לתחומים אלה בספרות ההלכתית.

המציאות הספרותית מעידה על תופעה עמוקה בהרבה, והיא התחום השני שעליו יש לתת את הדעת. ניתן לומר כי בפסיקה ההלכתית נדחו בדרך כלל עניינים שבין אדם לחברו מפני אלה שבין אדם למקום. במקרים שבהם ניכרה התנגשות בין החובה המשותפת לקיים את מצוות הא-לוהים ובין ההגינות החברתית כלפי היחיד – דחתה הראשונה את השנייה. נדיר מאוד למצוא בספרות השו"ת תשובה המעדיפה את החובה כלפי ה"אחר" על פני החובה מול ריבונו של עולם, אף שכאמור יש מקורות רבים להעלות אפשרות זו על הדעת. כאמור לעיל, קל להבין עמדה זו מנקודת מבט דתית, שכן על פי תפישת ההלכה כל בני האדם מצווים בסופו של דבר לשמוע את דבר הא-לוהים, ועל כן

בלבד, אלא גם לסידור העולם ולתיקונו. אולם מנקודת המבט של מרכז התודעה וקדימות סדר העבודה סביר להניח כי ישנם נימוקים כבדי משקל לקדימות הקשר המיוחד שבין אדם למקום על פני זה שבין אדם לחברו. העובדה שהנביאים נאלצו לשוב ולהתמודד עם הנטייה ללכת אל המקדש מלמדת על מיעוט הצלחתם. דבריהם החוזרים ונשנים בניסיון לשכנע את שומעיהם כי סולם עבודת הא-לוהים שלהם מוטעה מלמדים על ממדי התפיסה ההפוכה.

לא רק משיקולים פילוסופיים או משיקולים ענייניים הנוגעים למערכת הערכים הדתית נבעה המשיכה המתמדת אל המקדש. מעבר לדיון הרציונלי בשאלת היחס שבין עניינים הנוגעים לתיקון העולם החברתי ובין מעמדה של עבודת הא-לוהים, מצוי העולם החווייתי. חלק בלתי נפרד מנטיית האדם לא-לוהות נובע מהחיפוש אחר החוויה הרוחנית העליונה של התקשרות בטרנסנדנטי. אין מדובר במסקנה פילוסופית סדורה העוסקת בהוכחות לקיומה של ישות עליונה שבראה את העולם או משגיחה עליו, כי אם בתחושת כיסופים עזה וברצון להתקשר אל המופלא מתודעת אנוש. האדם מחפש את החוויה העמוקה של המפגש עם מה שאין בכוח העולם הממשי להעניק לו. הוא פונה אל מה שמעבר לעולם, ותר אחר תשובות קיומיות לשאלות המהות והתוכן. חיפוש זה אינו מתחולל בתודעת האדם בלבד, ואין הוא מכוון לחוויה פנימית ותו לא, כי אם לכלל תחומי החיים, לרבות החוויה הממשית והרגשית. אחד היעדים שבו מוצא האדם את אשר מבקשת נפשו הוא המקדש, ואין ספק שהמקדש משמש מקור השראה עז ועמוק יותר מחתירה לתיקון החברתי העוסקת בענייני הממון של החלשים מבחינה כלכלית.

שכן המקדש נחווה כשער שבין עולמנו ובין השמיים. שמו הראשוני של מקדש ד' הוא "אוהל מועד" והוא האתר בו נועדים א-לוהים ואדם: "ונועדתי לך שם, ודיברתי אתך מעל הכפורת מבין שני הכרובים אשר על ארון העדות..." (שמות כה, כב). זו למעשה חוליית החיבור שבין המציאות הסופית לאין-סופית, ונקודת ההשקה שבין העולם המופשט לעולם המוחש. למקום זה עולה הציבור כולו כדי לבטא את קשריו המיוחדים עם מה שמעבר לו, הן בבואו להעלות קורבנות ומנחות, הן בבואו להתפעל מהשראת השכינה. המקום המקודש ביותר, קודש הקודשים, מוסתר מעין רואה, והוא מבטא את ההתאחדות בין האדם ובין השכינה. כחלק מעולם הדימויים המקראיים, שבו משמשים יחסי איש ואישה כמשל ליחסי א-לוהים ואדם, מכונה קודש הקודשים "חדר המיטות". בחלק חיצוני יותר של המקדש ניצב המזבח, המאפשר לאדם לממש את קרבת א-לוהים שבו באופן מעשי.

לעומת כל אלה, קשה לדבר על עוצמת חוויה בעסקנו בתשתית המוסרית והמשפטית ובבניין החברה על אדניה. בהיכל הצדק אין מקום לחוויה כי אם לשיקול דין ממוקד וקר; במאבק כנגד מפקיעי מחירים שאותו ניסה עמוס הנביא לנהל אין מדובר בהתעלות רוחנית כי אם בניסיון לשכנע שאין זה מוסרי ואין זה חוקי לעשות כך; בציפייה כי בעלי העבדים ישחררו את עבדיהם ביום הצום כדברי ישעיהו, לא ניתן למצוא את אותו זרם רוחני עמוק השורה על האדם הבא בשערי המקדש ביום צום, ורואה בהימנעותו מאכילה חלק בלתי נפרד מכפרתו; המחאה כנגד עושקי הגר היתום והאלמנה אינה מלווה בתחושת שגב עילאית כי אם בתחושת סחי ומאוס כלפי דמותם של בני האדם שהשחיתו

לידידי היקר
הרב אבי וייס הי"ו
שנושאים אלה מעסיקים אותו מאוד מאוד

החוויה הדתית שבמצוות החברתיות

יובל שרלו

מן המפורסמות הוא שנביאי ישראל מחו בעיקשות ובהתמדה כנגד סולם ערכים מוטעה של עובדי א־לוהים. הנביאים ביקרו את המשקל הגבוה שהוענק לקורבנות ולעבודת המקדש, בשעה שהתשתית החברתית והמוסרית רעועה. ירמיהו הנביא בז לדרך הבאת הקורבנות וראה בהם אכילת בשר תאווה: "כה אמר ד' צ־באות א־להי ישראל, עולותיכם ספו על זבחיכם ואכלו בשר" (ירמיהו ז כא); הושע הנביא שלח את העם לעשות חסד במקום להביא קורבנות: "כי חסד חפצתי ולא זבח, ודעת א־להים – מעולות" (הושע ו, ו); הנביא ישעיהו כיוון את ממלכת יהודה לסולם ערכים נכון ולמהותו של יום הצום: "הלוא זה צום אבחרהו: פתח חרצובות רשע התר אגודות מוטה, ושלח רצוצים חופשים וכל מוטה תנתקו. הלוא פרס לרעב לחמך ועניים מרודים תביא בית, כי תראה ערום וכיסיתו ומבשרך לא תתעלם" (ישעיהו נח, ו־ז), ועוד ועוד. המסר שבפי הנביאים תאם מאוד את הסדר שבו ניתנה התורה, היינו קדימות ענייני המשפטים שבין אדם לחברו למצוות המשכן והקורבנות.

דברי הנביאים אינם מובנים מאליהם. להפך, מבחינה פילוסופית סביר שתימצא בתודעת האדם המאמין מחויבות עמוקה יותר כלפי הא־לוהים מאשר כלפי בני אנוש. בראש ובראשונה הוא יקצה את משאביו להסדרת יחסיו עם הבורא, ורק לאחר מכן יפנה אל העולם הממשי. העולם הדתי מדגיש תמיד את היות הא־לוהים מעל ומעבר לכל סדר גודל אנושי, ואת המחויבות אליו שהיא טוטאלית ובלתי ניתנת לחלוקה. על כן טבעי הוא שבראש סדר העדיפויות של האדם המאמין יעמוד ריבונו של עולם. אמנם, תיקון העולם הממשי והחברתי אינו עומד בסתירה לעבודת הא־לוהים, שהרי אנו מוצאים בתורת ד' מצוות רבות המכוונות אל העולם, ולפחות מחצית מעשרת הדיברות עוסקות בכך. אחד המאפיינים של תורת ישראל הוא שאין היא פונה להסדרת יחסי ארץ ושמיים

Rav Cherlow is Rosh Yeshiva of Yeshivat Amit Orot Shaul in Raanana, Israel. He is a graduate of Yeshivat Har Etzion and a retired major in the IDF. He has served as a teacher in Kibbutz Tirat Tzvi, and as a Rav at the Hesder Yeshiva in Chispin. Rav Cherlow was amongst the founders of the Tzohar Foundation, a central Modern Orthodox foundation which works to build bridges between the religious and secular worlds. Rav Cherlow is a member of Governmental Ethical Committees, and of the Presidential Press Council of Israel. He is the head of the religion and ethics department in the Jerusalem ethics center. Rav Cherlow also answers halakhic questions via his website; as of 2015, he has published over 60,000 such responsa.